Multicultural Education

Multicultural Education in
A Global Society

James Lynch

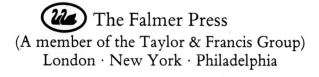

The Falmer Press
(A member of the Taylor & Francis Group)
London · New York · Philadelphia

UK   The Falmer Press, Falmer House, Barcombe, Lewes,
      East Sussex, BN8 5DL

USA   The Falmer Press, Taylor & Francis Inc., 1900 Frost Road,
      Suite 101, Bristol, PA 19007

First published 1989

British Library Cataloguing in Publication Data

Lynch, James
    Multicultural education in a global society.
    1. Multicultural education
    I. Title 370.11'5

    ISBN 1-85000-557-5
    ISBN 1-85000-558-3 pbk

Jacket Design by Caroline Archer

Typeset in 11/13 Bembo by Morley Harris Typesetting, 36 Cotham Hill, Cotham, Bristol BS6 6LA

Printed in Great Britain by BPCC Wheatons Ltd, Exeter

Contents

List of Figures   *vi*

Introduction   *vii*

1. Planning a Global Approach   1

2. Making the Multicultural Curriculum Global   34

3. Human Rights: The Core of the Curriculum   67

4. Delivering a Global Approach   104

5. Resourcing a Global Multicultural Approach   132

6. Learning for Teaching   150

Appendixes

I   List of Useful Organisations   171

II   List of Development Education Centres   175

III   List of ActionAid Education Services   178

IV   List of Journals and Periodicals   180

Bibliography and References   182

Index   189

List of Figures

1.1   Levels and Dimensions of Curriculum Goals   4
1.2   Educational Aims and Social Category Salience   13
1.3   Evolution of Concepts of Global Multicultural Education
      in the Twentieth Century   15
1.4   Objectives for World Studies: A Summary   20
1.5   Goals for Teaching Global Multicultural Education   35
2.1   Group Teaching/Learning Responses   42
2.2   Curriculum Responses to Cultural Diversity: A Phase
      Typology   44
2.3   Category Salience and Curriculum Planning   47
2.4   Components and Levels of Knowledge   53
3.1   Human Rights Education and Whole School Policy   82
3.2   Facilitative Approaches for Human Rights Education: An
      Evolutionary Approach   93

Introduction

Rationale for the Book

This book should be seen as a successor volume to my previous work on multicultural education, but one which is aimed at extending the horizons within which multicultural education is viewed and its objectives achieved. As with my other books, it has been written to encourage educators in all kinds of institutions to adopt a multicultural approach to their teaching. Thus, as in my previous work, the commitment to attacking prejudice remains central, as does the aim of empowering teachers and pupils to acquire the knowledge, develop the skills (including those of social actioning) and internalize the values and attitudes, which will enable them to feel comfortable with cultural diversity. Underpinning this is the continued belief, on my part, that both teachers and pupils must come to see cultural diversity as a creative momentum to their own development throughout their lives, influencing the relationships they forge, the professional and personal judgments they make and the social transactions they negotiate.

I also continue to recognize, of course, that multicultural education addresses more than the needs and rights of the individual and that it must often draw fine lines between the rights of some and the social responsibilities of others, seeking to facilitate creative and satisfying citizenship in an evolving, democratic society. Thus, in addition, to the empowerment of the individual, multicultural education also has social, economic and environmental goals at community and national levels. As in my previous writings, all three form central and complementary dimensions to the concerns and thrust of this book. Equally, I remain convinced of the need for legislative and political change, including the urgent necessity of providing more accessibly at national level what already exists at regional level, namely a national charter of rights and freedoms, such as already exists in Canada, for all citizens and, in particular, one which explicitly recognizes the rights of children. Finally, I am conscious that legislative and political progress, necessary though it is, is insufficient without the education of all for the exercise of freedom and responsibility in the form of participatory, democratic citizenship of a culturally diverse society. All of these commitments are consistent with my previous work, and have already been subject to explicit advocacy on my part.

What is new in this book is the way in which multicultural education is set within a broader world or international context, recognizing that a commitment to respect persons cannot halt at Dover! Nor, indeed, can it exist at the same time as economic and environmental exploitation of one of the parties is being exercised by the other party. We are interconnected and indeed interdependent; the two concepts imply both sides of a single coin – rights and responsibilities. It is this interrelationship at community, national and international levels, across *cultural*, *social* (including economic) and *environmental* dimensions, which gives the interpretation of multicultural education contained in this book its sharper focus. Put in a slightly different way, I am not only asking the question, for what kind of a society we are educating children, but for what kind of a world.

The interrelationship, implicit in this question, and referred to above, is fundamental to a number of curriculum development fields, which have traditionally been viewed separately – and some of them until recently not all – within the school curriculum. Thus, just as there is an increasing consciousness of the indivisibility of responsibility for the ecosystem within which we live with a growing appreciation of issues such as the destruction of the ozone layer, decimation of the tropical rain forests and the consequent greenhouse effect so, similarly, human rights are little by little being appreciated as indivisible, in the sense that infringements of one person's rights, or those of citizens of one country, are regarded as the concern of all. The logic of this process of internationalizing issues is that those democratic societies which have sought to introduce policies to respond to their own cultural diversity (and with *glasnost*, some other societies which have not) are now faced with the need to respond to a more newly perceived diversity – world cultural and social diversity. In other words, the basic ethic of multicultural education and the human values which draw upon it are beginning to be seen as applicable to all peoples everywhere.

In its struggles and efforts to be born, and its skirmishes and battles to survive, multicultural education has somewhat paradoxically manifested a predominant tendency to parochialism, narrowness and introversion, even chauvinism. Its goals have been seen, by and large, within the context of one nation or region, and advocates have tended to restrict their consideration of common humanity in such a way that a global dimension was almost regarded as superfluous and irrelevant, even for the marshalling of evidence and good practice. This ideological restriction has led to a narrowing of the conceptualization of multicultural education, such that its advocates have failed to perceive, let alone exploit, the way in which other educational reform movements and strategies also espouse common values and aims with those of multicultural education. Global education, World Studies, human rights education, development education, law-related education, peace education and environmental education, all share many common aims and objectives, concepts, and much content and vocabulary with multicultural education. Yet they strive separately to achieve their goals. The result is a lack of synergy at a time and in an area where increased effort and effect is urgently needed if education is not to lag behind the dynamic of cultural diversity in the wider societies. Just as, at the macrosystem level, there is a lack of appreciation of the way in which the world functions as one system of interconnected parts, so, at the micro-level, there is a failure to appreciate the interconnectedness of these variously labelled reform movements in the unity of the school curriculum.

Moreover, multicultural education has also over-emphasized differences (and anti-racist education more so), and has consequently augmented social category salience or 'categorization', when it should have been stressing those things that unite humanity, the similarities and commonalities, thereby seeking to achieve 'de-categorization'. Further, multicultural educationists have strayed far beyond the primary goals of education, inflating their quest into educational imperialism and failing to recognize that the multicultural aspect is only one dimension of the overall goals of a school and that change can only be mediated by re-attaching multicultural education to those goals.

To briefly summarize the arguments, there are nine major reasons why, at this time, it is essential to build a more global commitment to multicultural education and to see issues of cultural diversity in a broader global context:

1. The non-viability of a commitment to multicultural education, which neglects those issues of human rights and freedoms that lie outside the boundaries of the nation state.
2. The need, at a time of considerable conservatism in western educational ideologies, to combine with and learn from other curriculum reform movements that have similar aims and objectives.
3. The spreading international recognition of the phenomenon of cultural diversity and a growing appreciation of the need to come to

creative terms with that diversity.

4. The urgent imperative to learn from the policies and practice of other nations and regions, and to find new sources of inspiration for flagging western values, which are based increasingly on material exploitation and rampant consumerism.

5. The pressing necessity for improved environmental conservation, requiring a view of education that comprehends social and economic as well as cultural dimensions, and can emphasize the interdependence of all the earth's communities and resources, in this way fostering a sense of 'environmental custodianship' for future generations.

6. The need for peaceful resolution of human conflict demanding that world citizens be educated with an awareness of the responsibility of each human being for all (and a sense of a single humanity with fellow humans) at community, national or international levels.

7. The necessity to counter the headlong rush to individualistic materialism in western society by an educational strategy that balances human rights and social responsibilities for all humankind through citizenship education for community, national and world membership, which takes account of cultural, social and environmental dimensions of human existence and activity.

8. The need to re-emphasize the similarities and commonalities among human kind rather than their differences.

9. The need to re-engage multicultural aims to the primary goals of education, in order to achieve fundamental change.

Purpose of the Book

It is for the above reasons that this book aims to extend the boundaries of multicultural education, making them more world-open as well as more culturally permeable to the influence of complementary educational strategies. The book is, in this sense, complementary to the author's other contributions to the multicultural curriculum field, and to the principles and practice of multicultural education and education for prejudice reduction. This book seeks both to project that work further and to broaden its purview, its conceptualization, its strategies, content and resources. The aim is to broaden the parameters within which the theory of multicultural education is articulated and the practice of multicultural education currently conceived, through the analysis and critical appraisal of contiguous 'curricular fellow travellers', their theory and practice in the United Kingdom and in other countries and the identification, through that process, of a global agenda for multicultural education and its reformulation. That global agenda will comprise those areas where the practice of multicultural education may be informed by developments in other disciplines as well as those foci which demand a more than national treatment, such as environmental education, moral education, development education, peace education and human rights education. It is this duality of concern which gives the book its overall structure.

The book is aimed at teachers and teachers in training and it supports and enhances the efforts of educators to improve their own professional practice in responding to the challenges and opportunities of teaching and learning within a multicultural society. It defines multicultural education as a global strategy for educational development and extends its basic ethic beyond national boundaries, but it draws on the teacher's existing professional practice as the springboard for that process. The book seeks to make an original contribution to the theory and practice of multicultural education in schools, but it does this in the form of a dialogue rather than through the stipulation of imperatives.

The book makes a contribution to pulling multicultural education out of the backwater, into which it is sliding, as ably supported by the excesses of some of its own advocates as by a political climate, both national and global, which seeks to come to terms with cultural diversity by denying its importance for education, even on occasions its existence. The aim is for educational coherence and excellence, focused on cultural diversity. In pursuit of this goal, the book seeks to identify common and overarching conceptual, theoretical and practical issues and strategies, focusing them on the improvement of professional practice through new insights, knowledge and skills. It seeks to support the construction of novel approaches in the battle for an education for creative citizenship, of community, nation and world, attentive to democratic processes and values, within a context of rapid cultural, social and environmental change.

Structure of the Book

In this Introduction, the reader is acquainted with the rationale for the book, its structure, the various traditions on which the book will draw, the aims of a global multicultural approach to education and, through a series of questions, its relevance to the professional practice of teachers and schools.

Chapter 1 brings together the discussion of the levels and dimensions of a global multicultural curriculum and focuses them on cultural diversity. Consideration is then given to the meaning of cultural and structural pluralism. Drawing on precursory traditions – multicultural education, development education including Global Education and World Studies, human rights, peace education and law- related education – various master aims and objectives, procedural principles and school-oriented characteristics are proposed.

Chapter 2 seeks to identify the content and criteria of the conceptualizations outlined above for the selection of knowledge for a 'global multicultural curriculum', which can address issues of ethnic, national and global identity across the levels and dimensions, as well as address knowledge, skills, values and attitudes. Some brief consideration is given to previous attempts to construct multicultural curricula and to their shortcomings and strengths. Content and learning experiences are proposed which can reduce social category salience and emphasize common values and attributes. The chapter concludes with a set of criteria, by which such a curriculum may be judged and according to which it may be continually monitored.

In Chapter 3 a sharper focus is adopted onto the issue of human rights, and a rationale is developed for their inclusion as the core of a multicultural education pervaded by a global perspective. A brief introduction is given to the field of international and regional agreements and covenants on human rights, including children's rights, and this is used to formulate a definition of human rights education, comprising both content and basic values for the curriculum. Particular emphasis is placed on a democratic classroom climate and the empowerment of students to begin to reconstruct their own values through skills of reflective thinking and action. An outline assessment and evaluation strategy is formulated, located firmly within the context of an ongoing professional development policy for the individual as well as for the institution. The criteria for assessment, first introduced in Chapter 2 are then 'stretched' to take greater account of human rights education. A bias review procedure is proposed for the continual monitoring of all aspects of school life and to test for their congruence with the aims and objectives developed earlier. The chapter includes reference to the work of the Council of Europe and similar efforts in Canada, Australia and the United States.

The central concern of Chapter 4 is the synthesis of teaching/learning strategies which teachers may adopt to construct their own teaching style. Four families of models of teaching are introduced: information processing, personal awareness, synergetic social and behavioural. These are then used to inform nine basic principles that underlie a personal and institutional philosophy of teaching and guide the implementation of a global approach to a multicultural curriculum. These principles are expressive of a commitment to human rights both as content and basic values of that curriculum. The nine principles are used to inform a series of teaching approaches, which are required to conform to certain explicit criteria. The chapter is linked to previous discussions in earlier sections on assessment and evaluation, and emphasis is placed on the need for a gradualist approach to change and for 'pre-assessment of pupils'.

The material resource implications of a more global approach to multicultural education, core-committed to human rights education, are discussed in Chapter 5. Criteria for their selection are proposed and strategies for tackling deficits are identified. Resources are identified and trace details given in the form of lists of organizations and periodicals. Chapter 6, the concluding chapter, aims to identify and clarify the competences, values and knowledge that teachers will need in order to adopt a more global approach to teaching in a culturally diverse community, society and world. These 'needs' are seen as a natural extension and improvement of existing good practice.

Precursor Traditions and Concepts

There are, as mentioned above, a number of traditions and approaches to curriculum development and renewal on which this book draws and to which it is deeply indebted. First and foremost is the approach that has come to be called, in the English-speaking world, *multicultural education*. This comprehensive marshalling strategy for curriculum reform came from different roots and circumstances. In the United States, as Banks has illustrated, it arose from the Ethnic Revitalization Movements, themselves linked to and motivated by the Civil Rights Movements which reached the peak of their influence in the 1960s and early 1970s. This is not to neglect prior influences before and immediately after the Second World War, which focused strongly on issues of prejudice and discrimination. They drew a large part of their motivation from the experience of the Holocaust, and from the persistent riots in Black, urban areas of the United States, during and after the Second World War.

In other western nations, such as Canada, Australia and Western

Europe, multicultural education owed its birth to the increase in cultural diversity arising from mass migration in the 1950s, 1960s and early 1970s. Here a dichotomy arose in the cultural perception and political response, with the francophone regions of Europe and Quebec in Canada espousing what came to be known as *intercultural education*, emphasizing the need for social inclusion within a context of cultural diversity. There were, of course, linkages across the various traditions. For example, the early wartime developments in human rights in some Canadian states 'feed' into the postwar movement to introduce multicultural education. This happened also in the linkage in the United States between advances in civil rights and the genesis of multiethnic education.

Regardless of the derivation of form in which it first appeared, however, multicultural education manifests a number of basic commitments, which are central to this book and to linkages to other areas. These concept characteristics are: a concern with issues of cultural diversity, including an appreciation of difference and the ability to creatively relate to all cultural groups; the counterpart concept of consensus through discourse; human justice, in the sense of equality of opportunity and an active commitment to combating prejudice and discrimination; and social inclusion, meaning education for full access to social rewards and resources and for responsible citizenship, including both political and economic citizenship, within a pluralist democracy. These concepts flow directly from the three major aims of multicultural education – the creative development of cultural diversity, the maintenance of social cohesion, and the achievement of human justice.

Clearly, even from the brief cameo of multicultural education given above, it is evident that it shares important concerns with *human rights education* and *peace education*. From the initial declaration of human rights after the end of the Second World War (notwithstanding earlier precedents) nations began to strive to incorporate a commitment to human rights into their educational systems, encouraged by the United Nations declaration in 1948 that

> Education shall be directed to the full development of the human personality and to the strengthening of respect for human rights and fundamental freedoms. It shall promote understanding, tolerance andfriendship among all nations, racial or religious groups, and shall further the activities of the United Nations for the maintenance of peace. (Universal Declaration of Human Rights, Article 26(2), United Nations, 1978, p. 3)

But, perhaps the major developments took place in the 1980s with a clear and unequivocal commitment by the Council of Europe to human rights education (Starkey, 1986) and, in Canada, as a consequence of the patriation of the Canadian constitution, a major thrust to establish at both national and provincial levels those structures and procedures, educational processes and curricula that would address human rights. At an international level, too, there was concern to establish an effective charter of children's rights, leading in 1988 to the birth of the International Convention on the Rights of the Child. The major concepts associated with human rights education are those of conflict, justice, freedom, equality, human dignity, reciprocity, solidarity, duties, obligations, and, of course, rights of all kinds (human, natural, civil, political, legal, economic, minority, etc.) within democratically agreed boundaries. Whilst 'multicultural educators' have not been unconcerned with many of these concepts, they have not dealt with them in such fine detail; they have neglected such concepts as solidarity and reciprocity and on the whole have been unable to marshall sufficient expertise for them to find their appropriate place within a multicultural curriculum.

It goes without saying that a full advantage of such rights and responsibilities can only be available to those who have the knowledge and skills to take advantage of their rights, carry out their duties and fulfil their responsibilities. Thus, in some countries there has been a longstanding commitment to political education for citizenship and law-related education. In France, *l'instruction civique* has a long tradition, while *politische Bildung* was strongly developed under the Weimar Republic in Germany. More recently, the United Kingdom established a Law in Education project in the 1980s (School Curriculum Development Committee, 1988) by which time almost every state in the United States had a project in law-related education, with the American Bar Association, the Constitutional Rights Association and State Bar associations amongst those organizations with longstanding structures and projects (United States Department of Justice, 1987). The basic concepts are those concerned with values, norms, rules, conflict, duties, obligations, fairness, creative citizenship, justice and constitutional democracy, but with a distinct emphasis on skills of communication, advocacy, and social and legal actioning, collaboration and co-operation, such as have not normally been included in multicultural curricula.

The rapidity with which news of human and natural disasters is now beamed across the world has focused increasing attention on *development education.* Many international relief organizations, ranging from Oxfam to United Nations agencies such as Unesco (not least through its Associated Schools Project) and Unicef, produce curricula and other materials. Both examinations and school activities have also manifested an increasing concern throughout the 1980s with issues of environmental conservation, pollution, economic exploitation, injustice, human rights, world citizenship and economic responsibility. Growing concerns about environmental issues and humankind's depradation of its own planet have alerted educationists to their responsibility for encouraging responsible consumerism as an aspect of schooling, appreciation of sustainable development and the environmental interdependence of all animal populations with their biosphere and ecosystem. Similarly, improved communications have thrust issues of conflict and peace into the consciousness of educators and students, highlighting the need for skills of conflict resolution and understanding of the roots of conflict, nationally, regionally and internationally. Once again, themes of interdependence, responsible citizenship, human justice, and intercultural and inter-environmental relationships are intertwined in the context of both cultural and political diversity.

Not without earlier, precedent-forming initiatives, a number of important curricular reforms movements came to fruition in the early 1980s, seeking to draw together most of the above concerns and to unite the domains referred to into a coherent strategy. Whereas international relations and comparative studies in higher education were already active by the turn of the century, at the school level, amongst the most successful, recent and extensive of these concerns with a broader world view were *World Studies* and *Global Education*. Both of these areas became well established in the United Kingdom by dint of major projects and the foundation of centres at Lancaster and York, respectively. Each of the projects has also established a wide network of link teachers and advisers as well as curricular provision, in some cases leading to public examinations.

A major distinction is that, whereas World Studies tends to be viewed as an additional subject area within the curriculum, Global Education is also seen as a whole curriculum strategy, permeating and adding to the existing parameters, not only of individual subjects but in a holistic way across all the school-organized learning experiences of the student. In both cases, however, major concerns with social responsibility, cultural diversity and conflict resolution, human rights and justice, and with political, economic and environmental interdependence, and other concepts similar to those already introduced above, are at the heart of the goals of both approaches. They also both subscribe to a skills development emphasis, similar to that observed in other areas, such as law-related education and education for citizenship.

Common Concepts and Common Goals

This curricular itinerary shows that there are many goals and concepts shared by the above curriculum reform initiatives, which they hold in common with multicultural education. In the interests of tidiness I propose to organize these under three dimensions: cultural, social and environmental. Each of these dimensions is permeated by the concept of interconnectedness. Under the heading of cultural commonalities are the concepts of greater tolerance, understanding and intercultural competence, cultural diversity and interdependence, human values, rights, duties and responsibilities. Under social commonalities are the concepts of human justice and equality, responsible citizenship and consumerism, fairness at local, national and international levels, constitutional democracy and economic responsibility. And under the heading of environmental commonalities are human-human, and human-ecosystem interdependence, pollution, conservation of human, animal and biosphere species, and economic–environmental interdependence and interaction.

These baseline concepts together forge the goals of multicultural education, as seen within a global context. More specifically, the goals may be described as follows:

(a) To develop empathy with other human beings, an understanding of human diversity, similarity, difference and interdependence and to foster sociacy, including the intercultural competence to feel creatively 'at home' with the diversity of human cultures;
(b) to be aware of the reasons for human conflicts at interpersonal, intergroup and international levels and, where possible, to be able to contribute to their resolution;
(c) to develop a commitment to combating prejudice and discrimination, and solidarity for human rights 'at home' and abroad;
(d) to value the worthy achievements of all individuals and human groups, and to seek to make a significant contribution to them;
(e) to internalize agreed moral bases for behaviour within a culturally diverse society and world, including a critical appreciation of one's self, one's community and society;
(f) to develop an appreciation of human–environmental and economic

interdependence, the role, aims and limitations of different economic systems, both within a particular society and internationally, and to foster responsible pursuit of economic satisfaction;

(g) to acquire practical abilities, knowledge, skills and attitudes appropriate to responsible individual, familial, community, citizen, worker and consumer roles within a democratic culturally pluralist society;

(h) to develop qualities of imagination, inquisitiveness and rationality, both judgmental and communicative, and their application to responsible cultural, social and environmental activity.

Implications for Teachers

What is being proposed in this book is, in many respects, an evolutionary process stemming from what already exists in some schools more strongly than in others. Nonetheless, the book seeks to build selectively on already existing good practice and to address individual teachers and groups of teachers, inviting them to reflect upon their current practice and to consider in what ways it could or should be amended to take account of the arguments and evidence presented here. It seeks to engage teachers in dialogue about the aims and assumptions of their practice, as well as about the means of achieving their goals. It is, thus, not intended merely to allocate to teachers the technicist role of implementing what exists. It is not a 'hand-me-down' prescription. If teachers take creative issue with the ideas, goals and methods which this book contains it will have achieved its purpose. The book is thus in a very real sense an invitation to educators to review and reflect back on their current practice and to ask basic questions such as:

1. Is the curriculum, which I currently help to deliver, planned and organized to include the kinds of concerns introduced above? Are they considered legitimate? How are they included? Fully or only partially? Not at all? Why? What extrinsic influences (for example, international, national, local and institutional policies), and intrinsic influences (for example, staff perceptions of the needs and aptitudes of students, the professional expertise and cultural composition of the staff), determine its goals, form, content and delivery?

2. What are the current intentions of that curriculum for the students? Do they cover the three levels (local, national and international) and the three dimensions (cultural, social and environmental) introduced above. Are there any underlying negative assumptions about other groups and peoples, of different race, ethnicity, creed or nationality?

3. What curriculum principles underlie the curriculum as a whole, and my part in particular? Is it culturally balanced, or are stereotyped pictures of some cultural groups or other countries presented? Does it have sufficient global breadth? Does it adequately address the knowledge, skills and attitudes dimensions? Does it provide for continuity of theme and student development as well as for conceptual and skill progression? Are there implicit or subliminal principles at work, which adversely influence the planning of the curriculum, or the chances of some students learning successfully?

4. How far do considerations of human rights feature in my curriculum area and that of the school as a whole? In what ways do human rights considerations impact on the school, its policy, structure, procedures and its ethos? Are details are the most important instruments, which the students should know about, contained in the curriculum? Do staff and students have opportunities to discuss reflectively major issues of contemporary human rights cases, at home and abroad?

5. What processes have I chosen as the most appropriate to meet my aims, and why? Do they address the need to balance information, processes, attitudes and values? Are they attentive to the kinds of values indicated in the introduction to his book and contained in the list of aims for a global multicultural approach? How far, and why or why not? What aspects of my teaching/learning strategies could be usefully changed in the light of the arguments advanced above and in what ways?

6. How do I assess my student's learning, and which aspects do I currently not cover? How do I cope with student diversity and difficulty, and how do I indicate ways to improve? Is my assessment strategy culture-fair and sensitive to the levels and dimensions introduced above?

7. What hard evidence do I have about the success of the education I provide for students? Are the criteria I use to make my professional judgments reflective of the global, multicultural concerns and aims outlined above?

8. Has the above brief process of review of my current aims, assumptions and practice enabled me to identify areas where change is necessary? What are my personal and institutional priorities for professional development? How can I set about implementing them? Do the changes imply that I need to steer my aims nearer to the aims and concerns advanced in this book? Will this imply new materials, as well as new approaches? What additional training is going to be necessary? What additional support and pressure will be needed and

who is likely to be the best advocate? Are there any potential rewards for participation in the innovation? How can I best share my concerns with my colleagues?

Summary and Prospect

To some extent, of course, you will not be able to answer the above questions fully until you have read the book as a whole. Moreover, each of the questions is really an abridged compendium of other more detailed questions, which are retrieved and considered in the chapters that follow. Nevertheless, the baseline questions, posed above, form the platform of issues for the rest of this book, and will hopefully keep us on professional course throughout the rest of our common journey. So let us look back, and see how far we have come in this Introduction.

I began by linking this book to my previous work in the field of multicultural education, so that we can take some of the contextual issues as read. Advocacy of the urgent need for legislative and political change, and active commitment to combating prejudice and discrimination, were cited. As part of the consideration of the rationale for the book, I mentioned the three major dimensions of concern – cultural, social and environmental – which, at community, national and international levels, give this book its structure and focus. Then, I suggested some specific arguments why the approach adopted here is needed at this time, and I summarized them under nine major areas. Following this, I discussed the purpose of the book and the audiences at which it is aimed. Next, I described the structure of the book and gave a brief summary of the content of each chapter. A consideration of what were called 'precursory traditions and concepts' led to the identification of common concepts and concerns, shared by many 'fellow-travelling' curriculum reform movements; this, in turn, led to the formulation of eight major goals for a global multicultural approach, based on the commonalities previously introduced. Finally, I proposed some ideas about the implications of such a global approach for teachers and invited readers to respond to eight major questions about their current practice, its aims and underlying assumptions, both implicit and explicit.

In Chapter 1 we shall be retrieving some of the material initially shared with the reader in this Introduction. We shall, for example, construct a common framework, derived from the sketch of common concepts, dimensions and levels, briefly referred to already, illustrate it diagrammatically, and discuss its major concept characteristics. Then, building on the aims proposed above, a set of more detailed goals will be suggested, covering knowledge, attitudes, values and skills. A list of principles of procedure and criteria will be advanced, to prepare the way for the issues of curriculum content to be discussed in Chapter 2. Throughout this process we shall be reminding ourselves of the difficulties and pitfalls in curriculum innovation and of the need not only to have a good product – global multicultural education! – but also of the need to choose the right time, place, methods, words and incentives, bearing in mind the need for a judicious balance of both pressure and support for one's colleagues. So, I wish you bon voyage on our shared curricular journey!

Chapter 1

Planning a Global Approach

In the Introduction I criticized the current state of multicultural education as narrow and ethnocentric. In particular I suggested that much that passes for multicultural education is academically parochial and intellectually isolated. I argued that a curricular strategy which sets the boundary of its concerns at the frontier of the nation state is not worthy of the central ethic of multicultural education, which is respect for persons. I suggested that multicultural education has failed to learn from, let alone make common cause with, other cognate curriculum reform movements, and has ignored academic traditions, some of them very lengthy, which could have informed it and improved its effectiveness. This failure to form a coalition with other curriculum reform movements that share common objectives has led to fruitless competition for scarce curriculum space and time, and has reduced the credibility of multicultural education.

In the Introduction, I identified three levels of focus for what, as a shorthand, I described as the global multicultural curriculum. I suggested three dimensions to each of the proposed levels. Out of these levels and dimensions, I proposed eight master aims for such a curriculum, which take into account the strictures that I have levelled above. I concluded the Introduction by suggesting a series of eight questions, against which teachers may wish to scrutinize their current policy and practice, although I drew attention to the likelihood that these questions could be better answered after reading the rest of the book. The questions were intended to set an agenda for the dialogue, which I hope this book will stimulate. In this chapter, I want to retrieve that groundwork about the levels and dimensions, together with the master aims, and validate them against the statements of aims of other cognate areas of curriculum development, to set us on our way to plan our new curriculum in a process of discourse with what exists already.

Some Starting Points

Making a start is always difficult, and making the right start even more so. To recoin an old phrase, All's well that begins well! And, in developing any new curriculum approach, the first steps are very important. Equally important is knowing where we wish to go and how. So, in this chapter, I want to start with the levels and master aims, which I pencilled in as part of the Introduction, and to enhance them by reference to some of those cognate curriculum areas to which I referred in the Introduction. I want to consider the meanings of cultural and structural pluralism and associated concepts, so that we know what we are formulating aims for. In particular, I want to discuss the levels and dimensions of a global multicultural curriculum, and to look in greater detail at the operational objectives such a curriculum should address, in terms of knowledge, skills and attitudes. Throughout this chapter I shall be drawing attention to the need to balance teaching for common values and similarity, and teaching for diversity and difference. This is one of the eternal dilemmas of education, especially in a culturally diverse society. So let us make a start.

The Swann Report in England clearly identified the three levels of focus as important goals for any multicultural education, when it argued, for example, that a good education must reflect the diversity of British society and of the contemporary world. The Report states this unequivocally:

> In our view, an education which seeks only to emphasize and enhance the ethnic group identity of a child, at the expense of developing both a national identity and indeed an international global perspective, cannot be regarded as in any sense multicultural. (Secretary of State, 1985, p. 322)

You will note the way in which this statement recalls the three levels of goals – community, national and international – I proposed in the Introduction for a global multicultural curriculum: I argued that each of these three levels could be perceived across three dimensions of focus – cultural, social (including economic) and environmental. Any goals we devise for our students will have to be geared to the complex interrelationship of these levels and dimensions, or they will be incomplete, and that will mean that the school, or individual teachers, or both, are failing to provide an appropriate education for students – appropriate, that is, to their needs in the latter part of the twentieth century and the first part of the twenty-first century. Moreover, any such lack, say in one dimension, will have a detrimental impact on the others, because of the close interrelationship between the dimensions and levels: economic with environmental, national with international, national/economic with international/environmental, etc.

This systemic unity and interconnectedness is sometimes argued to be the most important characteristic goal of a global approach, and, thus, one of the most important concepts for students to grasp. It is also reflected in the interrelationship within an individual of personal, community, national and global identities – namely, the levels introduced above. As Banks (1987) argues, it is only possible to build a healthy national identity on the basis of a healthy personal and community (he calls it ethnic) identity, so that we are faced with a cumulative but not necessarily sequential process. Similarly across the dimensions, it is only where education has fostered such capacities as creativity, imagination and curiosity in the individual that the process is likely to produce the good citizen, the effective worker and the good custodian of the environment, which are alternative labels for the social, economic and environmental dimensions.

I have tried to portray this global, systemic interrelationship of goals in Figure 1.1, which illustrates the interdependence among the levels and dimensions. I have also given a few examples of concepts which need to be seen at all the levels within a given dimension, and in a number of dimensions within a given level. The opportunity to learn one's mother tongue is only valid if one has a right to use it. Equally, within a state where the national language is other than one's mother tongue, one has the responsibility to learn the national language and to be able to use it as part of the economic interdependence of all citizens. The economic interdependence or interaction may, however, be frustrated by environmental policies, over-exploitation of the source of livelihood of fellow citizens, pollution of their environment, or even deliberate environmental degradation for economic, even tourist purposes, or policies such as the 'ghettoization' of housing. Perhaps you can add further concepts and ideas, using the typology to facilitate your discussions, or better still amend the typology to better suit your own needs.

Clearly, our goals will be influenced by our basic assumptions about teachers and their teaching, students and their learning, about contemporary society and the world, and the way in which they are changing, as well as about any concept of knowledge and its transmission. Some of these areas can be very sensitive and so it is central to our plan of campaign to 'start on the right foot'. The reception of the goals will be influenced by their congruence with current ideas, policies and provision, and how traditional or innovatory they are. Put another way, our approach will have to take into account what already exists. Too revolutionary, and the goals may fail to carry conviction with our

Figure 1.1 Levels and Dimensions of Curriculum Goals

Levels ⟩⟩⟩⟩⟩⟩ Dimensions	Community	National	International
Cultural	intercultural communicative competence mother-tongue, national language, foreign language intercommunication		
Social	human rights, responsibilities and justice social interconnectedness		
Economic	responsible consumerism and exchange interdependence and interaction		
Environmental	sustainable development and non-exploitation spatial and ecological interrelationship		

colleagues, the students, their parents, the community or local or national politicians. Too traditional, and we run the risk of the classic defence response, 'but we're doing that already'.

So, a lot depends on the way in which we express and introduce our ideas, that is the words we use and the context in which we use them. An idea whose time has really come can be frustrated, or its implementation held up, by an inappropriate choice of words and location. Remember too, that people tend to implement those policies and practices about which they are convinced, and they tend not to be very enthusiastic about those that have been forced upon them. So the process of thinking out, constructing and implementing a global multicultural approach to the curriculum has to be one which is strong on discussion, persuasion, participation and justification. In that way any changes introduced will carry greater conviction and, thus, more chance of success.

The Context of Cultural Diversity

Before we begin to formulate educational goals to address issues of cultural diversity, nationally and globally, it is important to be sure what we mean by the term cultural diversity and how it differs from cultural pluralism. In this book, the term cultural diversity is used to describe the presence within one geographical area of a number of different cultural, linguistic, credal, ethnic or racial groups. Looked at against these factors, the composition or profile of individual districts, regions and nations varies very considerably, as it does internationally. Moreover, cultural diversity is not only a global phenomenon, it is also one of great longevity: it has existed for a very long time. We might say that it has been a fact of life in countries of East and West, North and South for a very long time. But it was really only in the period after the Second World War that the coincidence of five major factors transformed the way that educators and policymakers perceived cultural diversity. These factors were:

- The economic expansion of western societies at the end of the war created a demand for a large additional labour force, and was brought together by mass migration. Consequently, social policies were proposed to cope with the greater cultural diversity.
- Improved communications and international transportation systems.
- Growing concern for human rights, as a result of the atrocities of the war, and the establishment of new international organizations dedicated to peace, conflict resolution and human rights.
- The resultant ethnic revitalization movements responded to the disparity between the declared values and those operative in society.
- Major new independent nations emerged, with in-built safeguards to take account of cultural diversity, for example, Lebanon, India, etc.

It is in the first and last factors listed above that the responses to cultural diversity that we call cultural pluralism are most evident. In short, cultural diversity is a factual, descriptive term for the phenomenon of many cultures co-existing and interacting within the same spatial area, whether district, village, town, nation, region or globally; cultural pluralism indicates the policy of attempting to respond to that diversity.

As Bullivant (1984, p. 99) has pointed out, there is a vast literature about cultural pluralism, drawing from many different disciplines. Many models of cultural pluralism have been devised, all of them resting on implicit or explicit ideological assumptions and expressive of the contemporary fashions of their time in the social sciences. To put it another way, they are ideologically, historically and theoretically located.

We may distinguish several different ways of developing a definition of pluralism according to the main referent or descriptor used. Thus, *democratic pluralism* is an essentially political concept relating in particular to western democratic societies, and the existence within one nation state of several political parties and many political ideologies (its other pole would be democratic centralism as practised in the Soviet Union and the socialist countries of Eastern Europe). *Economic pluralism* is a concept relating to the type of economic system which predominates, along a polarity, for example, between capitalist or socialist, market or centralized systems.

Then, there is *structural pluralism*, which refers to the way in which society is stratified. Stratification may be on the basis of such referents as caste or social class or birth into monarchic and aristocratic groups, as in the United Kingdom. It does not necessarily imply that there is a different set of vertical structures in society (for example, armies, financial structures such as currencies, legal systems etc.) to match the horizontal stratification – a kind of social Balkanization. Nevertheless, social and economic stratification are usually closely related and allocation of life chances, jobs and economic satisfaction within society usually takes place on the basis of social stratification. Not many members of the aristocracy are to be found in the ranks of private soldiers in the national army, and not many working-class people become generals. Social stratification is a universal phenomenon, however, and it should not be assumed that it is to be found solely in western societies.

Finally, there is *cultural pluralism* where, as indicated previously, the descriptors are such factors as religion, ethnicity, race, language, etc. These descriptors are what Bullivant calls 'markers' for inclusion or exclusion, and are used by the groups themselves to advance their claims to rewards, status, powers etc. in society. But, such a cultural descriptor is not the exclusive cultural capital of any individual, or complete apartheid would rule and most societies would disintegrate. Individuals may have many roles in a structurally pluralist society, but their first encountered cultural identity is likely to persist most strongly, and, incidentally it may also predispose them to pre-judge members of other cultures, stereotyping them as a group to the extent that makes social conflict inevitable.

In the context of this book, it is important to realize that the cultural demands advanced by individuals, acting as a cultural collective, may include access to knowledge, including certain curricula, or to certain forms of education, for example university or prestigious graduate school. Economic demands may also be levied on the basis of people's group appurtenance (for example, when they are acting collectively as members of a particular cultural group, where such descriptors as ethnicity may be used to mark the boundary of the group and to demarcate their claim for social satisfactions against those of other individuals or groups by reference to particular political, educational or other ideologies.

In practice, of course, no society is organized on the basis of only one of these dimensions, although some group descriptors, such as 'caste', may predetermine group occupancy across the range of structures, circumscribing, for example, access to the economic rewards and other human satisfactions available in society. In western society there is usually much overlap, with individuals occupying several different kinds of groupings simultaneously, and using them as means of advancing their claims to satisfaction of their economic, political, cultural or other demands. Even there, however, there are fairly constant elites, supporting and dominating the existing social order. These groups exercise hegemonic control not only over society, 'sorting out' and influencing life chances and the distribution of rewards and resources, excluding and including differing 'realities', but they also allocate (or not) high status to knowledge, curricula and educational institutions.

Of course, each structure has its own culture, including the norms aand values, ideologies and assumptions, myths, meanings, symbols and language, and other cultural capital which hold it together and enable it to function, interact and exchange with other structures and, thus, to secure its own survival. But the culture of the overall social-structure, or indeed its component parts, does not necessarily coincide exactly with that of the elite groups in society. The picture is much less rigid than this, with certain components of culture remaining fairly static and others changing dynamically, just as the expression of that culture, its language changes and moves in response to need and creativity.

In any case, however constant those groups may be over time, their culture is inevitably changing and adapting to enable them to accommodate to changing environments, and to maintain their position vis-à-vis other cultural groups. They do this by resorting to the use of ideologies (ie. collections of beliefs, values, symbols, rituals and attitudes), which enable them to persuade themselves and others in society that their case of demand is natural, obvious and legitimate. Minority groups may challenge this cultural hegemony of the dominant groups in society by reference to the same or similar ideologies, or by challenging the ideologies as unjust, unfair, irrational or contradictory, or by proposing an alternative constellation of beliefs and values, in other words by proposing a new and assertive ideology competing for recognition

7

(Brown, 1988). So, there is never a situation of total cultural closure, and thus there exists the scope for creative change.

When we speak of cultural pluralism, then, within a nation state or globally, we are speaking of the extent of openness of the structural dimension of society to alternative values and norms. Put another way, the cultural membrane surrounding structures has to be permeable enough to absorb the values and beliefs associated with alternative cultural appurtenance, without becoming totally permeable so that the structure dissolves completely and the cohesion of society is destroyed. Therein lies the dilemma of structural pluralism. But, it is not an insuperable dilemma. It is one which has to be subject to continual re-resolution, or the cohesion of society is threatened by alienation and withdrawal of political consent to the social covenant that locks it together, and ultimately perhaps to the disintegration of that society. Put more simply, we are not faced with an either/or situation, but one which implies both cultural and social balance and accommodation. Firmly embedded in that balance is the concept of social justice.

A helpful distinction is made by Gordon (1964), when he distinguishes between liberal and corporate forms of cultural pluralism. By the first, he means a society where cultural diversity is tolerated but not officially recognized (for example, for the allocation of rewards and resources). By the second, he means a society where there is explicit recognition of cultural groups as a basis for the allocation of social and political power and access to economic resources. We might term the one passive cultural pluralism and the other active cultural pluralism; and of course there could be hybrids. So, it is probably more realistic to think in terms of a polarity along the line between active and passive forms. For, whereas it is necessary for different cultural groups in society to have some of their own structures, in order to survive, total adherence to that principle would lead to an impossible state, where all social, economic, military, legal and educational systems were split according to cultural criteria. That would clearly be unworkable.

Once again, we are faced with the need for an accommodation between structural pluralism at the one extreme and total exclusion of cultural diversity from any structural implication and impact at the other extreme. At several points between these two extremes are a number of forms of democratic cultural pluralism, such as can be legitimated, ensuring maximum justice to the maximum number, without society fragmenting and distintegrating. These two poles, let us call them total cultural and social heterogeneity and total social and cultural homogeneity, represent, at the same time, tensions and dilemmas in the aims and practice of multicultural education at all levels, in its attempts to provide, at the same time, for continued social cohesion and the creative development of cultural diversity.

Thus, one of the major problems faced by educational systems (and political systems as well) in East, West, North and South is that of inadequate interaction and accommodation between cultural and social systems, and between majority and minority groups. This failure to grasp the nettle of the 'pay-off' within a democratic society of interaction between cultural and social goals, and between those tending to unity and those supporting differentiation, has resulted in an absence of shared ideologies which would enable the legitimation of new accommodations with consequent crises in different parts of the social systems. In particular, there has been a blatant avoidance by educational and other structures of the need for coming to creative terms with an attenuated cultural pluralism, as a response to the imperatives posed by cultural diversity, in a way that can be sufficiently socially inclusive and legitimated with the bulk of the population.

This is the real world crisis in education and the broader society. Nations such as India, the Soviet Union and the United States, developed and developing countries alike, and even single religion societies such as Pakistan, suffer acute manifestations of the failure to construct and legitimate appropriate strategies for structural inclusion and, as appropriate, differentiation. It goes without saying that the actual profile of the policies and strategies will vary with the cultural and ideological contours of each society. Nonetheless, they will have much in common, not least the overall aims as set out above. And that leads us to the question of the goals and objectives to be pursued by educators, who are seeking to implement policies of cultural pluralism, which are responsive to structural pluralism in whatever form, but also aim to maintain sufficient social cohesion to avoid anarchy and disintegration and to secure social justice for all.

Setting Our Master Aims

I have referred above to the two major centripetal tendencies within a multicultural society and its educational and broader social policy aims, that is to social differentiation and to social integration, and the way in which the concept of social justice draws them into a creative balance, equilibrium and accommodation. In the pursuit of social justice, ideologies are marshalled and arguments deployed by groups in society in support of their goals. It is in this way, in a democratic society, that pressure for conservation or change is exerted and the balance between goals of diversity and unity is continually renegotiated.

Let us call these aims addressing the enrichment of cultural diversity and addressing shared values and ideals, the latter aims being the ideological adhesive that holds society together and prevents it from falling apart. In writings on multicultural education these tendencies are usually represented, together with social justice, as the overarching master aims. Master aims are goals of broader scope, around which more specific institutional or systemic goals of narrower scope can be articulated; they are important indicators of where an institution or organization wishes to go and what it wishes to achieve (Schmuck, Runkel, Arends, and Arends, 1977, p. 147ff). They are, in other words, important guides to decision making. So let us formulate the overarching goals in such a way as to move us from where we are now to where we wish to be as an individual, as a group or as an institution, and then let us seek to devise operational goals that can indicate more closely the means as well as the ends of a global multicultural approach. The master aims, we could describe as:

- The creative enhancement of cultural diversity (not solely the maintenance of existing cultures).
- The achievement of social justice in the form of equality of educational opportunity for all regardless of sex, race, creed or ethnicity.
- The propagation of a sense of shared values, rights and access to political power and legitimate economic and other human satisfaction.

In my other writings, I have typified these aims under the labels pluralism, equity and cohesion. These three master aims will imbue the goals for educational provision to respond to cultural diversity at the community, national and global levels, across the three dimensions (cultural, social and environmental), with regard to knowledge, skills, attitudes and values. These aims, together with their tensions and dilemmas, will also inform our operational intentions to achieve behaviourally consequential cognitive and affective improvement; one might say increased sophistication in thought, judgment and action, leading to more open, less prejudiced behaviour. Too much emphasis on difference and, in spite of what we declare to be our aims, we shall inadvertently increase the salience of cultural difference and social categories encouraging what Piaget referred to as 'transductive reasoning', or overcategorization, stereotypical judgments and prejudice. Too little attention to, and support for, cultural diversity and we shall stifle initiative, individuality, and, incidentally, bracket out an important source of social change and cultural adaptation.

Figure 1.2, which draws on the work of Miller and Harrington (1988), where this thesis is argued in greater detail, seeks to illustrate and exemplify this tension between commonality and diversity. In particular, it alerts us to the danger of adopting approaches that accentuate difference and augment rather than decrease category salience and, thus, inadvertently encourage stereotyping and prejudice. Such approaches undermine social perspective-taking and objectification of decisions and encourage overcategorization, de-personalization of judgment-making and overgeneralization; they also endorse and strengthen stereotypical thinking, prejudice and discrimination, inter-ethnic anxiety and even intergroup conflict. Many of the early attempts at multicultural education, such as ethnic studies, and some of the more recent initiatives, such as anti-racism, have fallen into this trap of emphasizing categorical thinking and action, albeit often with the best of intentions, aimed in exactly the opposite direction from that which was intended. Sometimes such failure has resulted in quite tragic outcomes of increased inter-ethnic animosity and violence (Manchester City Council Education Committee, 1988).

This intellectual 'balancing act' between common values and diverse values is the very fulcrum of education: its aims in a culturally diverse democratic society are fraught with difficulties and dilemmas for both teacher and taught. Only through encouraging our students to think autonomously, and empowering our educators to deliver the requisite knowledge, skills and attitudes, can we hope to achieve goals which involve the internalization of a kind of moral 'auto-pilot', enabling students to think out for themselves the resolution of difficult personal, social, cultural and environmental issues, in this way closing the gap between democratic ideals and social realities.

So, our task is to encourage all pupils to ascend the ladder of sophistication from the acquisition of knowledge, through the comprehension and application of that knowledge, through reflective thinking, to morally autonomous but socially responsible, evaluation and action. For it is only in behaviour (or manifest performance) that we can evaluate how far we have achieved our overall aims of creatively enhancing cultural pluralism, social justice and the acquisition of a shared heritage and values, let alone the more detailed operational objectives, which we shall be formulating a little later in this chapter. In short, the success of the global multicultural curriculum will be

Figure 1.2 Educational Aims and Social Category Salience

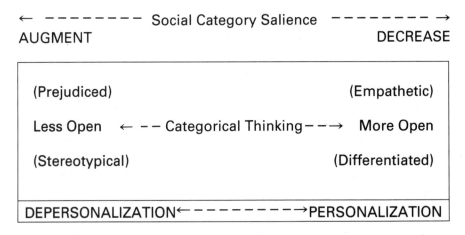

← − − − − − − − − Social Category Salience − − − − − − − − →
AUGMENT   DECREASE

(Prejudiced)   (Empathetic)

Less Open   ← − − Categorical Thinking − −→   More Open

(Stereotypical)   (Differentiated)

DEPERSONALIZATION← − − − − − − − − −→PERSONALIZATION

evidenced by behaviour, such as the ability to perform physical, intellectual and social skills.

I intimated in the Introduction that we need to learn from other curriculum development areas, and how the goals of multicultural education can be steered towards a more global dimension for all children in all schools. It is important to realize that most children in the world who have access to education attend schools which do not espouse such goals. They still receive, or received until recently, an education founded on the implicit assumption of cultural homogeneity (not least in the ex-colonial nations) and sometimes on the explicit assumption of cultural superiority. Most children, too, grow up fairly isolated from direct experience of other cultures in their own countries and not least in other countries, except for the vicarious, sometimes skewed scenarios which they receive from television.

Children in western society grow up even more isolated from the consequences of their own consumerism and its relationship to 'sustainable development'. Even where issues of development education, conservation and pollution are raised, or fashionable fund-raising for famine is organized by educational institutions, spurred by the immediacy and poignancy of tele-induced compassion, there is rarely the knowledge or insight to realize the connection between the children's own life-style and expectations and the plight of those in that other Third World, on whose shoulders they stand. Nor, indeed, is there the long-term and sustained commitment which would be generated by the inclusion of such items in the institution's goals.

Of course, in some geographical areas, and in some components of the curriculum, the situation has improved since the turn of the century, as an article by Capps (1986), based on a survey of contributions to the journal *Social Education*, convincingly argues. Whilst lamenting the lack of broader penetration of a global dimension in social studies, Capps points nonetheless to the undoubted expansion of 'curricular world-mindedness' as the century has progressed, consequent on the establishment of such international organizations as the League of Nations, the World Court and, after the Second World War, the United Nations. In this latter period, and according to the National Council for the Social Studies Position Paper from 1982, such a dimension became a major goal:

> to develop in youth the knowledge, skills and attitudes needed to live effectively in a world possessing limited natural resources and characterised by ethnic diversity, cultural pluralism, and increasing interdependence. (National Council for the Social Studies, 1982, p. 36, quoted in Capps, 1986)

This view of the aims of education offers a coherent rationale for our 'bifocal' approach, although it appears not to acknowledge, let alone seek to build on, the existence of the natural powers of learning which we all possess from birth and add to throughout life, as our cultural biography develops and changes. But the position paper does link together both global and multicultural aims and perspectives, in the way proposed in this book. Moroever, it focuses strongly on the concept of interdependence, identified in the Introduction as one of the fundamental concepts involved in such a global multicultural approach. This increasing interconnectedness can also be seen in the growth and both qualitative and quantitative improvement of the aims envisaged for global studies in a development, which has been described as 'accordion-like' in nature, with a rather narrow meaning and goals in the early years of the century and a much broader one today, as illustrated in Figure 1.3, amended and adapted from Capps' work.

Figure 1.3 is not intended to be finely accurate, but merely to illustrate the different developments and their approximate time phases and the historical and contemporary precursors upon which global multicultural education can draw. It is certainly not intended to imply co-operation among and between them! For, in spite of the apparent escalation of such innovations, they have usually occurred on a fairly discrete basis, and have not had as their focus the whole curriculum

*Figure 1.3: Evolution of Concepts of Global and Multicultural
Education in the Twentieth Century*

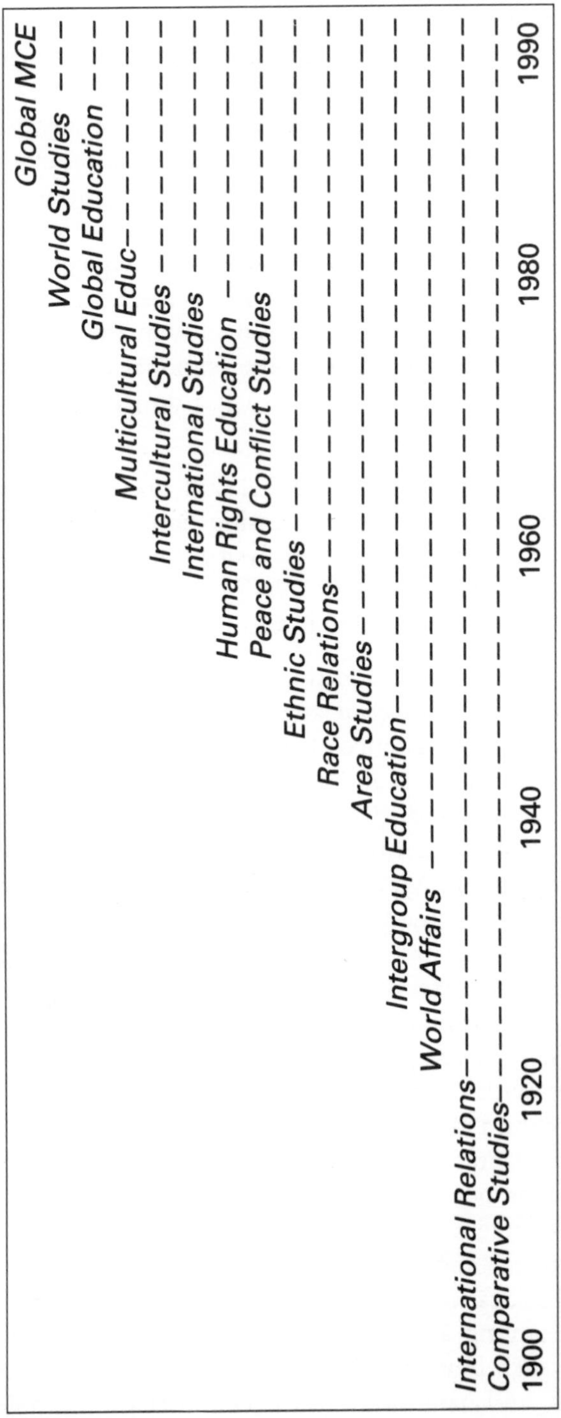

1900	1920	1940	1960	1980	1990

International Relations
Comparative Studies
World Affairs
Intergroup Education
Area Studies
Race Relations
Ethnic Studies
Peace and Conflict Studies
Human Rights Education
International Studies
Intercultural Studies
Multicultural Educ
Global Education
World Studies
Global MCE

(Adapted from Capps, 1986, p. 91)

approach as advocated in this book. There has thus been a lack of co-ordination, and therefore also effect, from such initiatives on the learning of all children. Notwithstanding, the escalation of disparate curricular reform movements portrayed above, addressing both multi-cultural education and studies, having a global or international perspective and goals. When the Swann Report in England surveyed the picture of developing countries currently held by schoolchildren, the results indicated that the views of many children were highly inaccurate, prejudiced and out-of-date. Similar surveys in other countries have come up with equally disturbing findings.

Faced with such evidence, the Swann Report argued that a good education should reflect the diversity, not only of British society, but also of the modern world (Secretary of State, 1985, p. 318). At an international level, and in similar vein, the so-called Brandt report expanded on the important role of education in fostering a better knowledge of international and not least 'North-South' affairs (Independent Commission, 1980). Its concern was for the widening of horizons and the fostering of a humane and active concern for the fate of other nations, as well as for common problems, which could motivate young people to perceive more clearly the dangers that they face, their own responsibilities, and the opportunities for co-operation globally and regionally, as well as in their own community and neighbourhood.

Further authentication of this gradual trend towards a more global and multicultural, less ethnocentric, concept of education is provided by official pronouncements at national level, which have also recognized the need for a wider horizon of cultural knowledge and social responsibility. In some cases, such pronouncements have explicitly linked together the aims of multicultural education with a recognition of international independence. One such document, published in the United Kingdom stated:

> Our society is a multicultural, multiracial one, and the curriculum should reflect a sympathetic understanding of the different cultures and races that now make up our society. We live in a complex, *interdependent world*, and many of our problems in Britain require international solutions. The curriculum should therefore reflect our need to know about and understand other countries. (Department of Education and Science, 1977) (italics added)

Such a recognition and acknowledgement of interdependence has been incorporated as a major aim for a nation's schools. For example, more recently, a national document, proposing goals for all schools in England, suggested that they should aim

> to help pupils understand the world in which they live, and the *interdependence of individuals, groups and nations.* (Department of Education and Science, 1985, p. 3) (italics added)

The linkage between multicultural aims and those of other areas of curriculum reform has also been recognized in the proposals of teachers' associations, coming, so to speak, from the direction of other curricular concerns and initiatives, such as peace education:

> . . . many of the areas covered by peace education will overlap with the family of studies which includes multicultural, environmental and development education and world studies. The Union believes that these fields should not be seen as competing for timetable space but rather as offering different, often complementary approaches. (National Union of Teachers, 1984, p. 8)

Powerful regional organizations have also picked up the relay of concern to link issues of inter-ethnic relations with those of international relations and interdependence. The Council of Europe, for example which has intensified its work in the field of human rights education in the 1980s, published a series of suggestions about human rights in the school curriculum, as an appendix to the recommendation of the Committee of Ministers on teaching and learning about human rights in schools. It included the statement that:

> The understanding and experience of human rights is an important element of the preparation of all young people for life in a democratic and pluralistic society. It is part of social and political education, and it involves intercultural and international understanding. (Council of Europe, 1985, Appendix 1)

At the more local level, too, institutions and development projects have evinced a concern with these dual objectives. The World Studies Project, organized by the One World Trust and the Centre for Peace Studies in Lancaster, for example, led to the publication of a handbook for teachers, which produced a very broad but succinct aim for world studies teaching, addressing both these issues.

> To help children develop the knowledge, attitudes and skills, which are relevant to living in a multicultural society and an interdependent world (Fisher and Hicks, 1985, p. 24).

Although it is not as detailed as the list of aims, which we encountered earlier in this book, nor indeed as explicit as the three master aims suggested at the beginning of this section, it has the virtue of briefly encapsulating the essence of our quest. It is easily grasped and remembered, and expresses our dual goals in the proverbial 'nutshell'.

You will recall that we encountered a number of questions in the Introduction about our current practices and their congruence with the approach advocated in this book. In particular, we raised the question of the intentions, assumptions and principles underlying current practice in our school. The broadly focused aims, which we have scrutinized so far in this chapter, are not intended to be immediately translatable into action, but they are indicators of directionality and they offer guidance to teachers and schools at the very first stage of reviewing their educational intentions and their underlying theoretical assumptions, before proceeding to a detailed examination of their existing policies, practices and procedures. Such statements of superordinate aims, even although they are usually expressed in a rather abstract way, are thus important for the cultural ambience and ethos of an institution and for individuals, as they embark on the professional task of reviewing their existing curriculum and its delivery.

They are, however, very limited in the guidance which they offer individuals for action, judgment and decision making in their daily professional lives. Furthermore, they tend to assume a common learning platform for all children, onto which the appropriate knowledge skills and insights have only to be deposited for learning to take place, and they naïvely assume a high level of predictability and steerability of the students' learning. For this reason, both individuals and schools need more operational statements of objectives, or principles of procedure, which are more clear-cut and specific in the guidance that they give, not only about aims but also about means and learners.

Embedded in such detailed statements will be tentative aims addressing some of the basic concepts which we have met already in the Introduction: interconnectedness, cultural diversity, interdependence, justice, social responsibilities, solidarity, reciprocity, and national, regional and global concern and co-operation. What, then, can we learn of the goals of such study from the work of others?

The next section of this chapter is concerned with the more precise and detailed objectives of a global multicultural approach to education across the areas of knowledge, skills, attitudes and values. These closer objectives will need to take on board the central concept of interconnectedness and retrieve our three master aims of pluralism, justice and

Figure 1.4 Objectives for World Studies: A Summary

Knowledge	Attitudes	Skills
Ourselves and Others Rich and Poor Peace and Conflict Our Environment Tomorrow's World	Human Dignity Curiosity Empathy Justice and Fairness Appreciation of other cultures	Enquiry Communication Skills Grasping Concepts Critical Thinking Political Skills

(Adapted from Fisher and Hicks, 1986, p. 25)

cohesion. We shall see in what way they can be expressed so as to provide us with a clearer and more precise set of yardsticks for policy and practice in our school and day-by-day professional activity, across the three dimensions and at the three levels. This interrelated complex does not replace the overall goals of education (our aim is not a *carte blanche* replacement of the existing curriculum), but rather provides us with a paradigm to set alongside the goals, on the basis of which revised aims can be prepared and implemented in such a way as to take account of the unique cultural biography of each child and the field of application for that which is to be learned, whether family life, work, responsible consumerism, leisure or further educational experience.

Setting Operational Goals

In the quest for more detailed objectives we shall continue the theme of learning from others in pursuit of a strong rationale for schools and teachers. So, let us have a look at something a little bit more detailed. The World Studies project, referred to above, also defined a list of objectives under the headings of knowledge, attitudes and skills. These objectives were, then, further subdivided as illustrated in Figure 1.4 and the labels expressed as operational objectives. The list is useful as an indicator of possible topics for thematic or project work; it also focuses our attention on the need to develop the active dimension of a child's cultural biography, concerned with communicating, advocating and engaging to exert legitimate political influence at local, national and international levels, as well as the development of basic skills.

An analogue project, The World Studies Teacher Training Project, which ran in York from 1982 to 1985, produced a statement of five aims, addressing four interlocking dimensions of globality: spatial, temporal, issues, and human potential. The aims were organized around five major marshalling domains: Systems consciousness, perspective consciousness, health of planet awareness, involvement consciousness and preparedness and process-mindedness. The aim was to assist students to:

- Acquire the ability to think in a systems mode.
- Acquire an understanding of the systemic nature of the world.
- Acquire an holistic conception of their capacities and potential.
- Recognize that they have a world view, which is not universally shared.
- Develop receptivity to other perspectives.
- Acquire an awareness and understanding of the global condition and of global developments and trends.
- Develop an informed understanding of the concepts of justice, human rights and responsibilities, and be able to apply understanding to the global condition and to global developments and trends.
- Develop a future orientation in their reflection upon the health of the planet.
- Become aware that the choices they make and the actions they take individually and collectively have repercussions for the global present and the global future.
- Develop the social and political action skills necessary for becoming effective participants in democratic decision-making at a variety of levels, grassroots to global.
- Learn that learning and personal development are continuous journeys with no fixed or final destination.
- Learn that new ways of seeing the world are revitalizing but risky (Pike and Selby, 1988, p. 34–5).

In the above list we encounter many of the concepts we met in the Introduction, such as justice, action skills (as in the previous example), human rights, and responsibilities, openness to other perspectives. In addition, concepts such as future orientation, ability to think in systems mode, and an interesting paradox of a 'world view' which may not be shared, are addressed. There is also an important element in the final aim, which emphasizes the unpredictable nature of the future, and avoids the impression of so many sets of objective that the future is all 'sewn-up'.

Heater, seeking to set down a tentative checklist of objectives rather than a definitive prescription, but one suitable for a course of study in human rights, proposed the following:

- Knowledge of historical developments.
- Knowledge of contemporary declarations, conventions and covenants.
- Knowledge of some major infringements of human rights.
- Understanding of the distinction between political/legal and social/economic rights.
- Understanding of the basic concepts of human rights.
- Understanding of the relationship between individual, group and national rights.
- Appreciation of one's own prejudices and the development of attitudes of toleration.
- Appreciation of the rights of others.
- Sympathy for those who are denied rights.
- Intellectual skills.
- Action skills (Council of Europe, 1984, pp. 7ff).

In developing the discussion of the objectives of human rights education further, Starkey draws our attention to the importance for effective learning of three elements: thinking, feeling and doing, otherwise expressed as knowledge, attitudes and skills. He emphasizes that the action skills needed to achieve human rights and democracy can only be learnt through doing (Starkey, 1986, p. 64). This democratic and participatory contextual ethos is of great importance in the delivery of any set of objectives, devoted to global multicultural education which we may devise. Unless there is a climate of justice and fairness, it is clearly unlikely that those objectives can be learned by pupils and the values associated with them properly internalized.

The emphasis of skills development encountered in the above example is very much to the fore in most law-related education. Projects devoted to this dimension of the curriculum tend to highlight skills of reasoning, communicating, problem-solving and decision-making. They also seek to encourage not only a knowledge of the law and its role in their own lives, but also to nurture an appreciation of the values underlying the law and a concern for social responsibility and respect for others. Within this latter aim are the concepts of solidarity and reciprocity; concern is thus not only for one's own rights but also for the rights of others on a mutual basis as well as 'solo', that is a willingness to engage for the rights of others even when our own rights are not threatened or at risk. Of course, it can be argued, as I suggested in the Introduction, that rights are indivisible, and that a threat to the rights of one are a threat to the rights of all. A British project on the law in education set itself the following objectives:

- To raise the legal awareness of young people.
- To deal with law-related problems and situations that are relevant to the lives of young people.
- To develop understanding of the role of law in society.
- To develop skills to discover and use the law in real-life situations.
- To encourage an understanding of and respect for values which underpin the law, including concern for justice, social responsibility and the rights of others.
  School Curriculum Development Committee/Law Society, 1986, p. 2)

The emphasis on skills, knowledge and values for action is also firmly rooted in the philosophy of global education, deriving from a social studies background. In the United States, for example, a widely read and used handbook for the social studies emphasizes the action dimension, arguing that the goal is to enable students to attain a sense of personal, social and civic efficacy to influence social and civic institutions, through experiences such as political campaigning, community service – and even through responsible demonstrations. Accordingly, the goals for the social studies are organized into four categories:

> The major goal of the social studies is to prepare citizens who can make reflective decisions and participate successfully in the civic life of their communities, nation, and the world. Goals in four categories contribute to this major goal:
>
> - knowledge
> - skills
> - attitudes and values
> - citizen action
>
> (Banks, 1985a, p. 7)

The National Council for the Social Studies purpose statement for global education reflects this emphasis in its guidelines for social studies in arguing that its goals must include four major areas – knowledge, abilities, valuing and social participation – if it is to become a reality in the classroom, and have consequences for the student in the wider society. Here, one encounters the element of citizenship education and its facilitation by democracy in school and classroom. Becker (1979, pp. 42–3) has proposed a more detailed set of objectives for global education and world studies programmes, which take account of this four-fold goal approach, and include the element of unpredictability and ambiguity encountered earlier in World Studies:

1. Provide learning experiences that give students the ability to view the world as a planet-wide society.
2. Teach skills and attitudes that will enable the individuals to learn inside their lives.
3. Avoid the ethnocentrism common in sharp divisions drawn between the study of 'us' and 'them'.
4. Integrate world studies with developments in other disciplines and fields of study.
5. Teach the interrelatedness of human beings rather than simply identify uniqueness or differences.
6. Explore alternative ways of resolving problems of a world-wide nature.
7. Recognize in the experience provided for students the likelihood of continued change, conflict, ambiguity, and increasing interdependence.

Coming at the question from another perspective and level, a Peace Project, based in a local authority in the United Kingdom, defined four contexts, coincidental with the levels previously introduced in this book: global, national, community and personal, where the objectives focused on knowledge, attitudes, skills and concepts. The knowledge objectives identified were: our society, other societies, socialization, communication, information, wealth and power, the environment, justice, discrimination, conflict, peace and differing perspectives. The attitudes were: self-respect, respect for others, curiosity, open-mindedness, justice, ecological concern and group concerns. Repeating some of the competence already encountered in other projects, the skills were: enquiry and research, communication and social skills, co-operation, affirmation, empathy, assertiveness, critical awareness, conflict analysis and resolution, political skills, consultation and counselling. The concepts were: causes and consequences, communication, conflict, co-operation, distribution of power, fairness, interdependence, similarities and differences, social change, values and beliefs (Manchester City Council Education Committee, 1988, pp 10ff).

The International and Multicultural Education Programme (IMEP), based at Jordanhill College of Further Education in Scotland and supported by the Consultative Committee on the Curriculum, sought to wrestle with the diversity of objectives embraced by the above projects, their varied levels and specificity, and the different traditions from which they came in order to initiate and coordinate a multidisciplinary teaching and learning approach in Scottish secondary schools. That approach sought to pull together five major areas: development education, environmental education, human rights education, multicultural education and peace education. It sought to express a composite list of possible targets (including understandings, skills and attitudes) that could facilitate the construction of a global multicultural perspective on the secondary curriculum, which was at the same time attentive to issues of conflict resolution, justice, economic interdependence and resource conservation. Those learning targets for the students that the project set itself were described as:

- Awareness of the world as a set of interactive systems.
- Appreciation that peoples have rights and duties towards each other and that even the pursuit of self-interest necessitates co- operation.
- Consciousness that one's own perspective on world issues and other peoples is biased by one's own cultural background.
- Empathy (viewing other societies from their own perspectives and one's own society from the perspective of others).
- Appreciation of others, sympathy for the plight of the unfortunate, regard for the achievements of the creative.
- Skills to understand a rapidly changing world and to make critical judgments from a mass of information.
- Ability to communicate with others across cultures without prejudice to oneself and also to combat prejudice in others.
- Readiness to act responsibly towards the environment held in common by the world's inhabitants (Dunlop, 1983, 3).

Picking up the relay of this latter aim, the British Environmental Advisers Association has argued that this is an area par excellence, where cross-curricular policies are essential in schools. They summarize the general aims of environmental education as:

- To teach and encourage learning about the environment in order to emphasize the interrelatedness and interdependence of man with other species and the environment.
- To use the environment as a source of information and for direct learning through practical involvement in a number of ways:

(a) by observation, measurement and analysis;

(b) by the development of environmentally related skills;
(c) by the development of an understanding of principles, concepts and generalizations about environmental processes;
(d) by the development of enjoyment and aesthetic awareness and appreciation of the environment, and by trying to involve pupils and adults in the protection, conservation and improvement of their habitat – both natural and developed.

• To develop social, moral, economic and political awareness of environmental issues, and to provide the knowledge and skills to make decisions and to take appropriate action.

Although the above statement is weak on the international dimension, it does highlight the interdependence of man and the ecosystem and of environmental and economic issues, as well as emphasizing the development of decision making and action skills, such as we have encountered previously in human rights education and law-related education.

Not explicitly included in the previous examples is the cybernetic or informational dimension, particularly the skill so essential in modern society, of interrogating data. But each of the above examples, in its own way, raises the issue of the usual building blocks of a curriculum: the knowledge, attitudes and skills dimensions of human learning. Some of the examples raise the issue of the field of application of learning, and a few refer obliquely to the learning experience components of the curriculum. All the examples are offered to teachers as starting points to their own thinking and curricularizing, and all provide insights for teachers of all subjects. But their effectiveness in doing this is limited by their lack of systematization of the definition and utilization of the essential building blocks, and their level of abstraction and clarity.

So, we are now ready to draw from these examples, and from the other traditions referred to in the Introduction, our own list of knowledge, skills, attitudes and values which we would seek to help our students to achieve. But, remember, these are only suggested ones and the best list for you and your school will be the one that you draw up for yourself and collaboratively for the school. Remember, too, that the objectives suggested are not intended to be refined behavioural objectives but rather beacons that can illuminate your progress towards a more global multicultural curriculum, when set against the mainline goals of the school. The objectives also carry a proviso, namely that we have not yet attempted to identify the learning experiences nor teaching/learning processes which can make these objectives real for our students, nor the 'lock-on' to areas of knowledge in the school timetable. We shall attempt this in subsequent chapters.

Knowledge

- To provide pupils with an awareness of the similarities and differences of human beings, their values, locations, languages, beliefs, styles of life and political institutions.
- To facilitate an understanding of how stereotypes originate and persist, and of their impact on relations between ethnic groups and nations.
- To cultivate an awareness of economic and power motivations in human relationships.
- To enable pupils to understand the variety and patterns of human settlement in the context of the physical environment.
- To nurture in pupils an understanding of the concept of human–human and human–ecosystem interdependence on a global basis.
- To develop in pupils an understanding of different forms and modes of production in developed market and non-market economies, and in subsistence, cash-crop and primary-produce economies in the Third World.
- To ensure an informed understanding of the problem of developing countries, the economic and cultural dominance-submission relationship of 'North and South', by providing accurate information and vicarious experience and by correcting for misinformation.
- To support and facilitate the growth of knowledge and understanding of international interdependence through the period of colonialism to the present day, including the work of international agencies and organizations.
- To encourage an understanding of the differential impact of technology on human beings and their biosphere.

Attitudes and Values

- To develop a commitment to the values of pluralist democracy and to civil and human rights.
- To nurture a sense of informed responsibility for all fellow human beings and for the total ecosphere.
- To foster a positive appreciation of the rich diversity of human

---

cultures and a willingness to judge each in its own context.

- To facilitate a sense of sharing common human values and ideals with all humankind.
- To stimulate the development of empathy with other cultures and peoples, particularly those in developing countries.
- To enable pupils to develop social commitment, and economic and environmental responsibility, as world citizens.
- To encourage an appreciation of the role and responsibility of all 'world citizens' for each other and for pressing human problems such as the achievement of peace, the abolition of environmental pollution, the guarantee of human rights for all and the cessation of the exploitation of poor countries.

Skills

- To foster international political literacy in pupils and the potential to engage in action in support of greater equity, justice and human dignity.
- To develop intellectual integrity in the collection, collation, utilization and evaluation of a variety of evidence as a basis for informed and balanced judgment.
- To develop visual, linguistic, aesthetic and other imaginative competences as a basis for dialogue and discourse within and across different cultures.
- To encourage the development of global political literacy and the practice of political skills such as communication, advocacy, problem-solving and conflict resolution.
- To reinforce and extend basic learning skills and develop advanced cognitive organization and functioning.
- To reinforce the growth of clarified and reflective values and attitudes and their applications as criteria for balanced, humanly sensitive decisions and judgments.
- To encourage critical reflexivity vis-à-vis the images of developing countries portrayed by the media.
- To develop decision-making, collaborative and participatory skills as a basis for reasoned judgments.
- To facilitate the ability to judge the history and contemporary place of their own country in the context of world history and development, and particularly in its relationship with developing countries.

As I intimated earlier, it is not a matter of instant implementation of the above goals *en bloc*. We are not talking of a completely new curriculum, but rather a penetration of the major aims and content of schooling with a commitment to a global, multicultural approach. In seeking to achieve that permeation, a balance has to be drawn between stability and change, tradition and innovation, reform and retention. Remember, too, that the adoption of new or amended goals demands, for many teachers, a reconstruction of their professional, and sometimes also their personal, reality. Striving for goals such as those proposed in this chapter will certainly influence the way that colleagues interpret and participate in social relationships with their professional colleagues and the children, for whose learning they have accepted responsibility. So they will need the maximum professional support and personal and cultural understanding. If they are to succeed, they will need to be 'empowered' to 'empower' their students. (This theme of professional support and development is the theme of Chapters 5 and 6.) For, as the old adage goes, curriculum development is first and foremost a matter of teacher development!

It is also important to realize that the goals at which we arrived are educational goals. They are not, in other words, macro–political goals, which assume a total omnipotence on the part of teachers and the school. They are neither utopian nor millennial! They acknowledge and encourage the teacher to accept that there is much that cannot be changed by them and by schools and education, but that conversely they are not impotent. There is much that they can change. Many of the broader issues are not susceptible to change through educational measures alone, as I have argued in the Introduction. But many attitudes, values, skills and knowledge *are* susceptible to change by educational means. These latter have been the concern of this chapter so far. But goals, such as we have enunciated in this chapter, tell us little about the way to reach them, so we need to prepare the ground for our later discussion of teaching approaches by saying something further about how we intend to achieve our goals and by linking that to the overall international context, within which we strive to deliver a global multicultural curriculum.

Procedural Principles for a Global Multicultural Curriculum

So, now we need to begin to run and focus more sharply on how we can put into practice the master aims and operational goals that we have 'won' from our consideration of multicultural education and cognate curriculum areas with similar overall educational objectives. What we are looking for is quite simply principles which will guide our procedures and help to keep us on our global multicultural course, in pulling together the planned selection of knowledge components and learning experiences which we call a curriculum, and achieving our objectives through its delivery. We are seeking guidelines, some might call them process objectives, which will indicate appropriate means (and implicitly also inappropriate means) to enable us to bridge from the curriculum to the teaching/learning approaches for its delivery, and which are meaningful, congruent with our overall philosophy of curriculum and open to both professional and lay judgment. In line with the earlier work of Stenhouse (1975, pp. 86ff), I want to call these goals procedural principles, although I mean something slightly different by my use of the term, as will be clear when we begin to list them.

The principles will derive from our master aims and objectives and must of course be 'in line' with them and the overall aims of the school. Each school may, consequently, develop a slightly different set of principles, on the basis of dialogue within the school and wider community. Moreover, any list will be provisional and incomplete insofar as it will mature and develop over time and trial. So, the list of procedural principles I propose are a tentative, illustrative list rather than fixed, definitive and comprehensive. Such an initial list might, however, include the following:

- The school curriculum will address the extent to which students can:

  > fulfil their full potential and accept responsibility for assisting others to do likewise;
  > gain critical distance on their own learning and experience;
  > internalize a commitment to social justice, solidarity and reciprocity in human affairs at home and abroad;
  > encounter and gain knowledge and understanding of other cultures;develop a sense of shared values and humanity;
  > learn and work with members of other cultures and, if possible other nations;
  > accept responsibility for their environment and ecosystem.

- The school staff will attempt to ensure that:

  > school curriculum and other procedures are fully consistent with 'respect for persons', their legitimate cultures and their

human rights;

their choice of language is non-sexist, non-racist and non-prejudiced;

the school curriculum will enable students to understand their legal and moral rights and responsibilities, and teaching methods will reflect those rights and responsibilities;

students should have opportunities for collaborative learning within a democratic school and classroom context, so that students of different backgrounds, experience and levels of knowledge may benefit from exchange and dialogue with their peers;

students are empowered to gain critical distance form their learning;

students develop a commitment to the peaceful resolution of conflict and to change according to democratic principles of persuasion and negotiation.

- Students will be encouraged:

  to develop social, physical and intellectual skills, as well as to acquire accurate, up-to-date and worthwhile knowledge;

  to develop their own reflective, internalized and autonomous moral values, which take into account those of others and the broader society;

  to express themselves freely, confidently and responsibly across the range of school activities, exercising care, sensitivity and absence of prejudice in their choice of language;

  to regard educational knowledge as provisional, and local national and global inequality and cultural diversity as problematic, and susceptible to change;

  to engage in discourse in order to explore differing cultural perspectives and ideologies;

  to negotiate emphases within the curriculum appropriate to their own community, culture and interests;

  to respect reasoned argument and discussion, and to analyse and critically review evidence from whatever source;

  to explore alternative perspectives on cultural, social, economic and environmental issues at international, national and local levels; and

  to critically question the aims and process of social and scientific change.

Naturally, the above list needs to be further spelled out more fully for each year and component of the curriculum and, through a process of broader dialogue, for different members of the school community. But, I believe that the style and underlying philosophy are sufficiently illustrated by my 'first shot' for readers to critically appraise, develop and amend the principles, using them also as a professional yardstick against which to judge and improve their current professional practice. That process of inter-learning is one of the principles of procedure this books seeks to foster, support and empower.

The Context of an Effective Whole School Approach

One final point is necessary before we conclude this chapter in order to re-emphasize the link between curriculum and the institutional context and between policies for academic excellence and social equity. I have emphasized the need for curricular reform and development to broaden the concerns and world view of multicultural education. I have also underlined the claim for equity and justice to be a central core concern of that curriculum, individually as well as institutionally, abroad as well as at home. As a consequence, it may have seemed to some readers that this emphasis has in some way represented a retreat from the 'whole institution' approach I have so strongly advocated elsewhere, as well as the commitment to excellence. I would like, therefore, to correct that impression by reiterating that teachers do not have to choose between excellence and equity. They can pursue both aims with mutual benefit to both goals and to all students, and indeed to all members of the school community. Such a commitment demands, however, a 'whole institution' approach, embodying those characteristics of a good school, which emerge from the literature on both sides of the Atlantic, and which I have collated elsewhere (Lynch, 1987). Amended slightly to take account of the more global focus of this book, but building on the essence of that earlier work, such characteristics would include:

- Good leadership at all levels, with the skills for and commitment to a global multicultural approach.
- A school climate (ethos) conducive to the physical, intellectual and social skills learning, essential to such a policy.
- High expectations of all pupils, regardless of gender, race, ethnicity and creed.
- A particular emphasis on excellence in basic skills.
- High time-on-task for students and teachers.

- A clear set of master aims and operational objectives, shared by and effectively communicated to all members of the school community.
- A clear and unequivocal policy statement against discrimination, including institutional sanctions in case of infringement by staff or students.
- A continual programme of evaluation and monitoring – self, collegial and institutional.
- An ordered, safe and disciplined environment, where the principle of 'respect for persons' is manifest in all facets of life;
- A collaborative regime, where there is a commitment to democratic teaching and learning, including the planning of improvements to institutional life, and a continual appeal to the moral judgment of members.
- A commitment to good communication at all levels and between all members of the school and its community.
- A coherent, institutionalized policy for staff development and its delivery.

This last point is particularly important, for it is evident that just as curriculum innovation necessitates a 'whole school' approach and institutional support, so it also requires the support and assistance of outside agencies. It needs access to outside ideas, expertise and resources, and whilst these are not absolutely indispensable to any innovation, one as fundamental and far-reaching as the permeation of the whole curriculum with a global multicultural perspective requires both individual and institutional professional development. Absolutely alone, even the self-critical school cannot succeed in achieving the goals described in this chapter. This theme is dealt with in greater detail in Chapter 5, but for the moment let us take stock of how far we have travelled in this chapter.

Chapter Summary

In this chapter, we retrieved the major goals and concepts we encountered in the Introduction, linking them to the levels and dimensions. We then considered what we mean by cultural diversity and how it relates to expressions such as cultural and structural pluralism. Next, we embarked on a consideration of the master aims of multicultural education of shared values, social justice and the creative enrichment of cultural diversity. We looked at the master aims proposed in national and other statements for contiguous areas of curriculum reform, exhibiting the same or similar aims and objectives, to provide us with a kind of international rationale for the triple aims of global multicultural education advocated in this book.

This theme of 'learning from others', or inter-learning, was then projected into the consideration of operational objectives which could address multicultural education, set in a global context. Once again the search for such objectives included a wide array of sources, intended to assist our review of the current intentions and assumptions underlying the curricular policies of school and professional practice. Drawing on this exploration of the objectives of others, a set of detailed objectives was proposed which focused on knowledge, attitudes (and values), and skills. A tentative set of procedural principles was then proposed to enable teachers to put the objectives into practice. Finally, we reminded ourselves of the need to set curricular aims, objectives, policy and practice within a holistic context which seeks to pursue both equity and excellence, and has high expectations of all members of the school community. We sought to do this by listing the characteristics of a good and effective school, which are naturally the characteristics of a good school also committed to a global multicultural curriculum.

In Chapter 2, I want to clarify what I mean by the term 'curriculum' and to indicate the building blocks we shall be using to construct a global multicultural one: learning experiences and knowledge components (knowledge, attitudes and skills). Then, I want to consider a number of the earlier attempts to provide a curriculum appropriate to a culturally diverse society and the shortcomings and strengths of those efforts. After which, drawing on the master aims, goals and objectives introduced in this chapter, I shall be seeking to identify the curriculum content across the traditional categories of knowledge components and learning experiences, but emphasizing in particular the active skills-based nature of the curriculum in question.

In addition, I shall be suggesting five major concept characteristics of a global multicultural curriculum: cultural balance, global breadth, cultural and social equity, economic responsiveness and environmental sensitivity. That curriculum will be constructed across the levels and dimensions referred to previously, which can address knowledge, skill and attitude goals appropriate to ethnic, national and international identities in the context of cultural, social, economic and environmental dimensions. I shall be emphasizing both content and delivery, which can reduce prejudice and social category salience and underscore a sense of shared values and attributes, conjoined with rights and responsibilities (in preparation for Chapter 3, which is concerned with human rights education as the core of multicultural education). I shall also be preparing the groundwork for Chapter 4, in the form of suggested procedural principles for the delivery of such a curriculum and an outline policy and guidelines for its assessment and professional evaluation.

Chapter 2

Making the Multicultural Curriculum Global

In Chapter 1 we considered the meaning of cultural diversity and associated concepts. We examined master aims and objectives proposed by a number of curriculum reform movements, which enjoy considerable commonality with multicultural education. Then, we used those common aims and objectives both to confirm the overall aims of a global approach to multicultural education and to furnish us with a broader and more international rationale for a global approach to a multicultural curriculum. Using the preceding material, I proposed a detailed list of operational objectives for such a curriculum, emphasizing the relationship of this exercise to the questions raised in the review section of the Introduction about our individual professional and institutional intentions and implicit assumptions, and restating the need for a holistic institutional approach and one which addresses both equity and excellence. Finally, I suggested a provisional set of procedural principles, as a means to guide the achievement of objectives and, in order to emphasize once again the holistic nature of global multicultural education, I reiterated the characteristics of a good, effective school, amended to take account of a more global multicultural education.

In this chapter I shall be addressing the questions raised in the Introduction about the epistemological shape and cultural quality of the curriculum, experienced by students throughout their period of formal schooling. I am using the word 'curriculum' to mean the sum of the normal building blocks of curriculum development as planned by the school, its knowledge components (information, skills, values and attitudes), and the complementary learning experiences planned by the school (Department of Education and Science, 1985, p. 13).

I shall be levying certain criteria against those components and learning experiences, related to their cultural balance, global breadth, cultural and social equity, economic responsibility and environmental custodianship. These latter I call the concept characteristics of a good global multicultural curriculum. They are not to be understood as separate components of a curriculum nor as addressing any single area of learning experience, but rather as permeative and co-existential criteria through the curriculum and school life of the student. Nor do they coincide with any single subject but are to be thought of integratively. The reader will note the relationship of these concept characteristics to the levels and dimensions of a global multicultural curriculum, as described in Chapter 1 and illustrated in Figure 1.1. I shall also be emphasizing the experiential nature of a global multicultural curriculum and referring to the skills-based nature of its delivery and assessment. Put in a lay way, it will be the major function of the school and its curriculum to enable students to think, talk, discuss, judge, relate and act in a reasoned way, by reference to evidence, including issues about which there is no final answer, across the four levels and dimensions.

In sketching such a curriculum I shall be using the building blocks referred to above. I want, for example, to retrieve the operational objectives, introduced in the previous chapter, to describe a number of earlier attempts to conceptualize, design and deliver a curriculum appropriate to cultural diversity. Then, I want to use what I see as the shortcomings of those earlier attempts to lead back to a more detailed description of the concept characteristics, referred to above, which I believe should help to set the parameters for a global multicultural curriculum. Next, I want to identify the profile of such a multicultural curriculum in terms of the levels, dimensions and learning experiences, encountered in the last chapter, appropriate to ethnic, national and international identities, as individual, citizen and worker. Throughout this 'curricular excursion' I shall be emphasizing the need to clearly define and deliver content appropriate both to cultural diversity and to cultural commonality, to divergent as well as to shared values, to social differentiation and to social cohesion, and the need to keep strongly in focus a commitment to justice for all as a means of keeping these goals in creative interaction and equilibrium.

Previous Curricular Responses to Ethnic Diversity

Effective curriculum reform is extremely difficult to achieve and demands, in a sense, a reconstruction of perceptions of curricular and broader social reality. Early educational attempts to respond to cultural diversity, often under the generic title of ethnic studies, tended to have poor purchase on the new social and cultural realities to which they sought to respond. Thus, the 'problem' was seen as susceptible to solution by the adoption of an additive approach to the curriculum, whether in making provision for additional language tuition (usually neglecting the non-verbal language dimension), or in the form of additional thematic subject areas, organized around what was seen to be the indigenous culture of ill-defined and generalized definitions of ethnic groups.

This curricular phenomenon can be observed in most European countries, Australia, Canada and the United States. Names such as Asian Studies, African Studies, Aboriginal Studies, Native American Studies, Italian Studies, Irish Studies, Caribbean Studies, and Mahgreb Studies proliferate. Departments under these headings have been established and specific appointments made. Majority children did not usually participate in such curricula. Alternatively, in some few cases, they were given no option but to participate in a component of the curriculum, which was seen by them as of low status and completely divorced from their daily lives or educational and narrower vocational objectives. A later variant of this movement was the term 'multi-ethnic education' which, in addition to the additive strategy, attempted also to influence the main body of the curriculum, teaching materials and strategies.

The aim of the additive phase was often said to be to correct for the poor self-image (Jeffcoate, 1979) of the minority children of particular cultural groups, who were perceived to be under-performing in the mainstream curriculum. No attempt was made to change the main curriculum for all children and majority children received the same traditional curriculum as before, with no attempt at emphasizing commonality with the other minority curriculum, let alone any effort to tackle racial and ethnic stereotypes and prejudiced values and perceptions. Indeed, the effect of such a curricular strategy may have been to strengthen the 'them' and 'us' perception of both or all groups, reinforcing status differential, exacerbating poor self-image and emphasizing difference and therefore category distinctions between students of perceived different kinds.

A second-phase response was what I have described elsewhere as folkloric multicultural education (Lynch 1987), where an attempt was made to introduce into the mainstream curriculum, knowledge of the customs, dress and festivals of any or all minority groups. Little effort was made to tackle prestigious sectors of the curriculum, nor indeed to provide for skill and attitude development, as well as providing a sometimes potpourri-like variety of diverse knowledge. The emphasis once again was on difference, the exotic, and commonality was usually neglected, with the in-built assumption that all values and practices were automatically justified by dint of being labelled minority. There was no 'bridging' to human rights issues, to provide a moral basis for such judgments, let alone broader global issues on a cohesive or systematic basis. Majority students sometimes reacted with resentment, and social category distinctions were sharply accentuated by mostly well-intentioned but often disastrously misguided, policies and practices.

A later phase of multicultural education, the permeative phase, sought to impregnate the whole curriculum and examination with a commitment to cultural diversity. Attempts were made to introduce appropriate content and to forge teaching materials and methods, which were fully attentive to cultural diversity. Criteria were developed to monitor the responsiveness of the curriculum and existing subjects, together with their attendant materials and methods, to cultural diversity. A balance was often sought by the introduction of an emphasis on similarity and commonality. A few empirical studies were undertaken, particularly in the United States, to evaluate the effects. The results of introducing ethnic content into the curriculum were sometimes mixed, but sufficient evidence of positive effects was provided to justify the assumption of worthwhile benefits to inter-ethnic relations. Theoretical weaknesses in this approach were its continued over-emphasis of difference, its lack of systematic evaluation of the effects and its lack of sharpness in the matter of teaching/learning strategies. It was also neglectful of previous empirical work and had a marked ethno-centric orientation, both vis-à-vis other areas of curriculum reform with common objectives in the same country and also vis-à-vis cognate developments in other countries, with each country tending to plough its own multicultural or intercultural glebe!

In a few countries, such as the United Kingdom, this latter phase was overtaken by, and in some cases moulded with, the anti-racist phase in the mid-1980s. This movement began as a high profile, manifestly political attempt to exert influence for major change in schooling as a means of combating the structural and systemic racism, seen as endemic in market economies. The movement appeared to many observers to be a political revolutionary aspiration vis-à-vis capitalist society. Its early, 'rough-shod' approach was to condemn white racism and, building on the guilt of the majority community, to train teachers and pupils out of their prejudice. It provided a well-deserved and cutting critique of the effectiveness in overcoming prejudice and delivering greater equity of the second, more mature phase of multicultural education, pointing to the illusion rather than the reality of change. The preferred means to this end was short, sharp racism awareness training sessions, which were neglectful of the literature and empirical traditions of prejudice reduction that could have sustained and made more effective the strategies implemented.

The effect of this early phase of anti-racist education was, in the case of the United Kingdom, a massive reaction by powerful majority groups in society, by all possible means, including public ridicule of the excesses and aberrations of the movement. In fairness, its advocates often offered juicy hostages to fortune, which were seized on for processing by those of whatever ideological orientation inimical to any concessions to cultural diversity. In some cases it was argued to have polarized ethnic relations in schools to the point of antipathy, conflict and grave physical violence. This phase also coincided with an upsurge in educational 'apartheid', including strident demands for separate schools on religious and sexists grounds and an outpouring of middle-class children from the state into the private school system. In its later phase, the movement began to propose more well-grounded strategies, but still without drawing on the extensive literature and empirical traditions in the field in other nations. No attempt was made to co-ordinate initiatives with other cognate curriculum reform movements, even multicultural approaches being condemned as palliatives in the service of dominant groups in society.

A fifth curricular response to ethnic and broader cultural diversity has been represented by a coalition of different disciplinary forces, led predominantly by social psychologists in the United States, Canada and Israel. What began the pre-war years as the intergroup education movement, gradually became in the post-war response to the Holocaust an attempt to understand the genesis of prejudice and to devise appropriate educational strategies and approaches to overcome it. This orientation was strengthened by the desegregration movement in the United States and the problems experienced by countries such as Canada and Australia in absorbing large numbers of immigrants in the post-war period.

In deference to the 'whole school' strategies, the movement concentrated on teaching/learning approaches which could improve inter-ethnic relations, particularly by the use of co-operative group work of different kinds. The effectiveness of these methods has been more rigorously monitored than any of the other methods or approaches indicated above. Sharan (1980) has categorized five different approaches to co-operative learning in small groups, describing them as either peer-tutoring (PT) or group investigation (GI) methods. In a later article

Slavin identified seven co-operative approaches, emphasizing the conditions for improved relationships through inter- racial contact defined by Allport (1954): equal status contact, pursuit of common goals and institutional support leading to the perception of common interests and the recognition of common humanity. These principles are essential baselines to our search for the criteria, content and shape of a multicultural curriculum, which is permeated by a global approach. But we shall return to them later in this chapter.

The five approaches described and analysed by Sharan were Jigsaw, Teams-Games-Tournament (TGT), Student Teams and Academic Divisions (STAD) and Team-Assisted Individualization (TAI), which were categorized as peer-tutoring methods (PT); and co-operative learning approach; and small group learning method, which were described as group investigation approaches (GI). (Slavin adds a further co-operative team method, which included collection, discussion and interpretation of information in heterogeneous groups.) Experimental work on each of the above methods was considered and evaluated in terms of its effects on three areas: academic achievement, students' attitudes and ethnic relations. The later analysis by Slavin (1985) adopted a slightly more extensive categorization, and this has been taken into account in Figure 2.1. The interpretation and outline description of results are my own.

It is important to emphasize that there is no reason why the methods portrayed in Figure 2.1 should not all be used by the teacher, depending on the goals he or she wishes to achieve. Indeed, other methods can also be combined and used to coach students towards better performance in more demanding co-operative group work, and cognitive groundwork preparation may be necessary for affective gains to be achieved. It is argued here that we need to select what is best in whatever curriculum area we are interested in, in order to build a systematic and valid response to cultural diversity and the need to attenuate prejudice and discrimination. In this process, although the identikit teaching style of each teacher will be different, it will be constructed of common components. Above all, it will need to include the components of the curriculum and learning experiences referred to at the beginning of this chapter, and to be attentive to the characteristics of cultural balance, global breadth, cultural and social equity, economic responsibility and environmental custodianship.

A sixth response to cultural diversity has sought to do just that, and provides a catalyst to the best that could be garnered from all the previous movements and approaches to produce a composite approach

Figure 2.1: Group Teaching/Learning Approaches

Label and Main Proponent	Approach and Distinctive Features	Effects/ Gains
Jigsaw (PT) (Aronson)	Peer-tutoring, syndicate work on a co-operative basis	low-level
TGT (PT) (DeVries)	Competition between co-operative groups	cognitive inter-ethnic
STAD & TAI (PT) (Slavin)	Competition and rewards on individual and team basis	social
Co-operative Teams (GI) (Weigel)	Co-operative collection discussion and interpretation	high-level cognitive
Investigation I (GI) (Johnson)	Co-operative teaching in groups	inter-ethnic
Investigation II (GI) (Sharan)	Co-operative learning in groups	Social

which might be termed 'prejudice reduction'. This is not, in effect, a single approach but rather an attempt to draw together into a coherent and well-grounded, strategic menu those methods that have proven validity and effectiveness into a coalition, albeit fitfully and inadequately at this point, with other innovatory areas of the curriculum, to deliver common objectives, knowledge and learning experiences. In this respect, it has evinced a concern with content, materials and pedagogy in a way that other methods have not.

Looking back over the six approaches, it is clear that each has some missing links in the strategic chain of building a curriculum which can deliver the components and experiences, achieve the aims and objectives introduced earlier, and meet the criteria listed above, across the levels and dimensions. Some of the earlier methods concentrated almost exclusively on content and neglected teaching/learning strategies, whilst some of the later ones concentrated on methods, and neglected content. All underplayed the criteria and their relationship with other curriculum areas, not least in the economic and environmental fields. Some have concentrated too much on difference. The excursion has not been entirely in vain though, because among them are many of the elements from which each teacher may build up his or her own identikit teaching style, as well as guidelines for an appropriate professional development to support teachers. A global approach to multicultural education, as formulated and advocated in this book, is firmly in this evolutionary tradition.

We have now briefly covered six of the major curricular response strategies, adopted to articulate to the perception of cultural diversity in education, whether brought about by such initiatives as the ethnic revitalization movements, by civil rights campaigns, desegregation or by mass immigration. Figure 2.2 seeks to illustrate the six curriculum responses to cultural diversity and to describe the causal phenomenon to which they seek to respond, what they consider to be the major means by which that cause is propagated, the preferred intervention strategy and what we know of the effects, if any.

Of course, it is not intended that the above approaches should be seen as discrete and isolated. Quite the reverse is the case, with early forms continuing to co-exist with late approaches, hybrid methods as well as misinterpretations, and continuing interaction and conflict in the ideological battlegrounds of different societies. Nor should it be assumed that because a particular approach has been counterproductive that this was the intention of the advocates and practitioners. Goodwill is not an automatic guarantee of good results. Above all, it should be

Figure 2.2: Curricular Responses to Cultural Diversity:
A Phase Typology

Approach Label	Defined Cause	Identified Mediator	Preferred Intervention	Effects
Ethnic Studies	Poor self-image	Socio-economic & racial experience	Additive curriculum	Unknown
Folkloric Multicultural	Curricular neglect	Curriculum	Curricular 'sprinkling'	Some cognitive
Permeative Multicultural	Schooling	Schools	Holistic policies	Some cognitive
Anti-racist	Structure of society	Racism	Radical political change (revolution)	Counter-productive
Group Work	Educational strategies	Classroom approaches	Groupwork	Both cognitive & affective
Prejudice Reduction	School & society	Both	Holistic policy & practice	Same as above

noted that later forms have benefited from the criticism and dialogue, even where it has been conducted at long distance! Finally, all the approaches are so recent – the oldest a mere fifty years, the youngest less than five – that final appraisal is not within sight. The situation is till very fluid and we have much to learn and do, not least from other curriculum areas not labelled multicultural but included in the analysis of this book.

Characteristics of a Global Multicultural Curriculum

What, then, can we learn from these earlier attempts to develop curricula for cultural diversity? In what ways should they be shaped so as to gain benefit from our own concept of a multicultural curriculum, attentive not only to global issues, but also generative of a commitment to the rights and responsibilities of world, as well as national citizenship?

It is apparent that early attempts were ignorant even of the basic literature on ethnic contact and prejudice reduction. Both ethnic studies and folkloric multicultural education, and anti-racism even more so, emphasized difference rather than similarity, categorization rather than de-categorization and thus contributed to stereotypical thinking, increased inter-ethnic anxiety and accentuated out-group rejection. We cannot say how far such categorical responses remained at the level of values and attitudes and how far they may have been translated into words and actions. One thing we can say is that it should be a fundamental principle of the global multicultural curriculum to de-emphasize such 'transductive reasoning' and competitive social response, and to emphasize the commonality and similarity of the human species in order to encourage personalization of decision and judgment, which is the treatment of individuals and the conduct of personal relations on the basis of individual rather than group merits.

Figure 2.3 illustrates that emphasis in curriculum planning, and from it is derived the first of our principles for the construction of a multicultural curriculum, namely cultural balance. This means that the aims and content of the curriculum, as well as the teaching approaches, should seek to draw a judicious balance between celebrating legitimate difference, by providing knowledge, skills and insights about unique individual, ethnic and national distinctiveness and distinctions. It should also be aimed to provide a basis of common knowledge, skills and insights about the things that all human societies should hold in common and, thus, seek to decrease rather than augment category salience. This goal would surely include a knowledge of what is shared by all in entitlement if not in actuality, including human rights and the agreed moral bases for action and judgment within an imperfectly democratic and multicultural society, and a commitment to improve and change it for the better. And it would be susceptible to achievement as much through the methods as through the content of the curriculum.

A major problem in devising a curriculum for the schools of modern industrial, democratic and multicultural societies in an interdependent world environment is the sheer weight of knowledge crowding to get into the curriculum. Not only does each major interest group feel that its centre of epistemological gravity should be represented in a discrete and unique way, whether it is industry or commerce, the unions, professional associations and subject organizations, parents and political parties, regional and international organizations, or whatever interest or pressure group. But the expectation is that only additional and separate content and objectives can explicitly respond to that group's demands. The school and its curriculum are regarded as a kind of convenient knowledge pantechnicon into which can be loaded all of societies' ills for remediation and all their desires for satisfaction. There is little understanding that there is overlap and duplication between their various 'legitimate' wishes, which can be responded to by the same content and approaches, and that even 'curricular omniscience' could not satisfy all their cumulative demands separately.

So, if I argue that the global multicultural curriculum should have cultural breadth, I am not arguing that it is possible to cover everything about every culture in the nation, not to mention the world. Nor, indeed, does it mean that every teacher or every area of the curriculum or learning experience will be expected to deliver the full expanse of that cultural breadth. What it does mean is that the curriculum experienced by each child in the period of compulsory schooling should cover learning experiences and the areas of knowledge, skills, attitudes and values, from the levels (individual, community national and global) and from the dimensions (cultural, social, economic and environmental) introduced earlier.

Final shape can, however, only be given to these components and learning experiences when we specify the focus of our curricular efforts (i.e., what students are being prepared for). Here, the answer in the case of the global multicultural curriculum must include preparation for *cultural* functions in leisure, work and educational spheres as an individual member of a local community; a citizen and member of a national and a world community, as well as a continuing learner throughout life. It must also include *social* functions in preparation for familial and

Figure 2.3: Category Salience and Curriculum Planning

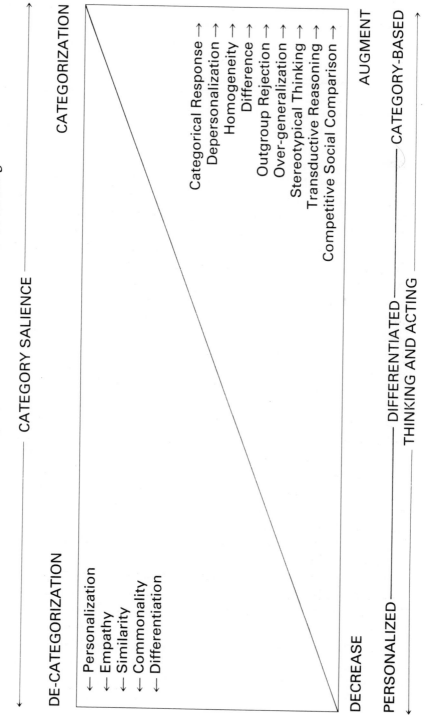

domestic roles and those of cooperative neighbourliness and creative and participatory, democratic citizenship; *economic* functions in preparation for roles of responsible worker and consumer, with a commitment to economic caring at the four levels; and, interdependent with the other dimensions, local, national and international *environmental* functions. Once again, this implies an emphasis on problem-solving and decision making and implementation skills, achieved through a process-oriented curriculum.

The concept characteristic of social and cultural equity derives directly from the master aim of global multicultural education, previously introduced under the shorthand label of social justice. It was described as the social adhesive, which prevented the other two master aims, cultural diversity and social cohesion, from straining out of balance. It is the major means by which policies responding to those needs are politically legitimated, that is explained and justified in such a way as to marshall a wide body of social support, endorsement and commitment. From a curricular point of view, it is a master aim that seeks to deliver the knowledge, skills, attitudes and values, which provide for equal access to the social economic, cultural and political rewards and resources of a democratic society on an equitable basis. In this sense it is the deliverer of the necessary cultural capital for social inclusion within a democratic society, whilst at the same time guaranteeing legitimate retention and creative enhancement of the individual's home-base culture. It should be present in all aspects of the school's functioning, its ethos, policies, practices and procedures and, of course, not least in the attitudes and values of staff in delivering the curriculum.

In this context, it will be clear that schools have a responsibility to foster equal opportunities for boys and girls, to prepare them for active involvement in family, community and civic life, and to provide a curriculum that can achieve these goals across its knowledge components and learning experiences. This may well, of course, not be the view of all teachers, parents or cultural groups, but that does not make it any the less a duty for the school to seek to deliver, sensibly and sensitively, that knowledge and those capacities which will enable girls to close the gap between the democratic ideals of society in this respect and the social reality of women and girls in developed societies, and even more so in many developing countries.

In the school, this means an end to both the overt and the covert sex-role stereotyping, in the curriculum and teaching/learning methods as much as in the staffroom. It means an end to the patronizing justification or acceptance of cultural or ethnic group appurtenance linked with gender as implicit justification for discrimination and disadvantage, through the limitation of the access of girls to benefits, services, facilities and learning opportunities available to boys. And, it imposes on the school an advocacy role vis-à-vis many parents. The unacceptable alternative is for the school to connive with parents to deliberately exclude and prejudice the girls' education and narrow it to fit prejudiced views of the capabilities and functions of the girls. But, it is no part of the function of a school in a democratic society to reinforce the gender prejudice and sex-stereotyping of the wider society or of particular cultural groups within that society.

It goes without saying that neither can it be the purpose of the school to connive at the infringement of the human rights of any segment of the student body. Rather, the school must seek to provide the knowledge, commitment and citizen action experience which will enable girls and members of minority groups to counteract the influences of whatever group or individual seeks to deny those rights. As a background to this struggle, but also as a means of empowering students to protect and attain their rights, all students should have a knowledge and understanding of the local, national and international legal instruments and covenants as well as the legal structures and processes which endorse gender, ethnic, credal and race equality.

Equally, this concept characteristic means that the school must ensure that the curriculum meets any special need that minorities may have, such as additional provision in the language area. Then, too, it must seek to culturally include the background of all students, in a sensitive way, but without skewing the delivery of the major social and cultural purposes of the curriculum. Less obviously, this concept characteristic means that the school must seek to provide the stimulus and opportunity for all pupils to gain legitimate access to the shared values and systems of the wider society, including the economic, legal and political ones of which they must have full membership in their adult life to gain economic satisfaction, to be able to defend their rights, to be able to advance and represent their interests in the political arena. Because they are minorities, ethnic groups need more than 'headcount' representation of social and cultural equity in the school curriculum.

The concept characteristic of economic responsibility includes but transcends preparation for the world of work. Of course, the school cannot be offering social and cultural equity if it neglects the provision of knowledge, skills and attitudes, which are conducive to all individuals to achieve economic satisfaction through work and a career. It cannot be contributing either to individual survival or that of the society if it is underplaying essential economic elements of modern life, such as the economic system, wealth production, saving and investment, international trade and human relations and local, national and international conflict in an economic context and in interconnection with other sectors. Once again, while accurate and up-to-date knowledge and information is essential, it is the process skills and attitudes which alone complete the achievement of this concept characteristic. The ability to obtain information, to interpret and evaluate information in a variety of forms and from a variety of national and international sources, and to work with others to utilize that data in a range of decision-making situations, including ones involving moral judgment, predicate a more than simply cognitive approach, which will need to emphasize the internalization of economically moral values and attitudes.

So, it must also include a curricular preparation for responsible consumerism, including the role of commercial and other pressure groups and an appreciation of the impact of western life-styles, expectations and power over the money and commodity markets on the life chances of minority children and communities in the developing world. Then, too the students will need to be well informed about the interdependence of social, cultural, economic and environmental factors in their own lives, the lives of their community, nationally and globally, and to be bale to use the above knowledge, skills and attitudes in formulating and implementing decisions in real local situations. Once again, we are not speaking of a discrete component, but of permeation of this characteristic across all knowledge components and learning experiences, into skills, knowledge, attitudes and values.

Finally, in this list of concept characteristics of a global multicultural curriculum, and strongly interdependent with the previous one, is environmental custodianship. here, we are talking of something much more than environmental studies, which could enable students to develop a knowledge and awareness of their immediate surroundings, although that is surely important, not least in combating the burgeoning of mindless environmental vandalism in modern society. But, both the expanse and the responsibility, implicit in this concept, are greater than that, and so the curricular skills, attitudes and social actioning components are commensurately greater.

The role of the citizen in a pluralist democracy is to advance other than economic arguments for action and to exercise creative guardianship over the irreplaceable treasure of our environment, during the brief period of time in which the individual has leasehold occupancy. For this goal of the environmentally active citizen, both the knowledge base and the provision of citizen action skills need to be broader than at present. They need to enable the student to think systematically and systemically about the environment, see its interrelationship with the other dimensions and concepts, and to handle a wide variety of both theoretical (i.e., vicarious) and direct practical environmental problems, including decision making and implementation situations, ranging from the simple to those where environmental decisions interconnect and chain with other decisions in other sectors and by other people.

These five concept characteristics together embrace knowledge, skills and attitudes. They contribute interactively to the overall profile of a global multicultural curriculum coterminously, progressively and continually with the school life of the student. They are not to be thought of as separate subjects, but rather interwoven and permeative criteria, which serve to ensure longitudinal and lateral coherence, progression and continuity throughout the period of formal schooling. They comprehend and are interwoven with all the learning experiences and knowledge components, and thus, cannot be delivered by any single knowledge component, curriculum area or traditional subject. In the next section of this chapter, therefore, we shall be considering the two major building blocks of curriculum: learning experiences and knowledge components, but bearing in mind the function and pervasiveness of the five permeative criteria, already described. In embarking on this task, I acknowledge from the beginning a certain variability, even arbitrariness, in the use of the terms in the literature, and I shall, therefore, do my best to define my usage of the terms as I proceed, without, I hope making the going too heavy!

Learning Experiences

One of the major building blocks of a child's learning at school is the learning experiences, designed by the teacher and participated in and influenced by the students in order to achieve the essential physical, mental and social abilities to equip the child to function effectively as a member of the local community, the nation state, and increasingly in the future, of the international community. We should not underestimate the extent to which students participate and influence the construction of their own curricular reality, but equally we should not underplay the role and importance of the teacher, and the mutual interlearning which this necessitates.

In Chapter 1, I suggested certain procedural principles that could guide the implementation of the planned curriculum, moving us from aims and objectives to the process itself. This 'process view' of the global multicultural curriculum implies an emphasis on skills (and this has been evident in the treatment of the five concept characteristics) with concomitant opportunities for both vicarious and direct practice, repetition and reflection. It also implies a particular view of an appropriate assessment and evaluation strategy, evinced in progressive changes in behaviour as the curriculum unfolds, and thus in terms of a longitudinal view of curriculum and its process and objectives. It means an active, open-ended and experiential curriculum but one that can be delivered by, and is thus complementary to, existing curriculum components or areas, such as those listed in Figure 2.4. Thus, once again, we are speaking of evolution from what exists rather than the mirage of a *tabula rasa*.

More specifically, because the global multicultural curriculum is intended to deliver the knowledge, skills and attitudes to empower students to active citizenship of their own community, their nation and the world, it is in its very essence an active curriculum. This kind of curriculum cannot be achieved by a 'banking' style of education, concentrating on the despatch of parcels of knowledge in the general direction of the learners, for such an educational methodology and philosophy cannot deliver what is needed, which is a problem-solving and decision-making approach that will encourage reflective and active, morally responsible engagement with the major issues of our time, locally, nationally and world-wide, culturally, socially, economically and environmentally.

The global curriculum has, in contrast, to be able to deliver the necessary strong orientation towards a wide range of learning through experiential means, because whilst knowledge is necessary for reflective decision-making, alone it is insufficient. Moreover, in the information-orientated society of today, with the rapid deterioration of the value of any given knowledge and its early redundancy, children need to acquire the 'how' more than the 'what'. And if this applies in the cognitive sphere, it also applies in the affective sphere, where the aim is not just autonomous learners but morally autonomous decision-makers. Thus, students need to develop skills of collecting, organizing, interpreting, evaluating and using information and sources of information, to learn and practice decision-making skills, rather than merely analyse them, and to be able to apply them in practise to a variety of problem-solving situations in family and local community life. In many cases this will involve direct purposeful activities outside the school, but it will also be

Figure 2.4: *Components and Levels of Knowledge*

Components of knowledge	Levels of Knowledge			
	Individual	*Ethnic*	*National*	*Global*
Human, social and economic				
Aesthetic and creative				
Linguistic and literary				
Mathematical, scientific and technological				
Moral, ethical and spiritual				
Physical and environmental				

(Department of Education and Science, 1985, pp. 16ff, amended by the author) necessary for the interrelated learning experiences in the school to be framed in such a way as to achieve this goal. Those experiences must certainly be such as to encourage the development of communicative and personal relationship competences, such as leadership, partnership and creative, principled yet critical followership. More specifically, each of the following, supported by appropriate practice, reflection, motivation and feedback, will make a contribution to the student's experiential learning:

- Relating, negotiating, co-operating, sharing, participating, leading, supporting.
- Challenging, advocating, resolving conflicts.
- Communicating verbally and non-verbally, orally and in written and graphic forms.
- Observing, analysing, interpreting, evaluating and making informed and balanced judgments.
- Acquiring, applying, synthesizing, assessing and interrogating knowledge, both formatively and summatively.
- Planning, collecting, collating, utilizing, reviewing, appraising evidence.
- Accessing, processing and presenting data.
- Developing visual, linguistic, aesthetic and other imaginative competences.
- Designing, making, testing.
- Selecting, categorizating, discriminating, classifying, generalizing and concluding.
- Formulating questions, posing hypotheses, validating and problem-solving.
- Imagining, creating, expressing.
- Measuring, estimating and formulating.
- Developing physical skills.
- Recognizing, analysing, evaluating and practising different kinds of decision and decision making at increasing levels of complexity.

(Department of Education and Science, 1985, pp. 39ff amended by the author)

The above list of learning experiences is no doubt incomplete, but it does seem to me to catch something of the reality of current best practice in classrooms, aiming to deliver an experiential and relevant curriculum throughout the period of formal and compulsory schooling. Moreover, it provides a yardstick, against which the teacher may begin to re-examine his or her own teaching and classroom, what is actually happening there now and what he or she wants to happen there in the future. It helps to direct the teacher's attention towards the necessary changes in teaching/learning strategies, methods and ways of working, which are at the heart of real curriculum reform. Moreover, changes to the balancing of learning experiences are changes that are well within the control of teachers, whether they work in an environment, where a national or local curriculum is prescribed or not. On the other hand, the learning experiences are clearly only one part of the intertwined helix that we call a curriculum. To complete the picture, we also need to consider the components of knowledge, which complement and amplify in interaction the learning experiences exemplified above.

Knowledge Components

As we have suggested above, the learning experiences are to be seen not as alternatives to the knowledge components of a curriculum, but rather as complementary to them, wherever possible representing coherent patterns, relationships and interconnections. Both are intended to contribute to enhanced cognitive, affective and conative sophistication, or put another way, to developing skills of socially responsible thinking, feeling and acting, delivered across the traditional subject categories of the curriculum in the case of many schools. Thus, for example, they will contribute to the development of thinking and other skills in students through activities centring around the commonly accepted components of human knowledge, skills and attitudes, including the dimension, introduced earlier in this book, at the four levels identified in the Introduction and now illustrated in Figure 2.4.

It is important to be aware that when we speak of knowledge, we are speaking of a range of complexity and human awareness, from simple factors to intricate chainings of principles, concepts, generalizations and theories. Concepts draw on knowledge and are particularly important to a multicultural and global approach, because they enable valid generalizations, categorizations and judgments to be made. They can also improve predictability and reduce the scope for misunderstandings, frustrations and conflicts in human affairs, or provide a 'common language' to make such conflicts creative and to resolve them where they occur. Particular care needs to be devoted to the development of valid concepts so that they do not become the epistemological haven where stereotypes and prejudiced views may reside and grow. Some categorizations of knowledge do indeed separate out concepts from other knowledge because the difference in degree of complexity and abstraction is regarded as a difference of kind.

For simplicity's sake, and because I see a continuum of complexity and potential usability of human knowledge, I intend to retain the categorization of knowledge, introduced at the beginning of this chapter, whilst at the same time emphasizing the interconnectedness of knowledge components and learning experiences, and, within the components, the interconnectedness of knowledge, skills and insights. *En passant*, I shall be exemplifying some of the concepts in the case of each knowledge domain, although, as with skills, many concepts overlap several components and require the students to draw on and collate information and mould it into principles and concepts. Moreover, it needs to be borne in mind that there are different levels of complexity of concepts and that the processes of observing accurately, classifying correctly and defining adequately are skills requiring practice and repetition as well as reflection. For, discriminating the characteristics of a concept requires the progressive development of both intellectual and verbal skills, such as discrimination, categorization and generalization, as does the connection of concepts, or variables so as to logically interrelate them in such a way as to form a reliable theory.

Even given that we know relatively little about teaching for theorizing (both building and utilization), particularly in the social sciences, the power of justification, explanation and predictability which this form of knowledge endows, makes it indispensable to the global multicultural curriculum, not least so that students can handle the limitations and potential of such theories as those of Marx and Freud, objectively, realistically and in an informed manner. In the scientific and environmental domains, in any case, students will have to encounter theories such as those of light, relativity and evolution and other grand theories in the natural sciences, and learn how to utilize them as a means of explaining and controlling their environment. So, although I shall be focusing on the knowledge domains, these are not to be seen as the acquisition of inert 'facts' as an end in themselves, but essential preconditions to the application of knowledge in daily life in a diversity of role, problem-solving and decision-making situations. In other words, they assist in empowering the students to gain greater purchase on his or her own life and environment.

Clearly, there is an almost endless list of factual information, which might be advocated for inclusion in a multicultural curriculum, which is at the same time permeated by a global concern. Even many ethnocentric curricula are already overburdened with factual content, acquired over the years on an accretion principle. Moreover, the exponential increase in the totality of human knowledge makes for the inclusion of an ever smaller proportion in the school curriculum. For this reason, it is essential that an integrative but highly selective approach is adopted to the permeation of the existing school curriculum with a global multicultural dimension.

To repeat what I said earlier, it is not part of the purpose of this book to assume a *carte blanche* for a totally new curriculum. That assumption would be unrealistic and, therefore, unproductive. Of course, the master aims and objectives act as a kind of intellectual yardstick for the selection of knowledge. That is why we spent so much time constructing them. What we can also do, however, is to use the typology, suggested in Figure 2.4, and based on a fairly widely-used categorization of knowledge components (see, for example, Cambridgeshire County Council, 1988), which can be taught through the whole curriculum, to exemplify an essential core 'portable valise' of knowledge, including concepts, principles, generalization and theories, that all students should legitimately be entitled to carry away on completion of their compulsory schooling as one of their student's rights.

In the human, social and economic domain, factual information will be necessary about the cultural composition and social structure of their own society, its economic and political systems, and the interrelationship of these with analogue systems abroad, not least in any regional or international organizations. This should include a map of the cultural profile of their own society and particular details about their own immediate community, its traditions and values. They should master such concepts as migration, democracy, totalitarianism, republic and monarchy, and understand the role that political systems and ideologies play and have played in human affairs. They will need to know of the economic problems of developing nations, not least in the area of international pricing of primary produce and currency, exchange rates and debt, and of the major inequalities of wealth and power in their country and the world.

They should know of the main human conflicts, their genesis and the way in which peaceful conflict resolution and conciliation can be achieved. They will need to know of the legal system of their country, how it works in outline, and of those areas with which they are most likely to come into contact, and where to go for further assistance and how to get it. They should know of different gender roles, but without stereotyping their incumbents. They need to be aware of their repsonsibilities as citizens, workers and members of families and their rights under the law. They will need to gradually master the ability to control concepts such as similarity and difference and to utilize them fairly. They will need to learn concepts such as supply and demand, capital and labour, wealth and poverty, family, kinship, ethnicity and community, social stratification, migration, power, justice and peace. They should be aware of prejudice in human affairs, how it arises and how it may be overcome, and that it comprises an emotional and cognitive dimension.

The aesthetic and creative domain is concerned with the way in which human kind has used its imagination, individually and collectively, to create aesthetic greatness to satisfy a deep-seated need for imaginative satisfaction through a host of different media. This domain should include the opportunity to learn of the outstanding contributions to world culture of members of their own community, their nation and other nations. They should gradually develop an awareness and competence in the ways in which they may contribute to those achievements. They should construct for themselves, but in interaction with their peers and teachers, their own criteria for sensory judgment, for aesthetic taste, beauty and responsible, socially acceptable creativity, being aware of alternative definitions of excellence in linguistic, musical, artistic, sportive and other recreational areas and in different geographical and historical locations, materials, media and traditions.

Students should develop aesthetic insights and construct their own concepts of what is good and beautiful in collaboration and in interaction with others. They should explore problems and decisions, involving the recognition, social location and cultural and moral justification or norms of taste, personal and social preference, and self and group interest, and their interconnectedness to the economic and moral domains. They should be able to differentiate and handle the difference between a statement of fact and one of value and taste, being aware of the emotional dimension of aesthetic and creative judgments, and be capable of recognizing it as a potential for bias, alienation and the stifling of the human spirit or, on the other hand, for greater humanity, sharing and the liberation of the human spirit.

In the linguistic and literary domain, more precisely, they should encounter their own community's literary and linguistic tradition and that of their nation. This should include some acquaintance, for younger children, with action rhymes, singing games, songs, sayings, puzzles and tongue-twisters. Knowledge of and sensitivity to paralanguage and kinesics should be included as important determinants of intercultural communication, as well as an understanding of the ways in which respect for persons can be conveyed through non-verbal cues, not least through such techniques as eye contact and smiling to indicate interest in a person and valuing of that person, not least in sympathetically dealing with cases of linguistic handicap of hearing or speaking. They should have an opportunity to learn another language, as a means of understanding alternative constructions of reality, and they should understand the function of language in establishing and maintaining relationships, as well as the strengths and weaknesses of different modes of communication, from direct to vicarious.

The linguistic and literary traditions may not always be located in the written word, and so other media such as film and television, archaeological remains, and at the other end of the time spectrum, information technology, will need to be encountered. But, they should also have an opportunity to gain a knowledge of the great world works of literature, both historical and contemporary, and to learn at least another language of their choice. Needless to say they must be encouraged to achieve individual excellence in the national language, speaking, listening, reading and writing, achieved through various media, including the learning experiences, referred to above, and to understand the fitness of purpose and audience of different registers of even the same language, including any local dialects.

The mathematical, scientific and technological domains may make a particularly important contribution to students' knowledge of relationships, patterns and generalizations, and of how they may gain greater purchase on their own lives and environments. In that sense, they are a major means to problem-solving and judging and thus central to the multicultural curriculum and its concern with peaceful and equitable resolution of conflicts and problems, locally, nationally and globally. This domain provides ample examples of both concepts and theories which can bridge cultures. Students should see the domain as comprising an international language and be aware of its presence and function in their own mother tongue and national language. They will need to appreciate the contribution of members of their own community and nation to scientific progress and those of other people's. They will need to be aware of the dangers as well as the advantages of such progress and the need for an ethical dimension. In particular, they will need to consider such issues as the consequences of 'irresponsible' science, such as space-related debris, chemical contamination, air-traffic pollution and the consequences of the travel and communications 'booms' for tourist host nations.

In the moral, ethical and spiritual domain pupils should of course learn of the different philosophical and religious traditions across the world and their impact on and contribution to contemporary morality. Particular emphasis should be placed on the commonalities of the major religions, including concepts such as justice and fairness, tolerance and humanity, and the reconciliation of individual and social rights and responsibilities. At the request of parents, students should also have access to more detailed acquaintance and knowledge of the religion of their own family or community. They should have an opportunity to discuss and internalize their own moral code, through encounter with both controversial issues and those problems to which there is no correct, right or wrong answer. They should know the difference between legality and morality and should also know of rules of custom and practice, which may be neither legal nor moral, but may control human norms and behaviour. They should be able to define concepts such as prejudice and stereotype, and know that such concepts can be immoral as well as have irrational universal consequences. They should know about reversibility, mutuality and solidarity, and be able to differentiate between fact and value statements and use practical syllogisms, principle-testing techniques and rules to test the validity of value claims and theories. They should be acquainted with the logic of value reasoning.

In the physical and environmental domain there is much for students to learn about the interdependence of people and planet, humans and animals, ecosystems and biosphere, not least their own contribution, through their style and volume of consumerism to pollution and depradation or unequal exploitation of the world's resources. They should know about such concepts as health, nutrition, sustainable development and conservation, approaches (local, national and international) to protect the environment, the major organizations concerned in the pursuit of these goals, as well as their own role in achieving them. They should acquire the capacity to help solve discomforting problems, arising from humankind's flagrant violation of its environment and malapplication of the results of scientific discovery. They should be equipped to become creative 'waste-watchers'! They should understand the importance of species preservation. From space, to air travel and sea lanes, human responsibility for weather changes, animal and plant extinction and other ecological disasters, such as the depletion of the ozone layer, to the neglect of their immediate environment, students should be exposed to knowledge of the consequences of humankind's cavalier and profligate treatment of the environment, often indeed of its neighbour's environment.

Of course, human knowledge represents an ever-increasing universe of almost indescribable complexity, and there is much overlap and interweaving of the domains of the knowledge components above. In any case, knowledge itself may comprise a wide range of states of awareness, from simple knowledge of a simple fact to comprehension of complex nexuses of principles or concepts. So, it is not suggested that the domains should be dealt with as discrete categories, but rather as webs of interrelationship, where, for example, economic exploitation of South by North leads to environmental disaster and often cultural and social disintegration, as in the jungles of the Amazon, or the forests of the Himalayas or the de-afforestation of Thailand.

But there is more to learning than information, facts and data centring around the above components, if students are to learn to review critically and reflectively their own actions and practices, scrutinizing them for their moral rectitude, factual correctness and social justice, and act accordingly. I have argued above that the multicultural curriculum is *par excellence* a skills-based curriculum, which can deliver physical, intellectual and social abilities acquired through reflection and practice interactively.

Skills usually nestle in a knowledge base, thus the term 'know-how'. But they are much more than knowledge and they include both reflection and repetition for practice. Moreover, the provision of a skill is no guarantee of the usage of that skill. So, for effective learning to be activated in the form of behaviour, attitudes have also to be nurtured. For this to be achieved, careful attention needs to be devoted to the development and integration of the various components of knowledge, seen coherently and holistically. Thus, in a sense, there is a kind of cyclical relationship between knowledge, attitudes and skills. I enter this as a small caveat at this stage, to remind us of the unitary nature of human learning, before embarking in the next section of this chapter on a consideration of the development of skills in the global multicultural curriculum, referring particularly to the crucial importance of thinking skills.

Developing Skills

There are basically two main areas of skill: cognitive skills, including both rational and intuitive; and, motor skills, which relate to physical movement. In practice, a skill may spread across both physical and cognitive areas, as is the case with basic skills such as writing. Skills are central in the educational enterprise and without them both knowledge and attitudes lose their efficacy. Of course, the reverse is also true, namely that without knowledge there can be no skill (although equally not all knowledge about skill is necessary to its performance), and without the correct attitude, the latent skill will remain unused. The essence of a skill is reflective practice, followed by internalization; when proficiency has been reached the skill becomes automatic. Because the global multicultural curriculum must aim to deliver cognitive, affective and conative learning, a reflexive capacity has to be built into the organization of teaching and learning. Such a reflexive approach demands a concentration on systematic development and improvement of skills throughout schooling, and nowhere more so than in the area of the thinking skills, which can support that reflexivity. Such a curriculum might concentrate on the accomplishment of the following thinking skills:

- Brainstorming ideas, including the generation of multiple imaginative solutions to problems (combined social and intellectual skills).
- Identifying sources of information (scanning and garnering skills).
- Obtaining information and requesting help from others (inquiry skills).
- Developing productive questions (integrative skills).
- Evaluating and analysing information and patterns (evaluative and analytical skills).
- Imagining alternatives (creative skills).
- Identifying consequences (interpretive skills).
- Determining values involved (ethical skills).
- Clarifying priorities (ordering and decision-making skills).
- Assessing consequences (problem-solving skills for divergence and convergence).
- Applying criteria (objectifying skills).
- Making judgments and inferences (inductive reasoning skills).
- Formulating valid conclusions (evidential skills).
- Reasoning probabilistically (estimating, hypothesizing and testing skills).

Of course, any such list must be articulated to the age and stage of development of the children, and the teacher's success in achieving skill development will be as much a function of the methods and approaches adopted, as of the content defined. Certainly for thinking skill development, a fostering of appropriately planned group work is essential, as is also an ambience within the school conducive to students taking increasing responsibility as they move up the school and developmental stages.

Attitude Development

A detailed list of the attitude objectives for a global multicultural curriculum has already been given in Chapter 1. That list concentrated on three major areas of attitude: person-oriented, for example, caring, mutuality, concern and respect for others, appreciation of a common heritage, empathy with those less fortunate or subject to persecution; societally-oriented, for example, commitment to civic values of democracy, to civil and human rights, at home and abroad, to peaceful resolution of human conflict; and, world-oriented, for example, concerned with world citizenship in the economic, political and environmental spheres, and particularly in relationships with developing countries.

Fundamental to that list was the basic ethic of respect for persons and the need for schools to take on board more forcefully an education to counter prejudice and discrimination, through the curriculum as a whole as well as through all aspects of the school's life. Such an approach presupposes a more deliberated, systematic and intentional approach to the cultivation of specific attitudes than has hitherto been the case, with some schools and teachers arguing that attitude and value development was not their responsibility, while others argued that it was inherent in every aspect of the school's life and did not, therefore, need to be addressed explicitly by the curriculum. I do not accept that either of these two positions is morally or socially tenable, but I do accept that most teachers are not well equipped by their training to undertake attitude education.

As knowledge and skills require the right attitude before they can be utilized, so attitudes require both knowledge and skills. Attitudes are the elements of our character which predispose us to think and behave in particular ways. In that sense, they are the expression of our personality and underlying value assumptions. They comprise both cognitive and affective dimensions, and some scholars (Allport, 1954) have suggested that the major problem in prejudiced attitudes relates to thought. Admittedly most work in this area has been undertaken with adults, but it is perhaps just as likely with children that when confronted with new, ambiguous or threatening social situations, the tendency is to respond categorically by using group characteristics, for the simple reason that it is easier to do so. Thus the emphasis above on thinking skills has to be seen, from the very beginning of schooling, as an essential and strong dimension of any curriculum which seems to attenuate and alter unhealthy social attitudes, expressive of racial, gender, ethnic or credal prejudice. This applies not least in the field of perceptual differentiation, where early training and acquaintance (for example with persons with difference features), directly or vicariously, can hinder the development of negative attitudes if linked with appropriate strategies and approaches to support it.

I have already referred to the problem of overcategorization and the need to develop methods of teaching and curricula which strike a balance between concern for similarity and difference, and I have emphatically stated the basic ethic of the global multicultural curriculum as 'respect for persons'. I have also flagged the results of those approaches which have, sometimes inadvertently, augmented category salience and there- fore reinforced prejudice. The alternative, it seems to me, is a curricu- lum which emphasizes similarity and common values, and enables students to examine their reasons for wishing to treat 'others' differently from the way they wish to be treated themselves. This implies an emphasis on thinking skills and the ability to reason things through to a morally tenable solution. Such an approach requires elaborative think- ing and reasoning competences to be cultivated in every student if early consolidation of cognitive and perceptual cues into inappropriate con- cepts are to be dislodged. Techniques such as those associated with principle testing, role exchange, reasons assembly charts, etc., may be found to be helpful in fostering attitude improvement (Association for Values Education and Research, 1978).

Assessment and Evaluation

Teachers need to appraise how far they are achieving the goals they have set themselves, and students and parents have the right to expect feedback on their learning from their teachers and guidance, based on that feedback, with regard to how they can improve. There are basically two aspects to this process: assessment of the student's performance and evaluation of the curriculum, within which I include the teacher's own professional appraisal of his or her own practice an the school's review of its performance as a whole. Both are essential and interactive aspects of the continual monitoring of the global multicultural curriculum.

The assessment objectives for such a curriculum will be both generic and synoptic on the one hand, and specific to tasks and timetabled subjects and activities on the other. The danger is that, because of epistemological boundaries, reinforced by timetable divisions and separation, the latter usually takes precedence, sometimes exclusive dominance, and the synoptic appraisal by the school of its holistic knowledge, attitude and skill objectives is forgotten and neglected. So, those wishing to plan and implement an appropriate assessment strategy for a global multicultural curriculum face a two-fold problem – of what balance and priority to give to each of the components of knowledge and learning experiences, and how to link that balance and priority to the assessment rationale for the school as a whole and its priorities and balance, currently dominated by an examinational-loaded, subject separated assessment philosophy. This latter philosophy could presumably support an assessment which would designate the acquisition of predominantly cognitively loaded examination results as more important by far than the acquisition of healthy, unprejudiced attitudes of the ability to work harmoniously and creatively as a member of a group – objectives which are central to a multicultural curriculum.

Thus, a 'whole school' policy for assessment and evaluation is necessary which does not exclude the importance of examination results, but can draw a balance between those and other important aspects of students' development, projecting a kind of ideal profile of performance across both academic and social dimensions, related to the objectives listed in Chapter 1. Those objectives propose a balance between the abilities associated with the obtaining and organization of information and those concerned with the social use of that information in problem-solving, decision making and the forging of satisfactory human relationships in cultural, social, economic and environmental spheres at the three levels. As in the case of the curriculum, so in the area of assessment, a set of procedural principles of assessment and evaluation are needed, which might address issues such as:

- The assessment policy for the school will seek to be as culture-fair as possible.
- The content, rubrics and procedures for assessments will be scrutinized for race, sex, ethnic and credal bias.
- Special arrangements will be made for those with special cultural or religious needs, including the handicapped.
- The pictures of other countries portrayed in examination papers will be balanced, up-to-date and fair.
- Examinations will be set that test judgment as well as factual knowledge, and where research, expert help and advice from others

as well as their interests and decisions may have to be taken into account.

- Emphasis will be placed on the demonstration of thinking and other skills, particularly in dealing with areas concerned with issues of taste, personal preference, self, family or group interest.
- All students will have a school profile, which will include details of their achievements in areas other than examinations, including any work in social action at home or abroad.
- Students will have opportunities for group projects and for involvement in their own assessment.
- A wide variety of opportunities for students to demonstrate performance in both discrete and integrated tasks through different modes and media will be offered.
- Students will have a right to see their own records, apart from any material provided to the school on a confidential and privileged basis.
- An annual appraisal of examinations and assessment against the school objectives will be conducted, which will lead to the normal process of feedback to all parties and agreement on action.

The above list is tentative and incomplete, seeking to illustrate and stimulate rather than prescribe or constrain. The issue of professional evaluation and techniques for professional appraisal is taken up in Chapter 5. For the moment it suffices to underline once again that assessment and evaluation are integral and interactive with the curriculum. In tandem with the progress of the students being monitored, the professional performance of the teachers and the school needs to be monitored. In the global multicultural curriculum, assessment and evaluation are equally evidential to success as the aims, objectives and content of the curriculum. Assessment and evaluation should be expressive of the same values and ideals, including lack of bias and prejudice, respect for persons, community membership and responsibility, and national and international citizenship across cultural, social, economic and environmental dimensions.

While I do not underestimate the challenge to schools to make their assessment congruent with their declared ideals for the kinds of individuals they wish to produce in a context of great diversity and student difficulty, failure to test out their own effectiveness in the pursuit of those ideals may frustrate their very goals, and nowhere more so than in the important area of human relations and rights, citizenship and moral responsibility. To retrieve the phrase used in the Introduction, when we were looking at the implications of a global multicultural curriculum for teachers, we need hard evidence about our students' learning and progress across the levels and dimensions. As good conscientious professionals, committed to continual improvement, we need hard evidence about our own effectiveness. Unwillingness or inability to produce it may alienate students and parents, reduce student achievement because of lack of feedback and it may, moreover, seduce others into seeking to impose unilaterally their partisan view of what should be assessed, and therefore what should be taught. Where that road leads has been amply illustrated in recent history, perhaps also in the contemporary world.

Chapter Summary

Following the closer identification and explanation of the master aims and operational objectives for schools, which we developed in Chapter 1, this chapter has been concerned with what we mean in this book by the term curriculum and what the building blocks are which comprise it: the knowledge components (information, skills, attitudes and values) and the complementary learning experiences. We have identified five major concept characteristics of the global multicultural curriculum: cultural balance, global breadth, cultural and social equity, economic responsibility and environmental custodianship. And we have described their implications for the process of curriculum development: knowledge and experiences.

En passant, we have had a look at previous attempts to develop a curriculum which responded to cultural diversity: ethnic studies, folkloric multicultural education, permeative multicultural education, anti-racist education, intergroup education, and prejudice reduction approaches. We have scrutinized them for their shortcomings and, in particular, for their unintended emphasis on social category salience. Then, we looked in greater detail at the learning experiences, highlighting the 'active' and skills-based nature of the global multicultural curriculum and the need to achieve reflective decision-making, judgment and social action, in order to empower students to gain greater purchase on their lives. After this, we considered the knowledge components of the curriculum in terms of the knowledge domains, at individual, ethnic, national and international levels, and emphasized the importance of concepts, theory building and usage, skills (particularly thinking skills), attitudes and values. We concluded the chapter by briefly referring to the need for continual assessment and evaluation and by suggesting a series of principles for an outline rationale for a school monitoring and evaluation policy.

In Chapter 3 we travel to the very heart of the multicultural curriculum, to the area of human rights and education for human rights. Whilst it could be argued that many of the initiatives advocated in Chapters 1 and 2 have already been initiated in some form in some schools, nowhere has that implementation been so slender as in the area of human rights, least of all perhaps in the area of children's rights. And yet, without human rights we lack a major moral yardstick, on a global basis, for human dignity, justice and fairness for society at large and even more so in the very fulcrum of cultural transmission, namely the school and its curriculum. And so, in Chapter 3, we present a rationale for the perception of human rights as the core of a global multicultural curriculum. Objectives are suggested as well as content, and teaching approaches are described with reference being made to the progress of countries such as Canada in institutionalizing their commitment to human rights within education and the school curriculum in the context of a multicultural society.

Chapter 3

Human Rights: The Core of the Curriculum

In Chapter 2 we considered ways in which the existing curriculum could be improved to include a greater commitment to global multicultural concerns, without making the same mistakes made by previous curricular and broader educational efforts at responding to cultural diversity. For this reason, and building on the definitions of cultural diversity introduced in Chapter 1, we considered a number of curricular strategies, which had been mounted to take account of that cultural diversity. I presented a brief typology of the major approaches: ethnic studies, folkloric multicultural education, permeative multicultural education, anti-racist education, intergroup education and prejudice reduction. I pencilled in some of their intended and unintended effects and consequences, and particularly the unfortunate contribution, which some of them had unconsciously made to the augmentation of social category salience, of greater perception of difference and increased prejudice. Then, seeking to learn from their strengths and weaknesses, I moved to consider the shape and content of a multicultural curriculum, centrally committed to a global perspective, particularly in its core are of human rights and responsibilities. (That core commitment and its implications for teachers and schools is the subject of this chapter.)

Next, I proposed five concept characteristics, which would typify and permeate a global multicultural education: cultural balance, global breadth, cultural and social equity, economic responsibility and environmental custodianship. The normal building blocks of curriculum development were then used to illustrate how a curriculum can be reoriented through evolution from what exists to a global multicultural perspective. Firstly, learning experiences were discussed and exemplified; then, the knowledge components were introduced in terms of knowledge, skills and attitudes. Emphasis was placed on seeing the components at the four levels (individual, ethnic, national and global), and each of the domains of content was illustrated and concepts from that domain were exemplified. Reference was also made to the important role of theorizing and generalization in human thought processes. Particular attention was given to the development of skills, especially thinking skills, which can contribute so importantly to attitude and behavioural change to correct for stereotyping and prejudice and to greater predictability of acceptable human behaviour.

Reaching back to the list of attitude objectives encountered in Chapter 1, the importance, difficulty and delicacy of teaching for attitude change was stressed, and the interrelationship and interdependence of attitudes, skills and knowledge was reiterated. Finally, the interactive nature of curriculum and assessment and evaluation was considered. Attention was drawn to the need for a 'whole school' policy, comprehending all aspects of school life and relationships, and a holistic overview of the extent to which individuals and the institution are attaining their objectives and, especially, those objectives which spread across several or all timetable slots and embrace one or more of the normal curriculum compartments. Elements for a rationale for assessment and evaluation were suggested and discussed. Examples of some procedural principles for assessment and related reported and recording policies were also suggested.

In this chapter I shall be penetrating my arguments for the introduction of a global multicultural curriculum to the very heart of education, namely to its moral and ethical generator plant that produces and secures the values which support it. I argue here that it is the field of human rights in a democratic society which gives to education its moral mandate and which prescribes the values that it should transmit. After a brief discussion, therefore, of the body of international and regional Human Rights Declarations and their implications for education, I shall focus quite sharply on the rights of school students, using them as a basis to inform the later identification of policies, procedures, ethos, structure, curricular principles and core content, which may facilitate a permeation of the moral authority of human rights throughout the whole school, its structure, processes, staffing and relationship with students and the community. I shall be defining what I mean by human rights education and emphasizing the process nature of such endeavours and the need to actively engage school students in dynamically and creatively constructing their own political reality in connection with human rights, rather than seeing the task as one of filling vessels with knowledge about human rights instruments and covenants. I shall be illustrating the relationship of human rights to the whole school ethos and underlining the need for a democratic school and classroom ethos to deliver an effective human rights education.

Human Rights: The Core Values

In the early hours of the morning of 10 December 1948, in the Palais Challiot in Paris, the Universal Declaration of Human Rights was presented to the General Assembly of the United Nations. It was approved *nem. con.* by forty-eight votes, with only eight abstentions. Henceforth, for education, that momentous and magnificent event placed an imperative on any curriculum and school, certainly in a democratic society, which seeks to prepare for 'respect for persons'. It forged an essential and indispensable moral framework that can never again be ignored. It was a kind of latter-day Ten Commandments, although much more complex, extensive and detailed and for all religions, peoples and for the whole of human kind. In a world, where, in any case, moral precept by religious prescription was giving way rapidly to instrumental and lay regulation, it provided an international yardstick for national and personal moral judgment and a global audience and 'lay court of appeal'. Its thirty articles cover freedom of thought, religion, expression and assembly. They include passages on discrimination, torture and unfair detention, and cover rights to life, a home, work, education and health.

In this chapter, therefore, we come to the very fulcrum of the global multicultural curriculum: human rights and responsibilities, and the kind of education which can help to make actual, in the school in the first instance, the vision, interpretation and reality of human worth and dignity contained in the ringing Declaration of Human Rights, and contained now in over fifty international instruments. Naturally, I accept that many of the Declaration's ideals are just aspirations and hopes rather than reality to the majority of the world's population. I acknowledge also, that the gap between what is meant by human rights in different parts of the world is enormous. It ranges from the freedom of imprisoned dissidents and the right to emigrate, through the right not to be homeless or hungry, discriminated against or uneducated, to the right not to starve to death and to have a fair price for the products of one's labour and freedom from arbitrary arrest and inhuman treatment and torture. I recognize, with particular shame, that in the contemporary world many children are subject to abuse, exploitation, abduction, slavery, torture, imprisonment, neglect, starvation, inhuman surgical practices, deprivation of education and summary execution. I concede that this code of acceptable human conduct has never found the secure place in the curricula of many of the world's schools which is so routinely occupied by analogous religious or political codes, and that many countries ignore it.

But that event, over forty years ago, had one immediate and direct consequence, and one longer-term and cumulative consequence, if only in the act of declaration itself. In the first case it took issues of human rights out of a purely domestic arena, brushed aside the cobwebbed protestations of those who would have secrecy to cloak their inhuman behaviour and denial of human dignity, and made human rights a global issue, a global concern, a matter for all the world's citizens and, therefore, implicitly, an essential part of the education of those citizens and their children. In the second case, by the customary law of nations it has become binding on nations, and together with the two covenants on civil and political rights and economic, social and cultural rights respectively, and with the optional protocol giving individuals the right to petition over the heads of their rulers, and the approximately sixty instruments which have grown up around these two covenants, it constitutes an interrelated body of international law, including codes of conduct and complaints procedures. In some instances, as for example in the case of torture, the important extra-territorial principle of international jurisdiction has also more recently been introduced.

Indirectly, too, even if 'policing' of that body of law has never been a high priority for governments (there is still no United Nationals Human Rights Commissioner), it has led to the establishment of world organizations such as Amnesty International, which now has almost a million members in over 150 countries. In 1985, a special rapporteur to examine matters of torture was appointed, together with two others with power to intercede. Many newly independent countries have incorporated some of its ideals in their constitutions; other countries, such as Canada, have accorded their citizens a Charter of Rights and Freedoms and established mechanisms, including educational ones, to implement it, while yet others, such as the United Kingdom, have found themselves pronounced guilty of human rights breaches at regional courts such as the European Court of Human Rights, with alarming regularity.

Of course, there are also Charters and Covenants at regional and national levels too. Canada has both a Human Rights Act, passed in 1977, and a Charter of Rights and Freedoms, dating from 1982 and attached to its constitution. It is interesting to note that Section 27 of the Charter specifically supports the preservation and enhancement of the multicultural heritage of Canadians. There is also a more recent Multiculturalism Act as well, which aims to give full legislative expression to the racial and cultural diversity of Canada, to provide for a race relations strategy, to engage the public in overcoming prejudice and discrimination, and institutions in securing equality, regardless of race, colour, age, religion or sex. There are extensive structural facilities at national and provincial levels for the enforcement of all these provisions. The United States also has Civil Rights legislation and a Commission at national level, with other organs at state and sometimes county levels. Countries such as Great Britain have legislation against racial and gender discrimination but not yet against religious intolerance or discrimination.

At a regional level, there is the European Convention on Human Rights, which was signed in 1950 and came into force on 3 September 1953. It is intended to guarantee at European level a number of the principles of the Universal Declaration. The main organs for the enforcement of the Convention are the European Commission and Court of Human Rights, the former with a predominantly conciliation and inquiry role, whereas the Court has the power to make judicial decisions, which are binding on member states. The main rights and freedoms protected by the Convention are the rights to life, liberty and security of person, fair administration of justice, respect for private and family life, home and correspondence, freedom of thought, conscience and religion, expression and the holding of opinions, peaceful assembly and association, membership of a trade union, to marry and found a family. In addition, protection in the protocols covers other items including certain rights to education, and the Court has pronounced on such educational issues as corporal punishment and compulsory sex education in schools.

Such instruments, to which most democratic countries are party, must have fundamental consequences for education in those societies. As Starkey (1986, p. 58) so eloquently states, there are some values which education in a democratic society stands for unreservedly, and, quoting the Director of the French National Research Centre, Mme Francine Best, he argues that human rights provide the core or the heart of the new moral and civic education. Indeed, in a pluralist world there is no other moral codification available to and commonly accepted by humankind to regulate relationships and to express and protect the worth and dignity of all human beings. Religions are partial, in the sense that they are accepted by some and not by others; in some cases they are even a source of bigotry, conflict and infringements of human rights. They are tied to particular traditions, even regions of the world. The same applies to political ideologies. So where is the area of moral values beyond diversity (Boulding, 1988, pp. 64ff), if it is not in human rights?

Only human rights chart the area above and beyond sectional

religious and political traditions in that they are universal principles and entitlements which should apply to all human beings without exception, explicitly because they are human beings. Whilst it is true that they were originally constructed under the influence of a Judaeo-Christian tradition, they now carry with them both moral international recognition and the overt support and authority of the world organization, the United Nations, that they shall not be subject to unfair or arbitrary limitation. Further, they represent an interrelated system, not a hierarchy or set of priority choices from which some are more separable than others. They are indivisible and mutual, for in the exercise of these rights there is the responsibility to be careful with the rights of others; furthermore these rights are not located in power.

Even the most powerful government does not have the right to withdraw these rights from the least of its citizens. As Singh (1986, p. 76) has argued, human rights are the value expressions which derive from the very fact of the humanity of human beings – a fact which cannot be altered. They represent claims, based on and deriving from that unalterable fact, to satisfaction of basic life needs and purposes, and, quoting Vandenberg, Singh argues that moral principles involving such universal obligations and unalterable rights should form the ethical foundation of the whole curriculum, and inform the whole process of education, including professional relationships and ethics. That balance of rights and obligations, entitlements and responsibilities as the fundament of all education is the ethical and practical position represented by this book.

In sum, human rights represent the only universally recognized code for the regulation of human behaviour across the levels and dimensions of the global multicultural curriculum; human rights go beyond cultural diversity to the domain of common humanity, common values and common entitlements. In this respect they reinforce the sense of similarity, of human unity, and attitudes of reciprocity and solidarity, which are at the heart of a global multicultural curriculum. They diminish rather than enhance social category salience. They alone embrace and comprehend all cultural diversity, including moral diversity, and extend it. They are normative statements about human life. They derive from the very existence of that life, they apply everywhere and to everyone, and are, thus, the only universal body of moral guidance on the relationships of individuals, groups and nations, and internally within nations.

Within no social system of the nation state is the existence of these normative ideals, or value statements, more important than in the very power-house of cultural transmission, namely the education system. In pluralist societies the education system, especially teachers, schools and educational administrators, are particularly vulnerable with regard to the ethical basis of their professional judgments and they are increasingly called to account for their decisions and assessments. But against what criteria can those judgments and decisions be accountable? The very pluralism of those societies has been a cause of their confusion, with some even asserting that it is not the task of the schools and teachers to transmit values, an argument I regard as being so naive as to be incredible. The very act of education implies the learning of culture, which comprises not only knowledge but also values, attitudes, symbols and language. So, in educating one is transmitting, implicitly or explicitly, overtly or covertly, consciously or unintentionally, subject to public scrutiny or subliminally, values as well as knowledge.

So, to return to our question of the criteria or norms against which educators and others may justify their educational decisions and judgments other than on a random basis, one is left with national and local laws and regulations, and/or human rights. But, in many cases national laws are inadequate. They can be used by majorities to impose settlements, which may be unjust to minorities or individuals and which are not mutual in the sense of being explicitly or implicitly discriminatory. In times of excess they may be used to infringe the fundamental values of humanity. They are too large meshed, and in any case law can only provide a framework and cannot be used to monitor the minute and frequent decisions which teachers are called on to make every day in their classrooms.

But the law of individual nations and provinces is a rough and unwieldy monitor for the multitude of interactions which take place every day even in a single school. There has always needed to be a moral code as well as a legal code, which could influence and guide human beings in their more secret and unobserved decisions, and to hold them rationally accountable for those as well as their more public judgments. The only such means available universally – and as a particular way to solve the conflicts of interest and moral dilemmas inherent in a culturally diverse society, and which can be legitimated amongst all cultural groups – is the body of human rights, that is the inalienable entitlement of all humans, and not least school students – without any further qualification.

Children's Rights

Before moving to the implications of the Universal Declaration and similar documents for education, and more narrowly the school curriculum and teaching approaches, it is perhaps apposite to remind ourselves that one of the major implications of these declarations emerges for children and school students. It is evident that they are no less human beings and no less entitled to their basic human rights because they occupy a transient and temporary status, that of childhood, and, for the lucky ones, 'schoolhood' as well. Indeed, they are surely entitled to additional rights, protection and care, although the progress towards the explicit acceptance of those rights has been painfully slow.

As early as 1924 the special status of children was recognized in the Geneva Declaration of the Rights of the Child and later in the Declaration of the Rights of the Child, which was adopted unanimously by the United Nations General Assembly on 20 November 1979. But these declarations have no legal force and they are only the first and easiest stage in securing the rights of children, which still continue to be so cruelly abused in so many parts of the world. In 1966, therefore, the International Covenant on Civil and Political Rights (in Articles 23 and 24, in particular) and the International Covenant on Economic, Social and Cultural Rights (in Article 10, in particular) underlined the need for special protection and care for the child. They were passed in 1966 but did not come into force until 1976. The need for extending particular care to the child is also enshrined in the statutes of such specialized United Nations agencies as Unesco and Unicef. Once again, however, these provisions are not readily or really enforceable, and they have, in any case, only been adopted by a minority of countries.

In 1979, twenty years on from the Declaration of the Rights of the Child, the United Nations designated 1979 as International Year of the Child, encouraging all nations to review their provisions and programmes for the well-being of children. That year also saw the first moves towards a new international convention, consequent on the adoption in 1978 by the United Nations Commission on Human Rights of a proposal made by the Polish Government to set up a working party to consider a new draft Convention of the Rights of the Child. Work on that Convention was substantially completed by 1988, with formal proposals expected by the end of the decade. Article 15 of the draft Convention states:

> States Parties shall take all appropriate measures to ensure that school discipline is administered in a manner reflective of the child's human dignity.

Article 15 has particular regard to the needs of developing countries in regard to the elimination of ignorance and illiteracy and the development of modern teaching methods. And a little later in the proposed Article 15, the Convention also includes the need to prepare children for life in a free society, in a spirit of understanding and friendship among all peoples ethnic and religious groups and for the development and respect for the natural environment (Children's Legal Centre, 1986, pp. 17–20).

Yet the United Nations Children's Fund (Unicef) in its yearly Report still continued into the 1980s to document the denial of basic rights to children, cataloguing over 40,000 young children dying of malnutrition and infection every day, and over a quarter of a million living in hunger and ill health, with millions lacking basic education, seventy million forced to work, drafted into armies, physically and sexually abused and sold or otherwise forced into slavery (Children's Legal Centre, 1983, pp. 11–14).

The situation for those in school is also more honoured in the breach of their rights than in their observance. Thus, as Brown (1983, p. 39) points out, the Universal Declaration itself affords them rights such as freedom and equality in dignity and rights (Article 1), freedom from discrimination (Article 2), protection against degrading treatment or punishment (Article 5), recognition as a person before the law (Article 6), a fair and public hearing (Article 10), and protection from arbitrary interference with privacy and from attacks upon honour and reputation (Article 12). But their rights are not restricted to these universal ones and certainly not diminished by their childhood. In fact the reverse is the case, with the UN Declaration of the Rights of the Child affording special protection to children, when it states in Principle 2:

> The child shall enjoy special protection, and shall be given opportunities and facilities, by law and by other means, to enable him to develop, physically, mentally, morally, spiritually and socially in a healthy and normal manner and in conditions of freedom and dignity. In the enactment of laws for this purpose, the best interests of the child shall be the paramount consideration (United Nations, 1978, p. 114).

Later, and in specific relation to the educational rights of the child, the same Declaration states that the child

> shall be given an education which will promote his general culture and enable him, on the basis of equal opportunity, to develop his abilities, his individual judgment, and his sense of moral and social responsibility, and to become a useful member

of society . . . [the child] shall be brought up in a spirit of understanding, tolerance, friendship among peoples, peace and universal brotherhood, and in full consciousness that his energy and talents should be devoted to the service of his fellow men (United Nations, 1978, p. 115).

Whilst the sexist language of the Declaration may jar in the world of the late 1980s, the sentiments, ideals and moral direction and authority are clear. School students of whatever age are human beings and have rights! Moreover, those rights are also explicit in regional agreements, covenants and conventions. The European Convention on Human Rights, for example guarantees to everyone, including school students, all the rights contained within it. Indeed, the European Parliament passed a Resolution in March 1984 emphasizing that the school system has no choice but to comply with the Convention (Children's Legal Centre, 1987, p. 53). The most important articles for school students are Article 3, which outlaws torture, inhuman or degrading treatment or punishment; Article 8, on the right to respect for private and family life, home and correspondence; Article 10, on the right to freedom and expression, including the right to receive and impart information and ideas; Article 11, on freedom of association; Article 14, on freedom from discrimination on the grounds of sex, race, colour, language, religion, political or other opinion, association with a national minority, property birth or other status; and Article 2 of Protocol 1 on the right to education.

And yet, in spite of the 'rights to the consumer' trend of the 1970s and 1980s, and the impetus given by the International Year of the Child in 1979, the establishment of organizations such as the Children's Legal Centre in London and analogue organizations elsewhere, there are many areas where school students do not have explicit rights and entitlements such as rights to participation, involvement in decisions which affect them, to consultation etc. Children are only rarely recognized as a group with the automatic entitlement to have their views considered, to whom those who take decisions affecting them should be accountable, let alone have a right of independent appeal to a Children's Ombudsperson, as in Norway. These gaps are particularly acute in areas such as the right to a fair hearing, freedom from discrimination, freedom from violence, the right to adequate and confidential health services, freedom of information and privacy. In this latter respect, there are still no rules limiting the disclosure of school records on a national basis, except those held on computer. These items form a tentative agenda to be taken on board as part of a whole school policy later in this section.

A Definition of Human Rights Education

Insofar as human rights provide us with a universal system of moral values, which should underpin all human relationships at whatever level, they are an essential part of all schooling, not least in a democratic society. Indeed, they are one of the guarantees of the continuation of that society, insofar as they lock in place many of the fundamental freedoms and entitlements which democratic societies accord to their citizens. However, those in power often take those rights out of the realm of the grace and favour of that society. An individual or group has a right to them automatically, and not at the gift of that society. They are, in other words, at the same time guarantors of those freedoms and facilitators of the system that supports them. In education they are both the cultural values which should underlie the structure and part of the structure in the form that we call a curriculum. Thus, reaching back to the definition of curriculum and its components as outlined in Chapter 2, human rights education is not simply a matter of the knowledge components, still less of knowledge itself. Nor are they indeed solely a matter of curriculum, but of the ethos and values procedures, processes, policies and practices in every facet of the life and functioning of school in a democratic society. Human rights education is thus a moral education about the way that human beings behave towards each other in the family, in groups, in their community, in their nation and globally. It is thus about thinking, feeling and acting or cognitive, affective and conative dimensions of education.

On the other hand, knowledge of the accepted body of international agreements, covenants and conventions, their genesis and implementation, and the organizations, structures and procedures involved must surely be a part of the curriculum of any school that claims to prepare active citizens for participatory democratic society. Such knowledge, built into what we might term a reasonable content and concept base, at some time during compulsory schooling, will be an important interlocutor with and vehicle for the acquisition of skills and attitudes. For, it must be the aim of human rights education to deliver the skills, attitudes, processes and activities, rather than to encourage mere recall of knowledge or even concepts for their own sake. So, additionally it demands and implies the acquisition of such skills as advocacy, petitioning and moral reasoning, attitudes of empathy, solidarity and reciprocity, moral values of respect for persons and their humanity, active commitments to protection and guardianship of those rights which are also essential components of any education, core-committed to human rights. We shall be returning to the reasonable knowledge and concept bases for human rights education later in this chapter.

Retrieving the levels and dimensions of a global multicultural curriculum, human rights education pervades the four dimensions (cultural, social, economic and environmental), explicitly mentioning the first three and implicitly involving the last. Further, they are not just a matter of individual rights but also of social responsibilities to communities, nations and the international community. They thus pervade the four levels (individual, ethnic, national and international). Moreover, human rights education also involves the five concept characteristics of a global multicultural education (cultural balance, global breadth, cultural and social equity, economic responsibility and environmental custodianship). Infringements of any of these characteristics can imply an infringement of basic human rights.

For example, environmental exploitation which involves taking away the environmental resources of populations in developing countries or exploiting natural resources such as minerals and then leaving the local population to clean up, may also take away their right to a livelihood and to health, and coincidentally their own and their family's right to life. The stripping of the rain forests in the Himalayas for fine furniture in the West, or sometimes for tourist trinkets, may not only uproot indigenous populations from their culture and homes, it may also result in the rains shedding too rapidly from the mountains onto the plains and causing flooding and climate change as well as erosion of agricultural land and soil, which may deprive others of food, security and life. The enforcement of a cash crop economy onto populations, which then have no means of feeding themselves when world demand for their cash crop declines and the commodity price crashes, may also result in starvation and death.

Tarrow (1988a, p. 1) has suggested that human rights education is a conscious effort through both specific content and process to develop in students an awareness of their rights and responsibilities, to sensitize them to the rights of others and to encourage responsible action to secure the rights of all. She suggests that a number of assumptions about both content and process underlie this tripartite definition, and I believe that there is much that we can extract from her statement which will assist us in our quest for strategies to implement human rights pervaded global multicultural education in our schools. Certainly, it very usefully alerts us once again to the individual and social awareness dimensions of human rights education on the one hand, and the social action skills dimension on the other. So, let us see what principles we may put together from the implications of that statement for our own definition and policy.

Firstly, it surely implies that the educational environment and teaching/learning strategies must be expressive of human rights principles, respecting human dignity and protective of legitimate difference. This must imply a focus on the whole school, whole classroom and whole curriculum levels. I shall return to these crucial variables shortly. Secondly, it also seems to me to imply an active process of students constructing their own perceptions and realities of human rights in action, involved in and managing their own learning, appropriate to their age and ability to do so, and not just involving passive learning situations. Moreover, there is an expanding universe of perception of human rights as not static but expanding and human rights education has to continually respond to a new range of aspirations and legitimate demands (Tarrow, 1988b).

Further, it means that human rights education is not the exclusive concern of any one subject or timetable slot, although it will, of course, be necessary to identify and allocate responsibility, otherwise everyone's responsibility soon becomes no-one's responsibility. Thirdly, by dint of this common thread function and in the context of increasing cultural diversity, especially in western democratic societies, it serves a central function in the implementation of an education, responsive to cultural diversity, nationally and internationally. It throws open the window of curriculum to a necessary global perspective. And, fourthly, it provides a common 'trunk', to the many disparate, uncoordinated curriculum initiatives, which would seek to grow in a similar direction but which are really only branches of that basic concern. We have referred to some of these in the Introduction; Figure 3.1 seeks to illustrate the relationship and mode of interdependence of human rights education, as a communicant of basic values and part of the whole curriculum.

In other words, and returning to our earlier definition of the building blocks of the curriculum, human rights education interweaves and underpins all knowledge components and learning experiences. It provides both a unifying moral base and a marshalling intellectual coherence and interconnection for a global multicultural curriculum, and of the circumambient educational context essential for its delivery. Moreover, because a global multicultural curriculum comprehends and underlies other cognate areas of curriculum development, as illustrated

Figure 3.1: Human Rights Education and Whole School Policy

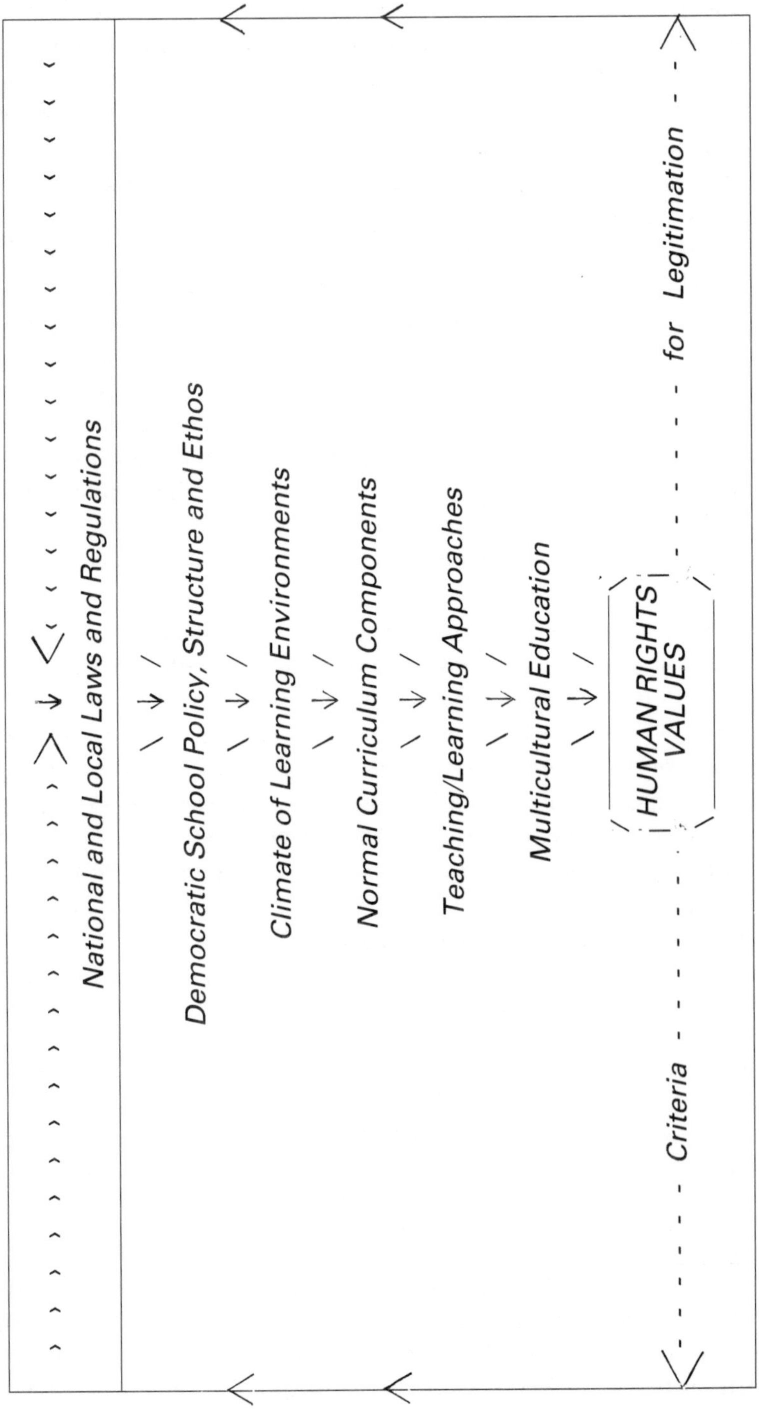

National and Local Laws and Regulations

Democratic School Policy, Structure and Ethos

Climate of Learning Environments

Normal Curriculum Components

Teaching/Learning Approaches

Multicultural Education

HUMAN RIGHTS VALUES

Criteria - - - - - - - - - - - - - - - - for Legitimation

in Chapters 1 and 2, human rights provides a useful tactical and strategic means of bypassing the proliferation of curricular initiatives, with which schools are currently faced. Many of these initiatives draw on human rights but adopt alternative curricular media to deliver the same values and content, with consequent content overload, confusion and dissipation of scarce resources and professional goodwill. Put plainly, it provides a legitimate basis for coalitioning.

If we define human rights education as the moral core of any education in a democratic society, it takes on a superordinate quality to which other more partial initiatives must be related and accountable, and with which they must comply. It has, in a sense, not only a kind of priority but a moral leadership authority as well. It offers a lay 'holy book' of humanity. As such, it provides a means of decision about the overall shape, ethos, content, aims and processes of education, and a resolution to the continuing dilemma in a pluralist democracy of what we should include in the curriculum.

An explicit commitment to human rights education at the systemic level also offers a moral authority to influence those schools which do not come within the direct control of the state system: a kind of legitimation of the persuasion that they also should include human rights as the core of their curricular and educational endeavours, that the education which they offer shall also be attentive to and congruent with human rights, not least those of its students. It thus helps to bridge the public and private sectors of education, and provides a means of detached and rational response to those (usually men) who claim that they should have the freedom to provide a separate, restricted, partly incarcerated education for their daughters . . . but not necessarily for their sons – a manifestly discriminatory policy.

Given the above considerations and arguments, we might define human rights education as:

> The basic moral education of all students, content and process, formal and informal, pervading all subjects and curriculum areas and providing ethical guidelines for the organisation of education, systematically, institutionally and individually, in all its facets, aims and intentions, content, procedures and processes, assessment and evaluation.

On the basis of that definition, we must now return to the issue of how it can be translated, packaged and implemented in practice in individual institutions, by teachers individually and corporately. This is the concern of the next section of this chapter. Let me, however, first of all recall the questions I posed with regard to human rights education in the Introduction. There were two major thrusts concerned with the question of how far human rights feature in the curriculum, and to what extent human rights considerations impact on the school, its policies, structure, ethos, process and procedures. As in the definition above, there are basically two dimensions: one is concerned with structural issues for the system as a whole or for individual schools; the other is concerned with cultural issues about the functions of those structures and, more specifically, functions in the transmission of a curriculum where curriculum is defined as both the learning experiences and content planned by the school and the intended processes. For simplicity's sake, and as a kind of shorthand, I intend to refer to the former of these dimensions as whole school policies and practice (the focus of this book is in any case on institutional rather than systemic issues). In the case of the latter dimension, I shall refer to curricular policy and practice.

A School Policy for Human Rights Education

This is not just multicultural education, but

At its 18th Session in 1974, the United Nations Educational, Scientific and Cultural Organisation (Unesco) adopted an important 'pathfinder' recommendation concerning Education for Human Rights and Fundamental Freedoms. That document set down a number of suggested major guidelines for educational policy, such as:

- An international dimension and a global perspective in education at all levels and in all its forms.
- Understanding and respect for all peoples, their cultures, civilizations, values and ways of life, including domestic ethnic cultures and cultures of other nations.
- Awareness of the increasing global interdependence between peoples and nations.
- Awareness not only of the rights but also of the duties incumbent upon individuals, social groups and nations towards each other.

The objectives and goals of such a commitment were also spelled out in greater details as:

- To develop a sense of social responsibility and solidarity with less privileged groups.
- To lead to the observance of principles of equality in everyday conduct.
- To foster the ability to communicate with others.

- To develop a critical understanding of problems at the national and international level.
- To encourage children to understand and explain facts, opinions and ideas.
- To encourage children to work in a group, accept and participate in free discussions, and to base value judgments and decisions on a rational analysis of relevant facts and factors (United Nations Educational, Scientific and Cultural Organisation, 1974).

Whilst the statement is a little bit of an intellectual and presentational hotchpotch, it does recall some of the major aims and objectives for a global multicultural curriculum and it firmly alerts us to the fact that human rights education cannot be solely about content. It is about a systemic approach, whole school commitment and a whole school delivery. Some countries, such as Canada have sought to institutionalize the commitment, not only through national and provincial bodies in a structural and judicial sense, but also through the provision of appropriate educational initiatives. The Canadian Association of Statutory Human Rights Associations, for example, concerns itself with efforts to combat discrimination through human rights education, including formal and informal programmes and post-experience training for teachers. Based on research carried out in the mid-1980s, the Canadian Human Rights Foundation has implemented a nation-wide human rights programme, which commences with grade four and has been classroom tested. It is prepared for and accompanied by intensive in-service provision for teachers. Most of the Provinces also have prepared, commissioned or endorsed human rights materials for schools.

Brown (1983, pp. 40ff) argues that there are certain inherent rights which schools should build into their dealings with students. Among these, he cites the right to due process, including:

- The presumption of innocence.
- The right to defend oneself.
- The right to witness.
- The introduction of an impartial authority.
- Explanation of consequences.
- The opportunity to appeal.

He suggests that, both in Canada and the United States, due process is very frequently denied, if not intentionally, then by ignorance and neglect on the part of teachers, and that generalization probably applies in many other countries too. And, indeed, it is not surprising, since it is also likely that very few teachers will have been sensitized to issues of the human rights of their students through a systematic programme of in-service training. He also affirms that teachers should not only eschew physical abuse, but that it is incumbent upon them, by dint of the human rights of their students, to avoid the use of psychological abuse as well. Students have at all times an inalienable right to dignity, worth and respectful treatment, but it is likely that many teachers feel that they have no other sanction than that of a 'psychologically sharp tongue'. He also points to the lack of privacy, which also often exists with regard to record-keeping practices, and the sometimes unauthorized disclosure of facts about students even to other students as a means of correcting recalcitrant or disruptive students in the classroom.

Tarrow (1988a, p. 9) sees other problems inhibiting the effective implementation of human rights programmes, including:

- Imprecise definition of the location of responsibility.
- Concern about its 'fit' with the existing curriculum.
- Dislocation between the content and the strategies.
- Paucity of suitable materials.
- Lack of networking of those involved.
- Absence of appropriate evaluation.
- Initiatives left to individual teachers.
- Inadequate preparation of teachers.
- Perception by some who see a clash between education for national and global citizenship (Tarrow, 1988a, p. 9, amended and summarized by the author).

This statement is very useful in prodding us to a realization of the intrinsic problems of incorporating human rights education into the curriculum, not to mention permeating the whole curriculum with such a commitment, as part of a whole school policy. But inevitably the question arises of what should be the knowledge, skills and attitudes associated with teaching human rights in school. Recommendation Number R(85)7 of the Committee of Ministers of the Council of Europe, adopted in May 1985, suggested that the skills associated with the understanding of and support for human rights include:

- Intellectual skills, such as those of advocacy, discussion and creative listening.
- Judgment skills, including the collection and appraisal of material from various media and the identification of bias.
- Social skills, including recognizing and accepting differences, non-

violent conflict resolution, establishing relationships. understanding the mechanisms for the protection of human rights, etc. (Council of Europe, 1985, p. 3).

It also contains suggestions about the knowledge which might be appropriate in the study of human rights, including the concepts of justice, equality, freedom, peace, dignity, rights, democracy; knowledge of the main categories of human rights, duties, obligations and responsibilities; and knowledge of the various forms of injustice and of the key events and people involved in the struggle for human rights. Appropriately, it has a particular section on the climate of the school and the involvement of the community.

So, it seems to me that we now have enough information to begin to construct a checklist against which schools may seek to measure the responsiveness and 'fidelity' of their current policies, ethos, procedures, structures and curricular policies, beginning with such questions as whether the various school policies have been formulated with human rights considerations in mind? How far have the publications and recommendations of the various bodies concerned with human rights on an international, national and local level informed those policies? Is the governance of the school reflective of all legitimate interests, particularly those of parents, staff and students? Are the staffing and staff development policies conducive to the achievement of goals of human rights education?

That checklist should include questions about even apparently abstract aspects of its life, such as the ethos of the school and the extent to which it is conducive to an open and democratic approach to education or, on the other hand, supports a traditional teacher–authority focused ambience. Recent research on both sides of the Atlantic emphasizes the fact that, intangible though it sounds, an effective school has a positive ethos (Mortimore *et al.*, 1988, p. 255; United States Department of Education 1986, p. 46). Are there, for example, structures for the involvement of staff and school students in discussing school policy? Is it an ethos, which values every member of the school for their basic humanity? Does it afford full dignity to all legitimate views and expressions of opinion, particularly minority ones? What proclaimed means are there for conflict resolution and conciliation? Does it actively encourage self-control? Is it an ethos which encourages care with language, written and oral? Are these procedures to counter bias in the various aspects of the school, its processes and materials? Is the school climate maximally conducive to the maximum learning for all its members? Is the school climate one which emphasizes self-control and responsibility, rather than the negative aspects of student's behaviour and attainment? Are there such items as human rights notices, displays, events and celebrations of anniversaries to raise awareness, generate an ambience and to inform staff and students about human rights? Is there a human rights 'club'? Is the school an example to its own members and the community of respect for the dignity and worth of the individual, for human justice and fairness?

In its procedures, too, the school will need to scrutinize its policy and its practice. Are they expressive of the principle of manifest goodwill? Is the use of physical and psychological abuse by staff in their dealings with students explicitly banned? Are there procedures to challenge school rules and regulations? Is there a school ombudsperson? Are there provisions for an impartial hearing? Are sanctions against racist, sexist of credal prejudice and discrimination made explicit? Are there bias review procedures for material, syllabuses, examinations and other policies? Are good personal relations with all members of the school community valued and praised in its reward system? Are there opportunities for co-operation across age ranges and backgrounds in both curricular and extra-curricular activities? Are the values of collaboration and mutual help safeguarded and reinforced? Are assessment, and examinations policy and practice, conducive to human rights? Do they accord with the democratic ethos of the school? Are there openly promulgated and fair procedures for appeal? Do students have access to advice and counsel? Do students have open or restricted access to their records? Are there any aspects which can be held in confidence to the students (as seems to be implied by the controversies surrounding the Gillick case in the United Kingdom. In that case, a mother's demand to know if her daughter approached a doctor for contraceptive advice was rejected as an absolute parental right.) Are staff available to discuss students' records with them? Are the students consulted about what happens to their records and to whom they may be transmitted? Is unauthorized data release explicitly forbidden? Are staff trained in making accurate, fair, just and non-ambiguous entries on students' records?

In terms of its structures, does the school manifest bias or discrimination of a racist, sexist or credal kind in its setting or grouping policies, in its offset policy for curricular options, or in its implicit assumptions about careers choice and advice? Does it take account of its annual timetable of the special needs of minorities? If it provides refreshments, do they reflect the diversity of school cultures by taking into account special dietary and food preparation needs? Does the structure and hierarchy of its staffing, and its policy and distribution of professional development opportunities, implicitly manifest discrimination? Is staff involvement encouraged and welcomed, even where it gives rise to varying viewpoints? What in-built structures are there for students to learn about democratic practice? Are there opportunities for the community to participate in the school and the school in the community, perhaps on a service basis? How often do issues of human rights feature on staff meeting agendas? Are new structural proposals scrutinized for their congruence with human rights?

A Curricular Policy for Human Rights Education

In addition to the overall context and positive climate-setting factors referred to above, a school will also need to ask more specific questions about its curricular provision and policy at classroom or learning unit level. The literature on classroom climate indicates quite clearly that more democratic classrooms correlate positively with higher levels of political efficacy and lower levels of disaffection and political cynicism. It is now widely acknowledged, that the way that the classroom is organized, and the way in which the teacher communicates with students, transmits to students a very powerful and socially and academically influential message about the teacher's intentions, assumptions and values, particularly those which the students are intended to 'absorb'. These factors may be even more influential than the formal knowledge and concept base in evoking learning in the crucial areas of skill development, such as oracy, as well as attitude and value learning. Evidence also indicates that good communication and feedback positively influence progress in all cognitive areas (Mortimore *et al.*, 1988, p. 227). A sharp focus on learning, on student involvement and the measured management of their own learning by students, together with maximum interaction and frequent and good feedback to students, are also shown to be highly correlated with positive and effective academic outcomes.

Moreover, the posing of higher order questions, intended to elicit answers involving problem solving, reasoning or imaginative responses from students, which are shown to be indicative of effective schools, are also indicators of effective classrooms and are, coincidentally, exactly the kinds of approaches essential to effective human rights education. So, a good 'human rights classroom' is also more likely to be a contribute to a good and effective school all round, and vice versa. A better human rights school is likely to be a better school by dint of that commitment, and to be a haven to better and more successful classroom learning. Equity and excellence can be pursued at the same time and in the same curriculum. We can have two (educational objectives) for the price of one! Thus, an essential prerequisite to the delivery of effective human rights education is a conducive classroom climate, including an appropriately planned and delivered teaching style.

It is in this context of the acknowledged and crucial importance of the classroom climate, and the characteristic components of that climate, that we now return to the curriculum as a whole, which is delivered within the cultural and structural framework of the principles inherent in that climate. I suggest, then, that we now retrieve the building blocks of curriculum, which I introduced in Chapter 3. It will be recalled that we labelled these as learning experiences, knowledge components (including information as the content base), concepts and theories, skills and attitudes.

Firstly, however, let us get our pedagogical bearings, and try to paint a picture of where we may possibly have to move from in terms of teaching approaches. A review of three National Science Foundation studies in the United States, which may also be indicative of a similar situation in other countries, discovered the following characteristics to teachers' pedagogical styles in the social studies classroom:

- Classroom reality is determined by the teacher's beliefs about the nature of their subject, and knowledge and available material.
- The teacher decides on the combination of these three factors alone.
- The dominant instructional tool is the textbook.
- There is little interdisciplinary work.
- Large group, teacher controlled lectures and recitation are the instructional norm.
- Memorization of information is frequent.
- Respect for others' views is 'expected' without question.
- Motivation is extrinsic.
- Content and instruction is uninteresting.
- Affective objectives are rarely seen as either important or legitimate (Reported in Evans, 1987, p. 550, summarized by author).

It will be apparent that such a profile will not be adequate for the delivery of an experiential, skills-based human rights education. For, knowledge of human rights declarations, covenants, conventions, instruments and agreements does not guarantee that students (or staff for that matter) are going to be more committed to the practice of human rights – and it is with the practice of human rights that we are here concerned. Moreover, the intention cannot be to merely process children in order to get them to reproduce a given stock of adult ideas, quite apart from the inappropriateness of such an approach for younger children.

Human rights education is *par excellence* about moral values and their incorporation into schooling. Moral values need to be internalized to provide for autonomous behaviour. Children will select appropriate information, skills and attitudes and use these to build up personal and meaningful constructs of their reality in interaction with their everyday lives. In this process, the more children themselves can be dynamic creators of their own new political meanings and values, the more the process of human rights education will succeed at the different ages and stages, as children progressively build up their own human rights biography of values, knowledge and competences. Concomitantly, the less chance there will be of an arid and boring banking concept of human rights teaching, based on an 'acts and facts' approach, as portrayed in the above research cameo.

So, the question arises as to what teachers can do in order to foster that knowledge, and those values, skills and attitudes nexus of human rights education, which will empower the student to be aware of, respect and seek to implement, human rights for all, but which will be subtle, flexible and dynamic enough to take account of the cultural background and cognitive development of the student as he or she travels through the period of compulsory schooling. Once again, as in posing a similar question in Chapter 2, the reply must be that human rights education must be a process-oriented, skills-based series of learning experiences, which are maximally attentive to the student's needs, background and culture, and which can encourage and facilitate interpersonal relations and co-operation in the joint construction of a new social reality by the students.

To polarize slightly, learning by living human rights is, in other words, preferable to learning about human rights. In any case, students' ultimate success in constructing their own 'human rights-responsive' reality is likely to begin to manifest itself first in the informal dimension of their schooling and extra-scholastic life – in situations such as the way they react to apparent unfairness, the way they talk about people who are different, the way they handle conflicts and disputes in the playground, on the football pitch, in the drama rehearsal, the way they respond to the needs of others, to famine appeals, to handicapped students and their special needs, and the way they interact with their peers.

As I have argued above, success in fostering human rights education will be a function of the context within which it takes place and the teaching methods adopted by the teacher. These two factors are interactive with the whole school factors referred to above and are likely to be much more powerful 'educators' than the content base. A more open and democratic classroom, with an emphasis on participation and responsible discussion and decision, good communication and feedback, will be more efficacious than one where the centre of all activity, objectives and knowledge appears to be the teacher. So, the teacher of any subject or curriculum area who wishes to embody a commitment to human rights education in his or her own classroom has to start rebuilding the pedagogical principles deriving from the major human rights instruments into his or her own practice. It is not even, in the first instance, a matter of any specific human rights content.

That reconstruction of new pedagogical principles involves, I will admit, a renewal and change of professional reality for the teacher. As I suggested at the beginning, this means reflecting on existing practice and trying to move it in an evolutionary way along a continuum, perhaps from the traditional pedagogy portrayed in outline above towards goals of greater co-operation, higher student participation, greater emphasis on self-control and less on negative, 'critical' control, more differentiation of learning processes, increased acceptance of student input and feedback, pacing, sequencing and choice, more intrinsic motivation, greater acceptance of the provisionality of knowledge, interpersonalization of skills, acceptance of multiple sources of valid knowledge, more intrinsic motivation, greater accountability of the teacher, more acceptance that learning has a legitimate affective/feeling dimension, and improved teacher/pupil and pupil/pupil relationships.

This evolution of one's teaching style is as much a question of process and directionality as it is of any finitely attainable and immediate goals. It will certainly involve a parallel and interactive staff development policy. For that reason, Figure 3.2 seeks to exemplify the evolutionary nature of the movement described above and to illustrate it. The issue of an appropriate staff development is taken up later.

It follows from what has been said about human rights education concerning classroom organization and process, and democratic ambience, in conjunction with the material in Chapter 2, which exemplified the kinds of learning experiences appropriate to a global multicultural curriculum, that there is a very high level of congruence between the two. Indeed, in view of the case that we are presenting for

Figure 3.2: Facilitative Approaches for Human Rights Education: An Evolutionary Approach

FROM← — — — — — — — — — — — — — — — — →TO		
Traditional Focus		Human Rights Focus
Climate	Closed/ authority-bound	→ Open/democratic
Objectives	Teacher-prescribed	→ Negotiated
Participation	Low	→ High
Control	'Critical'	→ Self
Pace, sequence and time	Unitary	→ Differentiated
Decisions	Given	→ Shared jointly
Methods	Few and 'frontal'	→ Varied and co-operative
Motivation	Grade induced	→ Intrinsic
Feelings	Irrelevant	→ Essential
Resources	Teacher selected	→ Multiple sources
Answers	'Right'	→ Provisional
Relations	Isolated/individual	→ Interpersonal
Evaluation	Student assessment	→ Joint appraisal

human rights as the core of the global multicultural curriculum, it would be surprising if this were not the case. Both emphasize an experiential approach to learning and the need for reflective decision-making. Particular attention will, however, need to be given to groups of learning experiences, such as co-operating, advocating, communicating, evaluating, problem solving, decision making at different levels of complexity and consequences, presenting a case, organizing a group, collecting and appraising evidence, petitioning, interrogating data and other information. Each of these can be commenced in the earlier phase of education and can be made more sophisticated as the student progresses through the years of formal education, moral maturity and developmental stages. The focus can also be sharpened from concrete local issues arising from the everyday life of young children, through direct purposeful experience, to more distant and abstract foci on a vicarious basis.

Having indicated the crucial importance of the classroom context and overall pedagogy, and linked that to the learning experiences, I want now to turn to the content base. I accept that there is an almost inevitable tendency to 'overdo' this aspect of the curriculum and to compile impressive, long and sometimes self-defeating lists of information. So the question has to be, in a crowded curriculum, what is the minimum reasonable content and concept base which will enable us to achieve our objectives. In terms of knowledge components, all students should at some time during their compulsory education have an opportunity to encounter, discuss and review the main categories of human rights, including obligations and responsibilities. They should also be aware of the main national, regional and international agencies concerned with human rights, and cover and discuss the main threats to those human rights in the form of discrimination, injustice, gross inequality and violence. Students should also learn about the historical development of humankind's quest to achieve human rights, of the continuing struggle for those rights and the main areas of abuse.

Some of this material can well come as part of existing subjects: science, history, civics, religion, social studies, etc. Some of it can be covered through the celebration of festivals and anniversaries, through displays and visiting speakers, through visiting theatre, drama productions and musical or sporting events, or as part of extra-curricular activities, etc. But there will need to be guidelines to make sure that all students do in fact have the opportunity to gain an acquaintance with these foundations. Needless to say, that process of awareness will need to be dovetailed with the maturing development of children, but some aspects can already commence at the earliest stages, a comment which also applies to concepts and attitudes.

Concepts are an important aspect of the human rights curriculum, both intrinsically and extrinsically. Intrinsically, they are essential means of gaining purchase on issues and thinking of them in the correct categories. Extrinsically, they also foster inductive reasoning, a sensitivity to alternative perspectives, a tolerance of ambiguity and a more subtle ability for logical reasoning in communication (Joyce and Weil, 1986, p. 39). But, we are once gain faced with the question of what would represent a reasonable concept base for a human rights permeated curriculum. Concepts, it will be recalled from Chapter 2, involve identifying items according to certain criteria and placing them into named classes on the basis of the applicability of those criteria. For this process, accurate definition and application of both essential and non-essential criteria is crucial, both for concept attainment, that is the acquisition of an existing concept. This is a crucial thinking activity, central to a human rights attentive curriculum, not least because of the political and sometimes highly politicized nature of claims (and sometimes counterclaims). Moreover, many concepts in the area of human rights involve value criteria.

Many of these concepts have already been covered in the Introduction, and in Chapters 1 and 2. In any case, they are probably not peculiar to human rights education, but are shared with other areas of the formal curriculum. They should certainly include democracy, justice, fairness, power, authority, interdependence, welfare, tolerance, self-determination, equality, civil liberties, legitimate diversity, equality, freedom, peace, dignity, duties, responsibilities, obligations and of course human rights. For ease of implementation, these concepts can be formulated as concept statements appropriate to the age of the children in the way this has been done, for example, by the British Assessment of Performance Unit's list of science concepts and knowledge (Department of Education and Science, 1988). Other concepts, such as injustice, conflict, discrimination, oppression, genocide and violence should not be 'shirked'. Once again, many of these can be covered as part of the normal curriculum or in connection with the teaching of other subjects, or extra-curricular activities, provided that the process is planned and monitored.

For example, as part of the science work on the interdependence of living things, concept statements which include the following could be used to raise issues of why we need each other, why we require human rights and why it is our own interest to secure the human rights of others:

- Living things depend on each other for their survival.
- There are many different criteria which can be used to classify living things.
- All living things produce waste.
- All living things need food as a source of energy.

Similar concept statements in other subjects can also be given their full human rights perspective and value.

When we come to consider the learning skills inherent in a core commitment to human rights education, it is important to keep in the mind the distinction, which was introduced in Chapter 2, between intuitive and rational cognitive skills, on the one hand, and motor skills, on the other. Important, too, is the emphasis on the need for skills to be practised and to have a reflective dimension, before internalization and automatization can be achieved by the students. The centrality of thinking skills, practised in active classroom involvement, once again underlines the experiential nature of human rights learning. Here skills of reasoning, questioning, making rational judgments, researching, brainstorming and thought reflection (thinking on a thought) will need to be measured against the age and stage of the students, but there is no reason why the process of skill development should not be fully coterminous with the school life of the child. As a shorthand way of ordering the most important thinking skills into coherent domains, a six-part categorization is sometimes used:

- General problem-solving (including problem identification, task selection and combination, resource application, monitoring, review, and revision).
- Comprehension of information (including establishment, appraisal of and inferential reasoning from 'messages' emanating from a variety of sources, listening and responding, etc.).
- Solving specific problems (including understanding, planning strategies, implementing and appraising success).
- Inter-communicating (including choosing an appropriate register and medium, understanding cues and other non-verbal communication).
- Researching (including topic identification, information and source discovery, collection and organization of data, report-writing, sharing, evaluating).
- Decision-making (including a range from simple decisions to multi-source and factor decisions on a chained and interactive basis) (Soloman, 1987, pp. 558ff).

This six-part categorization may be viewed not as a comprehensive list, but as an abbreviated, more readily understandable and recallable formulation. Concepts sometimes appear too abstract or vague, and teachers encounter difficulty in thinking of the translation of concepts into concrete skill forms for teaching and learning objectives; this shorthand formulation may be useful in identifying the basic core. Thus, the basic skill domains given above can be thought of as task areas to be accomplished and demonstrated, and of course they can be broken down into smaller or more specific tasks as well as amalgamated into hybrid ones.

Clearly, skills will only become effective if supported by the appropriate attitudes, expressive of our personal and deep-rooted values and personality, which in turn lead to actions that reinforce our self-respect. Attitudes, it will be recalled, predispose us to think, feel and act in particular ways. They comprise both cognitive and emotional dimensions between which there is interaction, emotion is bridled by reason and at the same time liberated to guide that reason through what we call intuition. Thus the curriculum needs to aim to educate students to develop from narrow, egocentric and irrational coping with emotions to the achievement of more rationally controlled, positive, self-transcending and sociocentric emotions, such as love, justice, respect, concern for truth, etc. Attitudes are, thus, crucial to the translation of morality from the 'ought' to the 'want', that is the movement from doing something because it is prescribed or required by the teacher, to undertaking that task or making that decision because one wishes to and feels one's self-esteem and respect enhanced by it. This latter is what I mean by being empowered to move onto moral auto-pilot, which for me is one of the main objectives of a human rights attentive, global multicultural curriculum, but which is also highly interdependent with the authority structure of the school and the classroom, and influential, in turn, with those structures, on the beliefs and perceptions which students and staff have of themselves as morally responsible humans.

The attitude objectives set out in Chapter 1 apply one hundred per cent to the core area of human rights learning, as does the tripartite categorization into individual, person-oriented, societally-oriented and world-oriented attitudes. Central to all the objectives is the basic ethic of respect for persons leading, as argued above, to enhanced self-respect and self-esteem and to the active dimension of that ethical attitude, commitment to engagement against behaviour, inimical to a human rights commitment, such as bias, prejudice, discrimination, racism, sexism and injustice. Additionally, an attitude of critical but firm commitment to pluralist democracy is also central to such a curriculum, encouraging specific attitudes consequential on that commitment and necessary for it, such as self-confidence in expression, responsible independence, sensitivity to justice and rights, and the willingness to stand up for what is right. A global curriculum should also seek to encourage attitudes of caring for fellow humans, animals and the environment, feeling comfortable with diversity, celebrating common human values and ideals, and empathy with other individuals and cultures (through such attitudes as reversibility and solidarity), not least with those in developing countries. Needless to say, a commitment to human rights for all across the levels and dimensions introduced earlier is part of the central attitude commitment of a curriculum core commit-ted to human rights.

Attitude/skill complexes such as a commitment to peaceful conflict resolution in their own lives, combined with the intercommunicative competence to achieve that goal, complement and extend the basic attitude repertoire. As with the curriculum as a whole, the core human rights commitment will require a much more deliberate, systematic and intentional approach to attitude development, and recognition of the emotional dimension of attitudes, than has usually been the case in our cognitively overloaded schools. This approach, in turn, will require a much more systematic process of appeal to the judgment of students than has usually been the case, for it is essential for students to construct their own attitude/values complex through a process of internalization, if they are to go onto moral 'auto-pilot' when the teacher is not present and their schooldays are past. Needless to say, care would need to be taken to adopt approaches to attitude development which would attenuate and not increase category salience, by emphasizing similarity and commonality rather than difference.

Evaluating and Monitoring

Already in Chapter 2 a series of tentative procedural principles for an assessment appropriate to a global multicultural curriculum were suggested in the context of an overall evaluation strategy, which recognized assessment as only one source of evidence about the effectiveness of the teacher, the curriculum and the institution. To summarize those procedural principles concerning assessment, it was suggested that they should address such criteria as:

- Culture-fairness of professional judgments.
- Absence of procedural bias.
- Special arrangements for legitimate special needs.
- Balanced, up-to-date and fair portrayal of others.
- Culture-fairness of professional judgments.
- Absence of procedural bias.
- Special arrangements for legitimate special needs.
- Balanced, up-to-date and fair portrayal of others.
- Orientation to judgment, problem-solving and decision making as well as factual knowledge.
- Emphasis on the development of thinking skills.
- Acceptance of an affective dimension in learning and performance.
- Recognition of a broad profile of learning achievements.
- Co-operative group work opportunities.
- Self-appraisal opportunities for students.
- Multi-media and resource approaches.
- Open and consultative policy on records and their transmission.

- Regular appraisal of examinations and assessment policy, and practice against objectives.

To that list would now need to be added more specific criteria related to the sharper human rights focus, introduced in Chapter 3, such as:

- Concern for due process.
- Eschewal of physical or psychological punishments.
- Concern for methods which support and enhance the human worth and dignity of the student.
- Emphasis on material which accurately reflects a global dimension on human rights issues.
- Concern with the moral education of students to a commitment to human rights, and to the corollary of their own duties and obligations.

In addition to the above criteria, there are also certain imperatives for the techniques of assessment, which arise out of the nature of a global multicultural education and which require a particular emphasis in the nature of the assessment. These might briefly be summarized under the headings of:

- Techniques that emphasize the centrality of oracy, in all its dimensions: social, including cultural sensitivity to different groups and contexts; physical, including non-verbal communication; psychological, including self-image and confidence; linguistic, including accent, audibility, clarity, register, vocabulary, for various purposes, such as problem-solving, decision making, exchanging ideas, eliciting information, narrating, clarifying, responding to others and building on their evidence and arguments; advocating and petitioning (BBC, 1987, p. 12 amended by author).
- Techniques that reduce the inequalities and potential injustices inherent in the more traditional procedures (these might include the reduction of time pressures, the timetabling of examinations, the rubrics and their universal comprehensibility, the extent of inclusion of *vivas*, opportunities to discuss the meaning of examination questions, exemplars from students' own cultural background, etc.).
- Techniques that test judgment, skill and ability to interrogate information; to work in teams and collaboratively; with questions and assignments being given in advance; more continuous assessment; reference material made available in the examination room; examinations held in a variety of contexts (e.g. the library, computer and information technology approaches); interpretation of experimental

results, data, social situations, real or simulated, etc.
- Techniques that assess the broader aspects of subjects or the interrelationship of subjects in the resolution of a problem, which require the acquisition of information or expertise from elsewhere, which require action in the community, the preparation of a position or information paper for a local community, or the school, etc.
- Pedagogical techniques to shift the emphasis of assessment to stimulus to learning and independent and co-operative study, such as projects, non-countable assessments, peer group assessment, etc.

It is evident that teachers need to be able to continually make professional judgments about the value and effectiveness of their educational goals, the processes and strategies they adopt to achieve those goals and the outcomes of their commitment to a human rights attentive, global multicultural curriculum. Sometimes, perhaps increasingly, they may be called to the bar of public or professional accountability, and asked to justify their judgments. Thus, whilst they will be asking themselves questions, such as those suggested in the Introduction about the kind of hard evidence they may have about the success of their professional endeavours, others may be asking them questions too, and they will need to be sure of the criteria against which they are making those judgments. These criteria are explicit in the master aims and operational objectives formulated in Chapters 1 and 2, but they should be considered as a basis for negotiation with the different parties concerned – colleagues, students, parents and the wider community.

Good teachers are, in any case, usually engaged in a constant process of negotiation, evaluation, review and improvements, consonant with their existing cultural and professional biography. That professional biography will result from a complex and interwoven relationship among a whole series of factors, the most important of which will be the teacher's personality, training, previous professional career and experience, the social system of which he or she is a part and from which the teacher gains professional sustenance and direction, and the political ideology of education, compendium and mix of teaching approaches that already make up that individual's teaching style. These factors, together with the aims and objectives, will, in turn influence the style, approach and methodology of educational evaluation with which the teacher feels professionally comfortable and effective.

What is required for a more global multicultural curricular commitment is the extension and development of the existing criteria, which derive from and are influenced by the teacher's professional biography, so that they are more attentive to the goals inherent in that approach, the objectives for which were made explicit in Chapter 2. That process of extending and developing the principles by which a teacher currently reviews and appraises his or her own professional performance is at the heart of the effective delivery of an appropriate curriculum. It is a process and not a state, and it may be seen as addressing three immediate levels of activity and focus – individual, collegial and institutional – with the community involved predominantly in the latter level. It is a demanding process of renegotiation of professional reality, requiring interpersonal, political and organizational skills. Ultimately, it is, as Adelman and Alexander (1982) claim, less a matter of sophisticated methodology and more a matter of the above skills where the challenge of an effective, skill-extending professional evaluation lies. Certainly, it is much broader than mere assessment of students, let alone a cognitively dominated assessment of them. Indeed, the success of the strategy proposed here is likely to be less manifest in such increments of knowledge than in the behaviours and relationships of staff and students in school and outside.

One thing is certain, namely that such professional evaluation can only come within the context of a sensitive and cyclical process involving staff development if it is not to descend into a fruitless formalism, or even worse, a witchhunt for non-conformity with what can be or appears to be measurable. Human rights are ultimately as much about obligations as about freedoms. Any evaluation of the acceptance of those obligations will probably have a much more important intra-institutional than extra-institutional dimension. Without a deliberate policy of staff development, aimed at both individual and institutional levels, there will be no prospect of the monitoring of such 'private' results. Because of this close and interactive relationship between evaluation and staff development, the issue of appropriate review and appraisal procedures is taken up again in Chapter 6, which is devoted to professional development.

Bias, Prejudice and Discrimination Review

There is one aspect of assessment and evaluation which merits more detailed consideration. Many teachers are concerned quite rightly about the presence of sex, race, and ethnic bias among their colleagues, in the educational materials they use in their curricula and not least in their teaching. They sincerely wish to help their students to acquire positive attitudes towards other social and cultural groups and to assist them in avoiding prejudice and bias. For this reason, it is important that what might be termed a 'Bias Review Procedure' is incorporated into the overall review and evaluation procedures for the institution as a whole so that materials, curricula, teaching methods, and other processes and procedures in the school are appropriate to the overall goals and objectives of an institution committed to the delivery of a global multicultural curriculum based on human rights. Thus, it is necessary to define what a biasing element may be which may have a negative or destructive influence on students, or may reinforce or create a prejudice or misconception detrimental to particular students.

> In this book, a biasing element in any aspect of the school's functioning including both verbal and non-verbal language is biased if it may reasonably be assumed to create or reinforce in a student:

1. A feeling of inferiority on the part of one group of students on the basis of their cultural appurtenance;
2. A prejudice against another group of people;
3. Direct or indirect inequality in access to resources teaching or opportunities for access to social or academic satisfaction;
4. A gratuitous and negative stereotype of a group of people or country;
5. Values, beliefs, or attitudes which are contrary to the notions of equality and equity enshrined in the body of human rights instruments adopted nationally and internationally.

Michigan Department of Education, 1979, p. 2, amended by the author)

Teachers will be aware, that bias may appear under a number of different headings and in a number of different forms, such as:

- *Slurs*. These are words, statements, innuendoes or other modifiers in spoken language, non-verbal communication, in written language, in illustrations or in other graphic forms of representation which are derogatory or insulting to or disrespectful of a member of any group or the group as a whole. (For example, the use of the word 'girl' to designate an adult woman, or 'Paki' to refer to a person of Pakistani background.)
- *Stereotypes*. These are biasing elements which fail to take note of a wide range of intragroup differences, or which conversely express the view that all or nearly all members of a group are the same. Stereotyping may occur with regard to occupational roles, family roles, personality traits, physical characteristics, ethnic background,

school roles, etc. (The use of secretary as an exclusively female designation, of 'breadwinner' to designate only fathers, of 'Jews' as being 'stingy', of all Blacks as having thick lips, of all Asian Indians as being Hindus, are examples of the categories given above.)

- *Erroneous Group Representation*. This may occur where there is under representation, when the context suggests that there should be representation, or where segregation is used by words or illustrations to separate or emphasize the differences between various groups. (For example, the exclusion of Blacks in the description of the population of a large city, or their representation in only one occupation, situation or location.)

What is required is an on-going procedure for bias review, which is neither repressive of individual and institutional creativity nor insensitive to the feelings and culture of individuals and groups both for themselves and towards others. Such a bias review procedures should be sufficiently fine-grained to detect racial, gender, ethnic, linguistic, credal, age and handicap bias in any aspect of the institution's functioning, yet flexible enough and humane enough to be part of the progressing life of the whole school community, and thus fully legitimated with staff, students and parents as a normal part of school life and improvement of the professional service offered to children.

Chapter Summary

Building on the materials and arguments deployed in the Introduction and in Chapters 1 and 2, this chapter has sought to adopt a sharper focus on human rights and education for human rights. After a brief introduction to the field of international and regional instruments and covenants, attention was drawn to the somewhat parlous state of children's rights, notwithstanding work on the initiative commenced in 1978 for an International Convention of Children's Rights. The point was made that such a convention, and the rights for children it contains, must be seen as over and above those rights that everyone should enjoy purely and simply because they are human beings. Reference was also made to the sections of other major agreements which afford special protection or care to the child, and to the annual catalogue of their abuse, published by Unicef. Then, I argued that human rights and particularly the Universal Declaration of Human Rights and consequential protocols and instruments, provide the only universally recognized, if not accepted and practised, code of values for schools in a democratic society, other religious and political codifications being partial in content and acceptability, if not restricted in geographical location.

Next, a definition of human rights education was formulated, which emphasized both process and content, as well as the role of human rights in providing basic moral values for all school policies and practices. The definition was then used to formulate a whole school policy for human rights education, which would at the same time inform the organization of the school and its life, provide a means to impregnate and pervade the whole curriculum with the values of human rights, and indicate where specific human rights curricular inputs were required and how that might be achieved. For this latter part of the exercise, the building blocks of curriculum were retrieved from Chapter 2, and the learning experiences and each of the components (knowledge, skills and attitudes) were briefly addressed as part of the formulation of a holistic curricular policy. Particular attention was given to the development of skills of reflective thinking; an abbreviated six-part formulation was suggested and explained. The case was also made for the achievement of a more open and democratic classroom climate, in which students were assisted in constructing their own social reality of human rights and slotting it into their own everyday experience and learning.

Then, and reaching back to the section on assessment in Chapter 2, which emphasized that assessment of students was only one aspect of a comprehensive evaluation strategy, an outline assessment and evaluation policy was formulated. The criteria introduced in that chapter were extended to take a greater account of the core human rights commitment, introduced in Chapter 3. Examples were given of five families of techniques of assessment which would be particularly apposite for the kind of curriculum policy and practice being proposed. Such a policy should emphasize the centrality of oracy; reduce the inequalities and potential injustices; test judgment, skill and informative ability; assess broader aspects of subjects; and, link teaching and assessing more strongly.

The evaluation policy proposed was argued to derive from the professional biography of the teacher and the institution. It would also need to be located firmly in an on-going process of professional development at individual, collegial and institutional levels. Finally, in the present chapter, a definition of a biasing element in any aspect of school life was given. Then, a bias review procedure was proposed, which could facilitate the continual monitoring of all facets of school life for possible racial, gender, ethnic, credal or other prejudice, and as a means of securing their congruence with the overall aims of an tion committed to the implementation of a human rights, expressive global multicultural curriculum.

In Chapter 4, I want to sharpen the focus on the delivery of the global multicultural curriculum and the teaching learning strategies which teachers may adopt to achieve the objectives set out in Chapter 2. Looking back at the questions posed in the Introduction, I shall be asking the basic question about what changes may be desirable in current teaching methods to accommodate a global multicultural approach, and what hard evidence we have of the efficacy of our current teaching on which we can build. I shall be reflecting back onto some of the material we have covered in this chapter on school and classroom climate, and the need for a more open and democratic pedagogy, which can involve students not only in discussing means but also in formulating appropriate objectives. I shall be proposing nine principles, which, I shall argue, should underlie an appropriate 'philosophy of teaching' to guide the implementation and selection of teaching/learning strategies. Then, we shall consider a series of teaching approaches for which we have validated evidence of their effectiveness and appropriateness for the delivery of a human rights based multicultural curriculum with a marked global dimension. The final two chapters consider questions of resources and professional development, which may be necessary to support such a movement in our professional reality.

Chapter 4

Delivering a Global Approach

Before looking in greater detail at the more specific teaching approaches which are necessary in order to deliver a global multicultural curriculum with a core commitment to human rights, I should like to review how far and over what kind of curricular terrain we have travelled to this point in our educational journey of pushing back the frontiers of the way in which multicultural education is currently conceived and locking it more firmly onto education for human rights, seen as both content and basic values to the whole curriculum. It will be recalled that in the Introduction a rationale was set down for the need for such a curriculum, and the intellectual and cultural parochialism of current efforts at multicultural education were criticized. Three overarching aims were proposed for multicultural education in pluralist democracies, highlighting the tension between diversity, common values and justice, and the dilemmas this generates for social policy, not least in the field of education. Then, a framework for analysis was proposed covering four levels and dimensions, and a series of questions was advanced about teachers' current practice.

In Chapter 1, and using the framework of levels and dimensions proposed in the Introduction, a series of starting points was proposed for discussion of the context of cultural diversity which makes a revision of the curriculum imperative, if it is to accord with a global multicultural perspective, building centrally on a commitment to human rights. A more extensive series of master aims was constructed, building on the three introduced earlier and drawing on the aims of a series of cognate curriculum reform movements, including multicultural education. From these aims a more detailed set of operational goals, addressing knowledge, attitudes, and values and skills, was proposed and accompanying procedural principles drawn up. Finally, in chapter 1, a profile of the characteristics of an effective multicultural school was described and the need for a whole institution approach underlined.

In Chapter 2 the relay of this groundwork was worked into a more definitive description of a global multicultural curriculum. A typology of previous curricular responses to ethnic diversity was constructed, and their shortcomings and failings were identified. Particular attention was drawn to the general weakness of most of the previous approaches, namely over-emphasis of social category salience, although some were also criticized for their parochialism and atheoreticism. Drawing on this analysis, specific learning experiences for a global multicultural curriculum were formulated and knowledge components, including information, concept, skill and attitude dimensions, were described in detail. Particular emphasis was placed on the active and experiential nature of the curriculum and the essential role of skill development, especially thinking skills. Finally, an outline assessment policy was proposed in the context of an overall evaluation strategy for the school.

The central chapter of this book, Chapter 3, had as its focus the concept of human rights as the kernel of the global multicultural curriculum. The argument advanced and more sharply focused in this chapter was that in a political context of democratic pluralism and cultural diversity there existed only one means of generating values powerful and acceptable enough to be embedded within the curriculum of schools of pluralist democracies. Particular attention was given to children's rights and the argument was advanced for consideration of these rights as an 'added value' to all other human rights. An acknowledgement was made of the parlous state of children's rights even in some democratic societies, but more particularly in the so-called Third World countries. The rights of school students too were also acknowledged to be inadequately defined and secured.

A definition of human rights education was advanced, which took account of the dual function of being both part of the curriculum and its major moral baseline and generative ethic, not least *vis-à-vis* the whole school ethos. The inclusive and generative aspects of human rights education were illustrated diagrammatically in a model. A school policy for human rights education was advanced and an appropriate curricular policy was described in detail, using the same curriculum building blocks introduced in Chapter 2. Once again, emphasis was placed on the central function and importance of thinking skills, if students were to achieve morally autonomous but socially responsible problem-solving and decision-making competences. Linking with the brief section on assessment and evaluation in Chapter 2, the importance of professional evaluation and monitoring, closely nestled into supportive and sensitive opportunities for professional development, was underlined, and flagged for further discussion in succeeding chapters of this book. Five families of assessment techniques were exemplified as being particularly appropriate to the kind of curriculum being proposed, including those emphasizing oracy, greater equality, the resting of judgment, skills and informatic competences, assessing broader aspects of subjects and drawing close together the teaching and assessment functions. Finally, and as part of that comprehensive evaluation strategy, a proposal was made for a bias review policy as part of the on-going monitoring of all facets of a school's functioning.

Drawing on the work accomplished in the first part of this book, I propose now to consider in greater detail what might be the components of an appropriate teaching philosophy, style and approach necessary for the delivery of a global multicultural curriculum. To achieve this goal I want to refer briefly to attempts to group major families of teaching models, and through this to make explicit that we all have a model of teaching underpinning our practice, but that it is often subconsciously held to a greater or lesser measure. Once again it is important to stress that there can be no assumption of a professional *carte blanche*. Rather, the approach has to take into account the existing professional biography and teaching style of all teachers, and to encourage the process of review and development which is central to the philosophy of this book. Thus, while the components of each teacher's teaching 'identikit' will be the same, the existing constellation and synergetic effect of those components will be unique. For that reason, the necessary professional development of each of these components will also be unique to achieve an effective style for the delivery of a global multicultural curriculum, which is at the same time centrally reflective of human rights education, seen both as part of the curriculum and as its moral powerhouse.

Important though a philosophy of teaching may be, the kinds of teaching strategies a teacher adopts are a function of a host of factors, including such powerful ones as that teacher's personality, previous professional experience, the professional social system to which the teacher belongs and which he or she uses as a professional and moral reference group, previous training and individual ideology of education. These factors working together produce different professional identities and perceptions of educational, school and classroom reality, according to the weighting and implicit generalizability accorded to that factor by the teacher. Thus, in order to provide some more objective assessment of applicability and generalizability, I propose, in the second part of this chapter, to work the principles of the philosophy of teaching into practical form in the shape of specific teaching approaches, which may be selectively adopted by teachers as part of their overall teaching style. As much as possible in that section, I shall be drawing on validated evidence of the effectiveness of each approach. I shall then be proceeding in the final part of the book to consider the material and human resource implications of the implementation of a global multicultural curriculum, which has at its core a commitment to human rights education.

Models of Teaching

All teachers have in mind a model of teaching, underpinned by assumptions about the way students learn, about society and its expectations of teachers and schools, and about knowledge. This theoretical framework, often unquestioned and unappraised, has a very powerful influence on the way they teach and relate to their students. Inherent and inexplicit, perhaps never communicated with spoken words, are attitudes about minority communities, about the world and about social issues, such as human rights. Because of the powerful communicator role of this conceptual framework, through which teachers make their professional reality coherent and controllable, it is very important that any review procedure seeks sensitively and gradually to begin the process of examination of the theoretical and practical justification of the models of teaching, which underlie the teacher's professional activity. One way in which that can be done is to look at ideal-type models of teaching that have been constructed by psychologists and to see whether we can locate our own theoretical position in terms of their constructs. For example, Joyce and Weil (1986) have produced a very useful compilation of four groups of families of models of teaching, which is as follows:

- The Personal Awareness Family, the major goal of which is greater self-awareness and responsible independence. These include nondirective teaching (Roger), synectics (Gordon), awareness training, and the classroom meeting adopting counselling approaches.
- The Information-Processing Family, the overall aim of which is to teach students to think effectively, through the acquisition of more complex intellectual strategies. These models include concept attainment (Bruner), inductive thinking (Taba), inquiry training, advance organizers (Ausubel), mnemonics, intellectual development (Piaget), and scientific enquiry (Bruner; Schwab).
- The Synergetic Social Family, which has as its goal the use of collective social efforts to co-operate in learning. These include group

investigation (Dewey), role-playing (Shaftel and Shaftel), jurispru-
dential inquiry (Oliver and Shaver), laboratory training and social
science inquiry.
* The Behavioural Systems Family, which sees humans as social
learners with a self-correcting capacity for learning from feedback.
These include mastery learning (Bloom, Becker, Glaser), self-control
learning (Skinner), skill and concept development, training and
assertive training (Joyce and Weil, 1986, pp. 5–15).

Each of these families – let us call them as a shorthand the intellectual,
awareness, social and feedback families – has characteristics that have
percolated into the folk theory of teaching of present teachers in different
ways, to different extents and to varying degrees of consciousness. They
are probably never utilized in an exclusive form either as families or as
individual styles within that family, but are combined into an overall
philosophy of teaching, held by every teacher even when they avow a
disinclination to theory; they are expressed through the action of
teaching. The point is that everyone's practice is underpinned by a
personally unique theoretical framework, which comprises components
that are consciously derivative from the families of models given above,
or are subconsciously held. These folk understandings are very influential and include a similar subset of assumptions about society and other
cultural groups, which may be overlaid with preconceptions and
presuppositions that need to be reviewed and critically, but professionally, appraised.

So, in the next section, I want to try to make more explicit what kind
of overall profile of characteristics might make an appropriate philosophy of teaching appropriate for a global multicultural curriculum,
expressive of human rights and attentive to the human rights of the
students. I wish to make clear that such an individual philosophy of
teaching will be unique to each teacher. It will be an amalgam,
deliberated to a greater or lesser extent; many components of it will be
held in common with other teachers in the same school. So the process is
to be seen as one of making conscious more of what exists, and of adding
to that further explicit components.

Towards a Philosophy of Teaching

If we reflect back on the implications of the aims, objectives and core
human rights commitment of the curricular reform proposed here,
certain basic moral and educational principles emerge quite clearly and it

is these 'ideological' principles, combined with the benefits of the characteristics of the families of models of teaching given above, which I intend to use as the professional markers for an appropriate philosophy of teaching. In addition to the ideological, psychological and social aspects, a philosophy of teaching combines both individual and institutional aspects and personal and group dimensions, insofar as it embraces those aspects of teaching on which agreement is necessary if a school is to function as a team. It must also provide a professional yardstick against which all teachers may make sense of their professional world, and may shape, implement and review their own teaching.

The baseline moral principle of respect for persons implies *respect for students* too, most of all in the teaching situation. It is a criterion that draws strongly on the awareness and social families of models of teaching, given above. Implicit in this criterion is not only the avoidance of physical and psychological pressure but, more positively, high expectations of all students and absence of bias and prejudice in materials, curricula and methods. It involves a spirit of positive acceptance of the cultural contribution of all students and an acknowledgement, indeed a welcome, of students as alternative sources of legitimate reality. This reality is seen as having an affective dimension. This means a recognition of alternative frameworks of human meaning and awareness, and the need to support these different frameworks in different ways, so that all can gain maximum benefit from the teacher's framework of teaching. For teachers, it means accepting the responsibility of empowering students to learn from their teaching and to inter-learn with the culture of the students.

It does not assume an 'anything goes' philosophy but one which imposes the highest standard of both social and academic conduct on all parties. It implies openness in decision making and professional judgments, and a willingness to discuss students' strengths and weaknesses with them frankly and in confidence. It implies consultation about the release of information about the students, and a readiness to negotiate classroom reality rather than to seek to impose it.

The second principle is closely associated with the first in the sense that it focuses on the teachers' responsibility to generate a *climate of acceptance and involvement* on the part of all students. It is strongly evocative of the social family of models of teaching. It implies recognizing that feelings exist and are an important component of the classroom culture and the individual student's construction of reality, in interaction with cognitive and rational components. It involves the construction of a classroom ambience and reality which can afford maximum 'social confidence' to each student as the basis of learning. It demands the development of a sensitive, humane, caring, warm and interested personal relationship between teacher and student and among students.

The third major baseline principle for a suitable philosophy of teaching arises directly from the need to educate future national and world citizens to be actively oriented to a *human rights commitment,* and to take on social responsibilities and duties. Underlying the acquisition of the necessary knowledge, attitudes and skills is the need for participatory and active learning, which emphasizes the student's own role in making decisions and solving problems, but also in developing active responsibility for less privileged groups. This means an appeal to the judgment of students in their own learning and in the assessment of that learning, which in turn implies the need to legitimate an appropriate pedagogy and assessment through persuasion and conviction rather than coercively through 'hand-me-down' authority and imposition.

The fourth principle is that of *democratic process.* The theory, deriving principally from the work of Dewey, is that education which claims to prepare students for democratic involvement and participation can only do that by direct involvement in the process. That process should include direct, deliberate engagement with problems of social significance. Since democratic process involves the ability to co-operate in pursuit of common social goals, it follows that the teacher should facilitate co-operative inquiry into meaningful and major social issues, which demand both social and reflective intellectual engagement. This does not mean an uncritical acceptance of whatever views are put forward, but rather a spirit of openness, integrativeness, inquiry and critical community, where such views can be tested out for their accuracy, applicability and validity through a process of disciplined, courteous and principled discussion and examination. For this, students need to develop the ability to reflect on the ways that they interrogate information, on their knowledge, values and attitudes. In terms of knowledge, this principle requires an acceptance of the provisionality and tentative nature of information and its cultural location, and of education as a continual process of negotiation and re-negotiation of reality.

The fifth principle embraces the teacher's *responsibility to provide creative environments,* not only of resources but also socially and morally. This principle implies the furnishing of a wide variety of information and research sources, addressing issues including human rights and other global issues at community, national and global levels. It owes much to the awareness and feedback models of teaching, but with a strong representation of the intellectual models. Here an emphasis on the acquisition of effective information processing skills is a central component of teaching. It does not imply that the teacher is the only arbiter of classroom reality but rather it aims for the joint construction of that reality by collaboration and negotiation between students and students and between students and teachers.

The sixth principle is that of *moral engagement*, that is an acceptance of the fact that the teacher has a responsibility to facilitate the movement of students from egocentric to socio-centric moral decision-making, while at the same time generating the competence and autonomy in the students to make and activate his or her own moral mind up by using rational appraisal of the social referents and moral precedents. A corollary of this principle is one which is often referred to as the principle of manifest goodwill, namely the presumption of goodwill on the part of all members of the school community until proven otherwise, and the opportunity for those who may have transgressed to return without recrimination, as soon as they accept the 'rules of the club' again.

A seventh principle addresses the function of the teacher in *facilitating more complex and sophisticated thinking* on the part of students, through such techniques as continually pitching questions that require reasoning at increasingly high levels, and facilitating problem solving and decision making at growing levels of complexity. It hardly needs saying that it draws predominantly on the intellectual models of teaching although, as we shall see later, it may also be the case that co-operative group approaches to teaching are also efficacious in enabling students to achieve more sophisticated thinking and moral perspective-taking.

An eighth principle is that of *communicative sensitivity* across cognitive, affective, moral and stylistic dimensions from expressive to transactional use of language. This breadth of concern means the teacher's function is to draw out the student's communicative competence along the continuum from expressive to instrumental use of language, evincing not just a concern with such matters as the forms, context and uses of language, but also coming to grips with issues such as equality of language, through the avoidance of discriminatory sexist or other biased or culturally offensive language. This also implies a concern – and hopefully increasing skill – in the area of using language to express feelings as well as facts and an appreciation of the important role of non-verbal communication. It means, too, a beginning with the deconstruction of the massive weight of negative images of women and girls in children's and young persons' literature, and an understanding that such bias may structure and limit the potential of those against whom it is directed, and their ability to proceed to higher level reasoning, where this is seen as outside the parameters of the stereotype. Finally, it implies encouragement of interest in linguistic diversity.

Finally, but crucially, the ninth principle is of *engagement with both aims and means* for students as well as teachers. This principle refers to the empowerment of students to engage in creative dialogue abut their own aims, individually and in groups, and to influence the formulation and achievement of their own goals. The corollary of this principle is that teachers must also be empowered to engage with their educational aims. Thus, just as the role of the teacher cannot be restricted to that of a technician, like an educational postman delivering pre-packaged, 'hand-me-down' knowledge, so also the role of the student has to be one that will encourage an increasing and legitimate concern with ends as well as means.

These nine principles form the basis of what we may call an outline *philosophy of teaching* for the implementation of a global multicultural curriculum. They are permeated by insights and influences from the models of teaching, but in different balance and weighting. Together they form the educational lighthouse which gives the implementation of that curriculum its momentum, directionality and legitimation. They provide both a yardstick for the choice and adoption of teaching/learning strategies and approaches, and an initial point of reference for the more detailed panoply of professional judgments which all teachers need to make, day-by-day, hour-by-hour and minute-by-minute in their professional lives. I propose to recapitulate the nine principles in shorthand form, before we move to a consideration of their linkage with more specific teaching approaches;

- Respect for persons, including students.
- Accepting and participatory climate.
- Manifest human rights commitment.
- Implementation of democratic process.
- Provision of creative environment.
- Moral engagement.
- Facilitation of more sophisticated cognitive processes.
- Communicative sensitivity.
- Engagement with both aims and means.

In the next section of this book I want to select a series of teaching approaches, which can achieve the aims and objectives introduced earlier, which draw on the models of teaching, and which are compatible with the above philosophy of teaching and which are also susceptible to use for the delivery of a human rights attentive curriculum with a strong global perspective. We are also looking for approaches which can attenuate social category salience and which can be implemented by 'ordinary' teachers without inflated expectations of revolutionary change, but rather as an evolution from their already existing style of teaching.

There are a number of criteria the teaching approaches will have to meet in order to be included in the overall framework, in addition to coming within the philosophy of teaching outlined above. Firstly, they must not detract from the efficiency of academic learning. In other words, they must combine both social and intellectual objectives. Secondly, however little, there should be some empirical evidence of their efficacy. Such evidence may have been assembled by ethnographic or by more positivistic methods. Thirdly, they should be capable of generalization. They should not be merely laboratory experiments, which could not, or could only with difficulty, be replicated in normal school situations. Fourthly, they should be manifestly reasonable, in the demands and expectations they place upon teachers. They should not be utopian or millennial, expecting some kind of overnight conversion of all teachers. Fifthly, they should be capable of implementation in normal schools with normal resources. Model schools are often lavishly staffed and resourced with materials and equipment in a way which could detract from the applicability of a method to more ordinary schools. Sixthly, they should be attentive to 'wisdom' to be extracted from the models of teaching. And, lastly, they should not be disruptive of the normal life and curriculum of the school, but should rather be capable of integration and application in such a way as to develop that which exists, without causing a negative reaction from staff, students or parents. In sum, the approaches chosen should meet the following criteria:

- They should enhance both academic and social learning.
- There should be some evidence of their efficacy.
- They should be generalizable.
- They should not place unreasonable demands on teachers.
- They should be capable of implementation in ordinary schools.
- They should not be overly disruptive, but should be capable of fitting in with the ordinary curriculum and approaches of the school.
- They should be attentive to the 'models of teaching', if not directly expressive of them.

One very well established approach to teaching and learning, which has now been replicated and validated in many different school and national contexts, is that described as *co-operative and collaborative group work*. As indicated in Chapter 2, there are six or seven different versions, emphasizing different perspectives, including both competitive and co-operative approaches, curricular and pedagogical dimensions, along a continuum from teacher-directed to student-centred. As shown in Figure 2.1 there are basically two orientations to co-operative group work, those inclining to a peer- tutoring approach, which have tended to address instructional but not curricular issues (see, however, Stevens *et al.*, 1987), and those which adopt a group investigation, or syndicate, approach, and have addressed both instructional and curriculum dimensions. To a greater or lesser extent they all draw on the strengths of the social synergy models of teaching, arguing that students working together can learn more and better both intellectually and socially. All of them have been shown to have a greater impact on cognitive and affective development than the existing whole class approaches. Some have also demonstrated an effectiveness on higher-order thinking skills as well.

The various co-operative learning methods adopted by the teams at the Johns Hopkins University in the United States use ethnically-mixed learning groups, which study material presented by the teacher; the students receive rewards according to the learning of the group as a whole. Fairly consistent effects on inter-group relations and on academic achievement of both minority and majority students has been shown to occur through the adoption of these various methods (Slavin, 1985).

One of the most widely-tested methods for small group, co-operative learning was that described as *Group Investigation*, which draws much from Dewey's project method, with students having a wide measure of freedom and responsibility in deciding the content and the process of their learning. Under this approach, a broad topic for study is agreed by the class and the teacher, the topic is then divided into subtopics, which are studied further by self-selected groups, with each student taking responsibility for an aspect of the subtopic on a kind of syndicate study basis and being responsible for reporting back on it to the group and through the group to the class. More recently this approach has been adopted by Sharan and his associates in Israel, with significant effects on both achievement and higher-level thinking skills, as well as on such behavioural outcomes as social interaction (Sharan and Shachar, 1988). Moreover, statistically significant correlations were discovered between the amount of co-operative behaviour and academic achievement, indicating what has been argued consistently in this book, namely that improved academic outcomes can be achieved by methods that also contribute to social goals, such as greater equity. Further, we also have details of the effects of the in-service preparation teachers received to undertake the new group methods, which show a significant attitude change on the part of the teachers (Sharan and Hertz-Lazarowitz, 1982).

The advantages of such group approaches for both minority and majority students are manifest. Their attractiveness for teachers is less manifest but also convincing. They not only comply with the outline principles of the philosophy of teaching proposed above, but they also meet all the criteria proposed. In sum, such methods can offer:

- Enhanced academic learning.
- Improved self-esteem, particularly of minority students.
- Better social-emotional and in particular inter-ethnic relations, including, in some cases, relations outside the classroom.
- Superior and higher order learning (in some variations).
- More and better oral participation (of minority students).
- Effective and synergetic combination of social and intellectual outcomes.
- Validated evidence, in a variety of settings, of the efficacy of different styles of group approaches.
- Practicability, in the sense that they are within the scope of most teachers in most schools (Sharan *et al.*, 1984; Slavin, 1985; Johnson *et al.*, 1981; Amir and Sharan, 1984; Sharan and Shachar, 1988).

Inherent within the co-operative group approach is perhaps the most potentially effective method of dealing with ethnic attitudes and relationships, usually referred to as *ethnic contact,* that is direct, purposeful contact between members of the different groups (Allport, 1954; Amir, 1984). Such contact has the potential not only to correct for prejudiced attitudes, misperceptions and for incorrect information, but also to the breaking down of expectations and stereotypes upon which those attitudes rest. It can also affect socio-emotional relationships. Naturally, just getting to know students from different ethnic and social backgrounds can help to commence the process of disestablishing prejudice and stereotypes, not least where most members of a society live in ethnic 'apartheid'. But ethnic contact on its own can be of little value and can even be counterproductive unless the conditions of the contact are carefully controlled and certain criteria are met. For schools thinking of adopting such an approach, it is important to undertake it under the most optimal conditions, with full legitimating and explicit authoritative backing of the school. The major conditions that must be met are:

- There should be equal status contact.
- There should be a common objective.
- There should be an opportunity for extra-curricular meaningful personal encounters and relationships on an individual basis.
- The contact between members of the ethnic group should be part of a continual regime rather than being transitory.
- There should be a similarity of competence and level between members of the contact groups.
- The approach should be manifestly backed by the full authority of the school.
- There should be a good chance of the objectives of the encounter being successfully accomplished.

Clearly, ethnic contact is susceptible to implementation in a variety of different forms and the strategies can be varied to match the ethnic composition of the school and its neighbourhood. Twinning, inter-visiting, exchanging, bussing, joint enterprise, excursions and field trips all offer scope for well-controlled inter-ethnic contact which could meet the criteria. Provided it is not on a merely transitory or 'exotic' basis, there is also scope for more enduring aesthetic encounters in the arts, music and theatre, through the utilization of community resources or visiting groups. Sadly, in the past, many schools and teachers have been unaware of the criteria and they and pupils have suffered great disap-pointment and even alienation when the method has been unsuccessful or counterproductive.

Many students may find difficulty in adapting to group techniques straight away, and the teacher has a responsibility to protect students from calamitous failure which could destroy rather than enhance self-confidence and achievement. The question, therefore, arises of how to best prepare all students for the difficult task of co-operative group work. Here techniques such as pre-preparation, coaching and expec-tation training are extremely useful ways of preventing groups being dominated by members of dominant groups, to the detriment of the social confidence of minority students and perhaps the reinforcement of the stereotyped views of majority students. In a sense, such approaches have much to do with enabling students to learn from particular types of teaching, of which co-operative group work is but one.

It goes without saying that good teaching will have its effect, and the advantages of co-operative group approaches over direct teaching should not blind us to the fact that *direct whole class teaching* can also be a useful method, although, used exclusively, not nearly as powerful as the two methods described above in developing affective and conative learning. On the other hand, if, in mixed ethnic classrooms, equal status is afforded to all students, teacher expectations are high for all students, the methods adopted are attentive to good teaching and learning theory, the tasks are well planned and graded to secure success for all, then there is a good chance of efficacious low-level cognitive increments of basic information and even the stimulation of higher-order thinking and some affective gains. In any case, even lower-order cognitive gains are essential to a global approach and to dislodging stereotypes and prejudiced attitudes, by correcting for misinformation and providing accurate, up-to-date data about other cultures and countries, not least about developing countries and those with a different ideological orientation. Moreover, while project work can provide lots of the information base needed to attain accurate, up-to-date and non-stereotyped views of other countries and global tasks and problems, whole class and often vicarious means such as film, television, pictures, computer packages, etc. are indispensable.

Firstly, however, the somewhat obvious point has to be made that there are a number of different ways in which interaction between teachers and pupils and among pupils themselves can be organized, within a whole class, heavily teacher-directed pedagogy. The particular strategy adopted needs to be related to the target population, the objectives of the learning session, the kind of task involved, the facilities available, the experience of both teacher and learners in different kinds of teaching/learning approaches, including group work, the conversational style desired by the teacher, etc. Nor does the strategy always have to be the same. Rather, through a process of gradual growth, an enterprising teacher can expand very considerably the teaching/learning situations managed in order to develop a global multicultural approach to the curriculum, which is expressive of human rights education.

And, of course, the teacher should not, however, assume that students only learn when the teacher is directing them nor that large whole class groups are always disadvantaged. Quite the reverse, for to be learned behaviour, behaviour must be self-maintaining (i.e., it has to adapt to situations where the teacher is not present and, as we shall be seeing later, a larger group affords a wider range of skills and opportunities for peer-group learning). Moreover, whilst it must be translated into other cultures with caution, studies have indicated that in British primary schools children in larger classes tended to do significantly better in larger classes than in smaller ones on tests of reading, arithmetic and social adjustment, thus confirming similar findings in the Plowden Report. There is, thus, some evidence that more traditional forms of organization help achievement in English, Maths and social adjustment. On the other hand, other factors such as time-on-task and peer group conformity and reinforcement can be maximized through a number of 'class segmentation' strategies, which do not go quite so far as to be called group work, as well as by treating the whole class as a unit for all tasks.

Any teaching which aims to be effective demands detailed advanced planning and this is particularly so where the approaches are to be innovatory in both cognitive and affective spheres. But there is a wide range of school-learning situations which a teacher may arrange and manage in the context of large-group teaching. There is a wide variety of strategies available, from keeping the class as one large group to breaking it down into groups for some tasks and individuals. Whichever is used, it is important to bear in mind the options of class control available to the teacher through the style and choice of communication, and of the interacting of the teacher. In this respect, it has been suggested that there are what might be typified as three distinct varieties of whole class discussion, each characterized by a different kind of conversational control employing:

1. Closed question approaches, where questions to which only one (factual) answer is possible predominate. These elicit one word or very brief answers directed to the teacher. The teacher answers pupils' responses, but does not respond to them; quizzes are often used in this way.
2. The teacher retains conversational control over the topic and of how and when and how much the pupils speak, and to whom, but there are more open questions, permitting a range of answers and the teacher responds to pupils' replies. There may be some encouragement to exploratory talk.
3. Conversational control by the teacher is reduced and not all comments need to be channelled through the teacher. There are fewer teacher questions and they are almost always open; pupil-initiated sequences and oriented responses are encouraged.

Generally speaking, the latter two styles are less frequent than the first one but are superior to it. Moreover, research seems to indicate that teachers often deceive themselves about which 'style' they are using predominantly and the proportion of pupils actually involved in verbalizing either responses or questions. Yet opportunity to verbalize is an important factor in achieving understanding and through that the kind of higher level cognitive functioning, which is essential to disestablishing prejudice and developing higher-order moral decision-making and problem-solving. Thus, the more teachers can enable pupils to be actively involved in verbalizing, the better the learning outcomes towards more healthy attitudes and greater global perspective-taking are likely to be. Naturally, that verbalization does not need to be 'pupil-to-teacher' – task related 'pupil-to- pupil' verbalization in dyadic partnership may be equally or indeed more effective.

Thus, teacher effectiveness, even in whole class, direct teaching situations, may crucially depend on the skills of questioning which the teacher can deploy, including the following:

- Use of the pupils' previously acquired knowledge, experience and skills as the basis of question-formulation.
- Sharing with the students information about what is to be learnt, performed or achieved.
- Relating the work in hand to other areas of knowledge of other activities/experiences.
- Post the initial questions, and/or make the first statements as *advanced organizers*, so that the class is interested in the work, stimulated by it and has an overview of it.
- Asking questions and/or making statements that are designed to help children to organize their thoughts, not simply ones demanding an informational response.
- Deliberately drawing from the class knowledge, experience and skills that are relevant.
- Focusing upon those aspects that are particularly relevant to the work in hand.
- Giving definitions to help clarify the issues.
- Emphasizing the key points, summarizing as appropriate.
- Helping the class to appreciate and understand the links between different aspects of the work, and between it and other areas of knowledge/activities or experiences.
- 'Equalizing' the distribution of questions and reception of responses.

But the style of questioning is only one variable in whole class approaches, which can with benefit be changed. While there are many non-alterable variables in a teacher's teaching/learning context, there are also many others, in addition to questioning strategy, which can also be changed. But, when considering the alterable variables, it is necessary to bear in mind that some have a stronger effect on learning than others, some are more susceptible to alteration than others, and the focus of the alteration may be different (for example, the teacher, the learner, the home environment or peer group). In a summary of the extent of effect of such variables, Walberg has listed the variables in order of the extent of the effect which they may have, and Bloom has quantified that effect (Walberg, 1984; Bloom, 1984).

Some of the variables will be more accessible and susceptible to change in some societies than others, but strategies which may, according to Bloom's work, result in increased learning if particular variables were changed, would include those which help pupils to improve their processing of conventional instruction such as:

- Encouragement of good study habits by pupils.
- Greater time-on-task and the improvement of students' learning skills.
- Provision of the cognitive prerequisites for each new learning task.
- Adoption of mastery learning/feedback-corrective approaches.
- Helping pupils to develop a pupil-support system in which groups of pupils study together.
- Use of advance organizers (e.g., statements of intention, advance notice of content, locking what is to be learned onto what has been learned, etc.).
- Provision of organizing aids during the lesson.
- Appropriate questions, summaries, etc. on completion of the lesson.
- Use of information technology approaches.
- Academic guidance and support given to the pupil.
- Stimulation to students to explore ideas, events and the wider environment.
- Opportunities for developing language use.
- Availability of a variety of interlinked extra-curricular activities.
- Equalization of teachers' interactions with pupils.
- Random distribution of positive encouragement arising from pupils' responses.
- Introducing more pupil activity and participation by more pupils in the learning process.
- Achievement of random but clear feedback by the teacher.
- Supply of additional clarifications and illustrations as needed.
- Teachers achieving a more accurate picture of their own teaching methods, their distribution of questions and praise, etc.
- Improved teaching of higher mental processes, such as emphasizing problem solving, analytical skills, creativity, application of

principles; teaching subjects as methods of inquiry; teaching subjects as ways of thinking; making use of observations, reflections on observations, experimentation, use of first-hand data and daily experience; reflection of the above approaches in both formative and summative assessment, materials, etc; use of first-hand experiences; utilization of primary resource material; and providing learning (and assessment) situations in which pupils apply principles in a variety of different problem situations (Bloom, 1984, adapted and amended by the author).

In sum, although direct whole class teaching has been shown to be a less powerful pedagogical strategy than some others in facilitating inter-ethnic friendships and improved attitudes, it has the advantage of providing pedagogical continuity with what exists. Moreover, given a democratic classroom regime, high activity approaches, rational methods of intellectually involving students, an emphasis on similarity rather than difference and material which stretches students conceptually and affectively, such methods can be very effective in promoting a human rights based global approach to multicultural education and in helping students to clarify their own value positions.

Either group or whole class methods or both may be adopted to the use of case histories to develop a global approach in the multicultural curriculum, where issues of human rights are central and human rights affords the moral direction and centrality of the curriculum. They may be used as:

- Illustrations of lifestyles of minority communities.
- Means of introducing eminent world citizens.
- A non-threatening way of enabling students to explore their own feelings of prejudice.
- A means of evoking empathy and reversibility.
- A useful means of introducing issues of human rights.
- To illustrate and investigate the good versus good dilemmas.
- A starter to other more active methods, such as role playing.

Case histories have been much used in the social studies and humanities curricula and in other subjects as well, to evoke empathy, to convey a commitment against injustice, to illustrate moral dilemmas, to provide material for dilemma discussion and material for dramatization. For the work of a number of authors and educators, some basic indications emerge of the principles which might govern the use of case studies, such as:

- The need for the inclusion of everyday characters, situations and information.

- The need to provide some 'same age' models.
- An inclusive 'us' rather than exclusive 'them' presentation.
- Illustration of inconsistency in value application.
- Indication of 'fight back' on the part of those victimized.
- Positive rather than neutral support for justice on the part of the teacher.
- An emphasis on similarity rather than difference.
- Consistency with previous material studied by students.
- Good but not intrusive de-briefing strategies.
- Assurance of confidentiality for individual students' notes, if they wish (Kehoe, 1984).

Each teacher will know his or her class best and, in particular, at what stage and in what ways case histories may be utilized. For some they will remain a source of factual information or historical study, perhaps with an illustrative function *vis-à-vis* human rights or the relationships of individuals and nations in a global context. For others, they may be used as part of role-playing or dramatic or musical presentation, or in dance or mime. One of the major advantages is that they may be deployed at all stages of education, from initial entry to school to adulthood. Used carefully, they may be used to evoke empathy with those suffering prejudice or discrimination, by those who harbour the same prejudice.

A further technique, which can be used either as part of group work or on a whole class basis, is that of *values education and principle-testing*. I propose to consider three approaches, which I shall label values education, principle testing and moral education, although each has a great deal in common with the others and all are concerned both with values and with moral education. Perhaps, also, we should reiterate at this point the essential 'morality' of the global multicultural curriculum, which has a core commitment to human rights education and rests on the basic ethic of respect for persons. Education within democratic societies has an intrinsically and inseparable moral purpose and obligation, or it is a futile exercise.

The theory behind the various values education approaches is that it is mainly by identifying, discussing and resolving values dilemmas according to rational criteria that students achieve greater moral responsibility and maturity. One of the major advantages of the material that has been developed for values education over many years is that it can either be used for discrete values programmes or it can be integrated into other subjects. While not underestimating the informal and incidental ways in which values education takes place, not least through the informal dimension of the school's functioning, material such as that developed at the Ontario Institute for Studies in Education (Beck, McCoy and Bradley-Cameron, 1980; Beck 1983) is specifically aimed at providing a reflective approach to values education, based on material that can be used by teachers with relatively little training. It rests on the explicit acceptance that students of differing religious and cultural backgrounds have a great deal in common and much to learn from each other in the joint study of values. It derives firmly from the tradition of moral education which asserts that students must internalize their own value system, which they should work out for themselves, rather than having it thrust on them. This approach does not, however, thereby underplay the important function of the teacher and appropriate materials in evoking the necessary insights, through appeal to the students' own judgment (cf. Stenhouse, 1975).

Values education approaches are particularly suitable for engaging with issues of human rights or injustice, including on a world stage. The basic method of the reflective approach, quoted above, rests on the identification of fundamental human values, which are then analysed and comprehended in the light of relevant facts, situations, ideas and other values. Further values and situations can then be discussed by reference to the clarified principles inherent in the fundamental values. Students are challenged by discussion techniques to attain consistency in the application of moral principles or to provide rational justification as to why there should be inconsistency of application of moral principles. To achieve these opportunities for values clarification, there is constant alternation between general propositions, key ideas and questions, on the one hand, and specific examples against which those propositions can be tested, on the other. The approach acknowledges the need for professional preparation of teachers for this work, and emphasis is placed on the qualities the teacher will need to exhibit, such as empathy, receptivity to the ideas of the students, understanding the children's ideas and interests and the ability to conduct a good stimulating discussion. But it is stressed that no additional formal preparation is necessary in order to get started, provided that the material is appropriate.

A subset of values education is the technique known as principle testing, which has been shown to be effective in altering and amending inter-ethnic attitudes (Kehoe and Todd, 1978), It involves the acquisition of certain 'rules of the game' by students, such as what an open discussion forum means in theory and practice, respect for the legitimate views of others, tolerance in turn-taking in discussions, appeal to rational criteria, reversibility of moral position-taking and consistency of application of moral principles. These rules rest on the same value assumptions as a global multicultural curriculum, committed to human rights, and are embedded in an acceptance of the worth and value of all individuals. The principle of dilemmas which are at the heart of the technique enlist pupils in an acceptance also of democratic process, of rationality in the solution of moral issues and involvement in such techniques as mutuality and reversibility. Above all the approach allows students to work out their own value positions.

Principle testing is sometimes taught through a method called discourse training. This approach rests on the assumption that students are being prepared for active citizenship and will therefore need to learn skills of advocacy, persuasion, petitioning and communication, which need to be extensively practised within a democratic context in the school. Notwithstanding the discussion approach to value dilemma material which burgeoned in the United States in the 1970s, much of the work on discourse training has been conducted but not extensively evaluated in the United Kingdom, where it has often been linked with community action or service. Indeed, community action may be one of the most potent methods of implementing the multicultural curriculum. Unfortunately, there is almost no independently validated evidence of its efficacy and thus this approach does not meet the rigorous criteria set down for detailed exposition in this chapter.

Allied with the work of values education is the approach to moral education, pioneered by Lawrence Kohlberg in the United States. The basic principles are based on a typology of moral development articulated by Kohlberg, and his contention that students must be taught at a level of moral engagement, one stage above their existing level (the +1 reasoning requirement). The process of challenge and response, involved in this dialogue can advance the speed of development and maturation of the moral reasoning of students. Again, the technique rests on the introduction of moral dilemmas, which can be solved by the application of reasoning at one stage above the existing level of moral reasoning of the students. While the detail of his work and techniques has been subject to much criticism, it does focus attention on the need for students to internalize values through a process of accommodation and construction of moral reality rather than merely assuming that the students will be able to absorb them through their pedagogic skins (Kohlberg, Levine and Hewer, 1984). Values development and moral growth need to be explicitly planned and worked for as does any other aspect of the curriculum, and the work on values education finally exposes the preciosity and pretentiousness of those who would argue that it is not the task of the school to transmit or propagate particular values.

Finally, there is the use of different modes of drama or theatre, including mime, dance and musical presentations, both 'off the hook' and 'made to measure' by the students themselves. Because it can extend the existing worlds of the students, it has the potential to push back the horizons of both factual reality and moral responsibility. It may be used in indiscrete form or as part of a scheme of work for another subject in the curriculum alongside other teaching methods. As part of simulation and role playing, it can be a major way of advancing such moral competences as mutuality, reversibility and reciprocity. It may also be used to help students aspire to higher levels of reasoning, especially as part of debriefing sessions. On the other hand, this technique needs careful preparation and practise by the students before they can become really proficient. They must also learn the rules of the game, which dictate that a role played is not reality, but make believe, and that such roles should under no circumstances be continued after the role play or simulation is over.

One of the big advantages of dramatic approaches, with or without script, is that they may be used from the earliest days of schooling, when children easily accommodate to dressing-up and puppet theatre. At that early stage, prejudiced or stereotyped preconceptions can easily be tackled and changed through a process of play in a way which would be very difficult later. The same point applies to the building-up of a positive image or greater self-confidence to which simulation and role play may also make a substantial contribution. Role play can also be linked very easily to the aesthetic dimensions of the school curriculum, through music, preparation of masks, shadow theatres, puppets and other artistic and expressive arts, and through exhibition of children's work or class or school plays, or other extra-curricular activities. Parents can become involved, can assist and can also be 'educated'. Visits to the theatre or activity museums by students, or visits to the school by itinerant players of theatre, music or dance, can also be fruitful and enriching occasions for developing new insights and broadening the cultural perspectives of students to make them more global or more attentive to human rights issues. For older pupils, voluntary playing of a role, which was previously unacceptable for the student, may move deeply entrenched negative attitudes and stereotypes.

Such occasions, however, need to be integrated smoothly into the longitudinal development of the student's learning and should not be seen as one-off events, or, as argued earlier, they may be counterproductive. They should also be integrated laterally into the broader curriculum and syllabus. They require good preparation and reinforcement, as well as follow-up and in the case of particularly controversial issues, debriefing as well. Used in an inexperienced or non-reflective way, drama can, however, be damaging to inter-ethnic relations and strict guidelines need to be set down by the teacher. Above all, the divide between play and reality must be clearly drawn, although at the same time, maximum opportunity must be taken to exploit drama for cognitive, affective and conative learning.

Once again, as with the models of teaching, there is no suggestion that any of these approaches would be used exclusively, although it seems clear that currently, the most widely and frequently used is the whole class, direct teaching approach, because it is traditional and is apparently the easiest to prepare for and deliver and is most included in initial teacher education. Conversely, the group investigation approach is the least used, because it appears to be the most difficult; it requires teachers with a good confident professional self-concept and is the least prepared for in courses of initial teacher education. But neither of these two approaches, nor indeed any of the others advocated in this chapter, need rule out children increasingly setting their own agenda, setting it within a widening context both substantively and geographically and setting it both within the school and outside. There is no reason why children should not be recognized as experts where they manifestly possess expert knowledge; conversely there is no reason why teachers need to pretend to be the ubiquitous and universal experts. By sharing their expertise, teachers and students can help to create a critical community, which is itself an opportunity for the living and daily practice of human rights and responsibilities.

Whatever mix of approaches is adopted by the teacher, each teacher, but hopefully supported by the school and colleagues, will have to assemble the unique profile, style and weighting of models of teaching and teaching approaches, which are suitable for the cultural context and the teacher's professional biography, but which will enable that teacher to deliver effectively an appropriate curriculum. Good, well organized and business-like classroom management, according to the philosophy of teaching set out above, will be a key feature and a key determinant of success. Teachers will need to deliver an imaginative and stimulating variety of different styles, motivational strategies and content, asking higher-order questions, rather than simply knowledge-level ones, being receptive of student's feelings, showing attitudes that facilitate effective learning and foster good human relationships, allowing students the time to think and to improve on their responses and making sure that the teacher's attention and services are well distributed around the class (Perrott, 1982). Further, as a major aim of the global multicultural curriculum is the empowerment of students to undertake citizen action, both vicariously and directly, teachers need to reflect on how their own preferred profile of teaching approaches can be linked into a meaningful community dimension.

The approaches should, of course, only be seen as one dimension – a major dimension it is true – but only one dimension of the total transactional scenario of the school as a whole. All planned interaction and informal contact, which is carried on 'in the name of the school', needs to be attentive to the principles, explicit in the philosophy of teaching, no matter where that interaction takes place – in the classroom, in the staffroom, in parents' meetings, in clubs and extra-curricular activities of all kinds. The same rules, deriving from the basic ethic of the curriculum, must apply. This moral ambience must also imbue non-verbal communications, such as displays, notices, events and activities, which are permitted in the school as well as any insignia or printed matter students are allowed to bring into the school. For the staff part as well, the philosophy of teaching implies carrying such principles as appeal to the rational judgment of students, non-coercion, respect for students' rights, facilitation of the student's own autonomous moral growth, beyond the frontiers of the classroom into all interactions and transactions where teacher and taught encounter each other. In this way there is a continual endorsement not only of appropriate modes of relationship and behaviour, but also of the fact that they are 'backed' by an authority beyond the individual: they have institutional legitimation.

The Need for Pre-assessment

Interlaced with the creative variety of the curriculum there will need to be a variety of assessment techniques, such as those set out in the assessment rationale and list of families of assessment techniques in Chapter 3, so that all students have as equal an opportunity as possible to learn from the teaching. In this respect, and when beginning the change from one curriculum to another with the concomitant changes in teaching approaches, the teacher will need to build in a period of pre-assessment so that overambitious expectations of students' ability does not cause learning frustration and thereby increase the very attitudes the teacher aims to reduce or eradicate. If students, who are unused to functioning at a more sophisticated level of cognition, and normally adopt a rather simplistic, single-factor dominated approach to processing information and reaching judgments, are suddenly confronted with rapid changes in teaching methods, which demand more complex modes of thought and problem solving, they will be more susceptible to social discomforture and intellectual anxiety, and thus less likely to be willing to undertake a more balanced and detached view of their own attitudes and prejudices. What is needed, therefore, is a gradual improvement in students' ability to use more information of a more complex type, in order to move gradually from simple decision-making to more complex decisions, involving the decisions and actions of others, combined with growing reflectiveness in making those decisions. Thus, through a strategy of pre-assessment, which can gauge the existing level of cognitive development of the students, the level of cognitive complexity of material and teaching approaches can be raised little-by-little and the student moved more and more from an egocentric stage of cognitive development to greater sophistication (Kehoe, 1982, p. 77).

In addition to this bench-mark pre-assessment, however, the teacher will also need to be continually vigilant for the observable indicators of the effectiveness of his or her teaching: the growth of knowledge, understanding and skills, particularly higher-order thinking skills and those of advocacy and petitioning, rational argument and intercultural communication, as well as more positive attitudes to learning, to the curriculum, the school, their teachers and their peers and to themselves as learners and advocates of the basic ethic of respect for persons. Remember, that it is the teacher who may decide whether learning has taken place and that, dependent on the choice of evidence, what will be the opportunities for students to demonstrate performance. Cultural factors may veil the teacher's choice of evidence, as they may also blur and even obscure the student's perception of the evidence the teacher requires of his or her ability to deliver that particular kind of performance. So, culturally sensitive monitoring is an essential accompaniment to the successful delivery of the revised curriculum.

It is important, at this stage to reiterate what I said in the Introduction about the powers of schools and the influence of teachers. There are those who tend to polarize the issue and to assert that the school cannot change attitudes and cannot change society. On the other hand, there are those who seem to believe that the school and teachers are omnipotent and have an educational panacea for all the ills of a sometimes desperately sick society. This book stands at neither of those two extremes. I accept that there are many matters that the school can do little about. Conversely, there are many which it can do something about and it is necessary, in this latter case, to know something about those which can be influenced and changed by the school. The school can change its curriculum and teaching methods to steer a closer course to cultural diversity, human rights and a global dimension. The purpose of this chapter has been to illustrate some of the ways in which that can be achieved by changing the teaching approaches adopted by educators and the criteria by which they themselves judge their own professional effectiveness. The process is an essentially democratic, collegial and professional one, where coercion is out of place and persuasion and discourse are at a premium.

How to move from the here and now of one's teaching approaches to that new more active, democratic and participatory profile teaching style cannot be solely a matter of content, nor indeed exclusively of personal choice. It is, in addition, a matter of reformulating one's own professional reality and, collegially, that of the institution as well. It will certainly involve a process of continually monitoring and appraising the existing and progressive state of knowledge, skills and attitudes of the students, and of measuring those against the objectives set out earlier in this book. As indicated above, pre-assessment can provide a kind of yardstick diagnosis of the quantity, range and quality of resources and pedagogical approaches that are likely to be most successful in order to get the cycle moving forward. But it is only a starter to the whole process and there are other factors as well, including essential resource and staff development 'launch pads' for curricular take-off. How to tackle that process of pre-assessment, diagnosis, collation of resources and gradual professional reformulation of reality is the subject of Chapters 5 and 6. Such a change demands considerable resources and investment of scarce time on the part of the teacher. So, for the moment, in Chapter 5, we turn to questions of material resources, and the sources from which they may be obtained, in order to assist teachers to launch a review of their curriculum practice.

Chapter Summary

In this chapter we have sought to construct the elements from which each teacher may, in turn, build his or her own teaching profile, appropriate to the demands of a curriculum which recognizes global as well as national cultural diversity as instrumental for decisions about both content and processes. An appropriate profile will still continue to comprise both explicit and subconscious elements. It has been the task of the chapter to increase the share of the former and to decrease the latter. At the beginning, four families of models of teaching developed by Joyce and Weil (1986) were briefly described. These were the information processing family, the personal awareness family, the synergetic social family, and the behavioural systems family. The characteristics of these four groupings of teaching models were then used to inform the identification of nine basic principles of teaching which would underlie a personal and institutional philosophy of teaching which could guide the implementation of a global multicultural curriculum, centrally committed to human rights education as content and value base for the whole curriculum. Those nine principles were respect for students, climate of acceptance, human rights commitment, democratic process, provision of creative environment, moral engagement, complex and sophisticated intellectual endeavour, communicative sensitivity, and engagement with aims as well as means.

The nine principles were then used to justify and describe a series of teaching approaches, which drew differentially on the models of teaching, were compatible with the nine principles of the philosophies of teaching, and were oriented to decreasing social category salience rather than augmenting it. Those approaches were required to conform with a set of practical criteria addressing the needs of students and teachers in the classroom. The criteria were that they should facilitate both intellectual and social learning, there should be some evidence of their efficacy, they should be capable of being generalized, they should not place unreasonable demands on teachers, they should be capable of implementation in ordinary schools, they should not be overly disruptive of the school's normal routine, and they should be attentive to or expressive of some of the models of teaching. The approaches described were group work, including group investigation approaches, ethnic contact, direct whole class teaching, case histories, values education including moral education and principle testing, and, lastly, drama including theatre in education. Finally, in this chapter I emphasized the need for a gradualist approach to changing one's teaching style and approaches and, linking with the previous sections on assessment and evaluation, I introduced the concept of pre-assessment as a means of benchmarking the existing level of cognitive development of students.

Drawing on the work accomplished in the Introduction and the first four chapters of this book, we now turn to issues of material and human resources. In Chapter 5, and drawing on the broad spectrum of cognate curricular initiatives referred to in previous chapters, I shall present a brief overview of material resources and the sources from which they can be obtained. It is not intended to be 'world-comprehensive', but to act as a starter pack for teachers to begin to collect their own institutional collection and catalogue. It is intended for all teachers, not just those involved in teaching subjects and levels most obviously involved in delivering the kind of curriculum advocated in this book. In Chapter 6 we shall consider issues of human resources in the context of the need for a coherent and systematic policy of personal and institutional staff development which can support the introduction of a curriculum pervaded by a global dimension and commitment to human rights within a context of democratic pluralism and cultural diversity.

Chapter 5

Resourcing a Global Multicultural Approach

In Chapter 4, and capitalizing on the groundwork achieved in the Introduction and the first three chapters of this book, we have been concerned with the development of appropriate teaching approaches to deliver a multicultural curriculum, which has a global attentiveness and a core commitment to human rights in its content and values. I have accepted that such a development must seek to build on what exists and that there can be no question of a utopian and millennial *carte blanche* curriculum exercise, which assumes a *de novo* change. I have emphasized the unique composition of each teacher's overall teaching approach and style, the components which comprise it and how these need to lock onto the components of the curriculum, learning experiences and knowledge. I have acknowledged that the changes I am advocating demand considerable resource and effort from teachers, and require a process of pre-assessment of students to match strategies with student need, competence and cognitive and affective sophistication.

Throughout this book I have laid particular emphasis on the need to learn from the experience of cognate curriculum development areas, with a large area of overlap in the goals they share with multicultural education. Equally, however, I have been concerned to point out that we must also learn from the shortcomings and errors of precursor traditions of curricular responses to cultural diversity and the overemphasis which many of them have placed on difference and, therefore, on social category salience, thus reinforcing prejudice and stereotype. This process of inter-learning with these other curricular activities has meant that I have necessarily drawn on a wide variety of diverse sources to justify my arguments and substantiate my case. This strategy inevitably has implications for resources and particularly for the selection of resources and sources, to which I refer in this chapter. So let us take a backwards glance for a moment, at the acknowledged debt this book owes to areas such as multicultural education, development education, peace studies, human rights education, world studies, global education, environmental education and law-related education. Our aims, objectives, procedural principles, assessment and teaching strategies and the content of our curriculum were derived from these sources and welded in the first part of this book into an overall curricular commitment to a globally sensitive, multicultural education which is expressive of human rights.

After recapitulating the process of reconstruction of the curriculum, necessary to achieve the objectives set out earlier in this book, Chapter 4 introduced a series of models of teaching derived from the theoretical and empirical literature. These were then used to inform a series of principles which should underlie a global multicultural curriculum. These were respect for students, climate of acceptance and involvement, human rights commitment, democratic process, provision of creative environments, moral engagement, complex and sophisticated levels of thinking, communicative sensitivity, and engagement with both aims and means. These principles were then used to inform a philosophy of teaching to underlie for both individuals and institutions a series of teaching approaches for the delivery of the curriculum.

The criteria for the selection of those approaches was that they should enhance both academic and social learning, provide evidence of their efficacy, be generalizable, not place unreasonable demands on teachers, capable of implementation in ordinary schools, not be overly disruptive of the normal routine and timetable of the school, and that they should be attentive to the models of teaching and the principles underlying the philosophy of teaching. The approaches discussed were collaborative and co-operative group work, including group investigation, ethnic contact, direct whole class teaching, including the use of mastery learning and advance organizers, case histories, values education, principles testing and drama approaches including theatre in education.

Each of these approaches, in its own way, has its own constituency of resources, on some of which I have drawn illustratively. Subsequently, I emphasized the need for the pre-assessment of students if new and sometimes 'strange' teaching approaches are to be successfully implemented. Without such a pre-appraisal, social anxiety and intellectual discomfort and frustration could alienate students and reinforce the very prejudices the teacher is seeking to eradicate. Linking with that process of pre-assessment, I shall carry that theme of scanning students into the arena of resources and 'hook it up' with the previous sections of the book which dealt with assessment and evaluation.

To sum up, in the first part of this book we have concentrated on the construction of a multicultural approach to education which is both 'world-open' and expressive of a commitment to human rights in its content and in its values and which, at the same time, can attenuate prejudice by reducing social category salience. This process has led us to engage in dialogue with a large number of curricular areas which are not normally considered together with (let alone interactive with) multicultural education. And yet, I have illustrated the way in which multicultural education and these other areas can learn from each other and achieve their common goals more easily through collaboration and coalition, rather than through senseless competition and strife.

Given this context of the great curricular diversity inherent in the cognate areas, we must now turn to the complex question of the great and confusing proliferation of resources which are available to teachers, whilst emphasizing that it is not the intention of this section to seek comprehensiveness. That would be unreasonable and impossible. What this section seeks to be is a fingerboard to the resources and sources that will enable teachers to develop their own collections and catalogues without undue additional demands being made on their already scarce time and energies, and which will enable them to exercise their professional discretion about what is appropriate and what is not, against explicit criteria, for which they may have to be culturally and socially responsible to their colleagues and controllers, to parents, the community and to their students. For, the selection of those resources and their use is a heavy responsibility and one for which the teacher may even be asked to be legally accountable. In this section we shall consider material resources and then in Chapter 6, human resource development.

So, in this chapter, I shall be emphasizing sources and access as well as the criteria for selection, rather than seeking to list all of what is available. Firstly, we shall consider how to access suitable material from libraries and standard works, and I shall have a word or two to say about computer searches. Then, I shall consider the kinds of useful organizations that may provide the kind of information, resources and support, which the teacher may find helpful, whilst at the same time emphasizing the distinction between those organizations that are intentionally beaming a single message, sometimes of a propagandist kind, and those that seek to provide a balanced service, looking at controversial issues from different points of view. A list of development education and ActionAid centres is given in Appendixes II and III, and a selected list of journals that contain information and ideas relevant to the global multicultural curriculum in Appendix IV. Next, the need for scanning and appraising materials for bias is emphasized and linked with the previous sections of the book concerned with assessment and evaluation. A set of seven bias review 'imperatives' is suggested, against which material could be appraised and reviewed. Finally, the issue of bias in tests and assessments is raised and a series of questions is posed about possible stereotypes and their impact, not only on the fairness of professional judgments, not least behavioural judgments, but also on the confidence and self-image of the students and the legitimation of educational decisions in the wider community.

Accessing the Resources

The resource implications of the process of coalitioning with other curricular areas and of seeking to permeate the whole curriculum with a global multicultural dimension, expressive of human rights, are at the same time complex and divergent. They are complex in so far as resourcing requires drawing together details from a wide range of subjects and curriculum areas in a coherent and comprehensible way, which will encourage colleagues to make use of the resources. But, conversely, they are divergent in the sense that teachers may reach out to those other areas for assistance with ideas and material resources to deliver the global multicultural curriculum, gaining sustenance and enrichment which would not otherwise have been available.

These initial caveats are necessary because this resource section does not aspire to be comprehensive or exhaustive in its coverage or even to collate materials from all of the contributory curricular areas, let alone from all the countries from which evidence has been cited in the first part of the book. It is intentionally eclectic and to some extent personal, and hopefully teachers will find or exchange other resources or material which might be used in addition or as an alternative to what is given directly here or indicated vicariously via the citations in the Appendixes. What this section seeks to provide is a kind of illustrative and portable 'starter pack' for teachers of all subjects who wish to link together their current concerns to deliver both excellence and equity in their present teaching with the growing need to respond to cultural diversity in their own society, to introduce a global dimension into their work, and to espouse a commitment to human rights in the content and process of their teaching. This is a tall order indeed, but then teachers are used to delivering on tall orders!

It is, however, important to bear three initial but major points in mind. Firstly, that there are not many resources that will exactly fit a teacher's precise purpose and match the particular needs of a school, the cultural and social profile of its population, and the development needs of its students and teachers. On the other hand, many existing resources can be adapted, amended or otherwise modified fairly easily for suitable implementation. Secondly, there is now a prolific outpouring of material of a controversial nature dealing with issues and subjects of a politically and socially sensitive nature. Some of it seeks to present a balance of perspectives and even to leave students and teachers to draw their own conclusions. But some of it is partisan, consciously aiming to propagate a particular political or commercial position, in some cases an extreme, naïve or anti-democratic viewpoint.

Teachers will need, therefore, to be sure of the criteria they are using to select their material and be willing and able to justify their criteria and choice if called upon to do so. In particular, teachers will need to make sure that they are not contravening any local or national policy, regulation or law such as, for example, Section 28 of the British Local Government Act, 1988. And thirdly, the kind of markets we use to commence our process of scanning and garnering resources will determine the results and the kind of teaching content and process we shall be able to implement. This indeed is a major difficulty, for there is no one descriptor that will open up the pantechnicon of all resources for global multicultural education, with a core commitment to human rights, in a tightly packaged, 'instant coffee' form.

So, what kinds of descriptors or parameters should a teacher be looking at? Some subject catalogues will recognize multicultural education and global education and human rights separately, but not link up the three together or recognize their interconnection or overlap. The same point applies to development education, political education, environmental education and human rights education. In the case of prejudice, discrimination, bias, racism and sexism the situation is equally complex, although I have mapped out a strategy for manual and computerized searches which will yield a comprehensive result (Lynch, 1987, p. 142). Additionally, there are some handbooks and bibliographies which provide a map of the majority of contributory curriculum concerns. The Marc Goldstein Memorial Trust of the University of London Institute of Education, for example, produces a catalogue of teaching resources for education in international understanding, justice and peace, which includes materials, as well as in the areas named, concerned with prejudice, human rights, racism, development issues and global and futures education, as well as teaching materials lists and an index, including highlighted subject areas (Marc Goldstein Memorial Trust, 1988).

Then, too, national organizations such as those listed below, including the Commission for Racial Equality, the Equal Opportunities Commission, Christian Aid, The Minority Rights Group, the Council for Education in World Citizenship, international organizations such as Unesco, Unicef, Oxfam, the World Bank, and national organizations abroad such as the Anti-Defamation League and the Association for Supervision and Curriculum issue catalogues of materials or bibliographies or both. The one by the National Youth Bureau is particularly helpful, having subsections on such areas as gender issues, challenging racism, international understanding, rights responsibilities, law, role playing, and gaming and simulation (National Youth Bureau, 1988). The user guide, prepared under the auspices of the Multiculturalism Sector of the Department of the Secretary of State in Canada, is particularly helpful, being both sectionalized and annotated (Machalski 1987). In some cases bibliographies on special topics are prepared and distributed free of charge. Some centres also loan or sell video tapes, films, posters and other materials (for example, Equal Opportunities Commission, Commission for Racial Equality and Anti-Defamation League). The guide to sources of information and material, prepared by the British Overseas Development Administration contains details of UK and UN agencies. It is sectionalized and includes details about each organization and the services it offers (Overseas Development Administration, 1986).

A few organizations, such as the Minority Rights Group and ActionAid (see the list of centres in Appendixes I and III) offer a limited but useful school support programme, including workshops, advice, in-service training, even where they do not have a local representation. Some local education authorities, most notably the Inner London Education Authority, also produce general catalogues of specialized material around topics such as multi-ethnic education, as well as providing both a resources and education library. While care is needed in their selection and use, pressure-group leaflets too can be a useful source of material for problem-solving exercises and they are often available free or at nominal charge.

One or two of the standard works in sub-fields such as multicultural education, global education, world studies and prejudice reduction also include extensive bibliographies and resource lists, including in some cases names and addresses of useful organizations (Council for Education in World Citizenship, 1980; Fisher and Hicks, 1986; Craft and

Klein, 1986; Lynch 1987; Ramsey, 1987; Pike and Selby, 1988; Banks, 1988). Similar bibliographical lists can also be found in the few books that exist on the teaching methods dimensions, such as Amir and Sharan (1984) and Joyce and Weil (1986). The compilation of practical activities for teaching and learning about human rights in schools compiled by Starkey (1988) contains much very useful material, although some of it is in French. There are also a number of excellent annotated selections of multicultural and multiracial books for the classroom (Library Association, Youth Library Group, 1985), for the under-fives (Commission for Racial Equality, 1978) and for the eight to twelve-year-old group. Another fairly simple way into the field is via one of the encyclopedias or dictionaries of education.

There are also one or two integrated curriculum packages available, although these are mainly addressed to teachers of history, geography and social studies. The former Schools Council projects in geography for the young school leaver, history, social science, environmental studies, general studies, humanities, integrated studies, moral and religious education, the Taba social sciences programme and the 'Man A Course of Study' materials, while now a little dated also contain valuable resource indications as well as much material which is still useful and details of teaching/learning approaches.

It is also possible to interrogate a data base fairly easily, if not from one's own facility, then from that of a neighbouring institution of higher education. Probably the most useful one of these for teachers is the Educational Resources Information Centre (ERIC), which can provide up-to-date annotated or non-annotated bibliographies, either on-line or off-line. The problem again is the choice of descriptors (parameters) within which the desired search can be most economically and successfully conducted. Several computerized searches were conducted for this book from ERIC, the Education Index (EI) and the British Education Index (BEI) against descriptors such as multicultural education, human rights, bias, development education, developing countries, environmental education, international education, peace education, global education, law and education, social sciences and social studies, although in each case the data base was asked for the total number of references in a particular category, before the descriptors were cross-related and a request made for printout. The printouts themselves would fill a book! More details on accessing suitable data bases and abstracting services are available in my publication on prejudice reduction (Lynch 1987, pp. 142ff) or from your local library services. The construction of a personal spreadsheet data base for retrieval purposes is also highly recommended and the interrogation of an existing one can assist in the definition of likely keywords for ease of access, when resources are needed for teaching.

Useful Organizations

Another way of beginning to collect information and appropriate materials on a personal and institutional basis is to assemble a list on card index, or better still for ease of updating, accessing, reproduction and sharing, on computer file, of information including the names and addresses of useful organizations and institutions. Clearly each person's or institution's list will be different, but as a 'starter', Appendix I reproduces an abridged version of my own list, having taken out a number of the international or foreign language centres and those concerned exclusively or predominantly with higher education and research and perhaps not involved with school education.

Development Education Centres

Approximately fifty development education centres (DECs) have been founded in the United Kingdom, mostly since the early 1970s, and consequent on the growth in the use of the term development education in the 1960s, arising from the first United Nations Development Decade. Their aim is to enable people to understand and participate in their own development and that of their community, nation and the world. It thus comprehends the four levels of application of global multicultural education, introduced in Chapter 1. Several of the resource centres are funded by overseas development and aid agencies, such as Oxfam, War on Want and Christian Aid, but others have no such external funding. Many of the centres include resources services, some of which produce and publish their own resources (broadly speaking) within the field of development education. There is also a National Association of Development Education Centres (NADEC), founded in 1980, which acts in a co-ordinating and mutual support capacity and from which a national overview is available. The facilities offered at the local centres vary considerably but usually include the opportunity to consult sources and resources and to meet and discuss with other teachers. Appendix II is an initial list of the DECs.

Action Aid Education Service

Action Aid is a charity which works with families and communities in the developing world, including many of the least developed countries. It offers a free education service through a network of education officers who are available to offer assistance and support to teachers working, teaching or studying in the field of development issues. There is a wide range of resources from developing counties, including slides, videos and photographs, in addition to written information and reports. There are fifteen regional offices in addition to the main one in London. (See Appendix III for a list of Action Aid Education Services.)

Journals and Periodicals

Another way of 'connecting' for material and new ideas is through the journals, magazines, newssheets and newsletters of the various organizations and pressure groups, and through the published journals appearing on a regular basis. Clearly, it is impossible for every teacher and every school to take every relevant journal or even to scan every journal. To that extent, lists will be a matter of individual choice or, better still, of collegial effort, depending to some extent on the differing levels, expertise and emphases of staff and the way they 'come at' introducing curriculum change to bring their teaching more into line with cultural diversity, a global perspective and human rights education. The list of journals and periodicals in Appendix IV is from my own files; teachers will no doubt wish to make their own additions or deletions.

Checking for Bias

In Chapter 2, a set of tentative procedural principles for assessment appropriate to a global multicultural curriculum was proposed in the context of an overall evaluation strategy, addressing the need for cultural fairness in professional judgments, absence of procedural bias, the need for special arrangements for legitimate special needs, the requirement of a balanced, fair and up-to-date portrayal of others, the recognition of a broad profile of achievements on the part of different groups and nations, the need for different modes of performance to be recognized and the acceptance of an affective dimension to learning. The case was made for a regular appraisal of examinations and assessment policies. Additional criteria were added in Chapter 3 to pull the list into closer alignment with a commitment to human rights education, and a set of appropriate techniques of assessment was proposed to reduce inequality and bias. Then, a bias review procedure was advanced to test out approaches and materials for their absence of sexism, racism and other forms of prejudice and discrimination, both direct and indirect. Definitions were given of biasing elements, including slurs, stereotypes, erroneous group representation, etc. and the need for a policy of bias review as an integral ongoing part of school procedures was reiterated.

Thus, building on the emphasis I have placed throughout this book on the need to keep the curriculum and the assessment of learning on course for human rights and positive human values, in this section I want to take a closer look at the content of bias review for reading and other materials, which are either used or sanctioned or supported for use by the school. What I have said for the curriculum and assessment also applies to resources and materials. Unless the teacher knows his or her resources well it is always possible for materials to be used inadvertently which carry a hidden negative message for and about particular students. The literature and textbooks used in schools carry a powerful message by dint of the authority that attaches to them because they are chosen by the school. Put another way, they appear with the imprimatur of the school and they give notice of the values which sustain the school. This point is particularly important in view of the detrimental effect that inappropriate material may have on both the intellectual and emotional development of students. But remember that it is not only what books contain that can be damaging. Books and materials can be offensive as much by what they omit as by what they include. So, we are talking about the baseline from which students are expected to learn, its equity, validity, completeness, balance and accuracy. Remember, it is the reality of the students which is at stake.

For this reason if for no other, on-going procedures for the continual scrutiny of all materials and resources, including library resources, are essential if the school is to be able to justify and maintain its stand for multicultural, non-prejudiced education committed to human rights. There are now a number of books and pamphlets, even regular bulletins, which deal with the issue of bias and prejudice in teaching materials, including books. Klein (1985) offers guidance on identifying bias and responding to it, as well as strategies for eradication. Her work is predominantly oriented to racial bias. There are also several books that recommend new dimensions of children's literature which are non-racist and conducive to the improvement of ethnic attitudes through literature (see, for example, Whitehead, 1988). Several State Departments of Education also published bias review materials, policies and procedures in the late 1970s, such as that quoted earlier for Michigan (Michigan Department of Education, 1979). The Council on Interracial Books for Children has published guidelines for selecting bias-free textbooks and story books, which include checklists as well as useful definitions (Council on Interracial Books for Children, 1987). It also publishes a regular Bulletin as well as an Interracial Digest, which contains many of the best articles from the Bulletin, and fact sheets on institutional racism and sexism.

A simple and speedy checklist for appraising books and materials (including tests, examinations and assessments) might include the following seven anti-prejudice 'commandments':

Check the date of publication of the book. Most educational and children's books published before the 1960s tended to represent a predominantly white male middle-class perspective. This stricture includes educational theory books which were very late in adopting a multicultural perspective. Even now the predominance of them is still Eurocentric if not downright ethnocentric or based on predominant North American concepts and perspectives. This, inevitably, has influenced not only the portrayal of women, minorities and developing countries but also the conceptual frameworks and cognitive schema, which have been used to apprehend, analyse, interpret and judge them. So date can be an important indicator of the care which needs to be taken in assessing a book for bias of a racial, credal, ethnic, linguistic, gender or global kind. Very rough date guidelines would mean that books published before 1960 would need very careful scrutiny with a gradual progression from that date in attempts to unload much of the historical bias.

Check the illustrations. This admonition may be particularly important for textbooks and library books but it also applies especially trenchantly to illustrative material such as pictures, displays, notice boards, slides, films, video tapes, maps and graphic representations, as well as to symbolic representations in clothing, sets, etc., when dramatic productions, musical evenings, Christmas stories, pageants, parents evenings and similar events are organized. More recent publications may adopt a tokenist approach where women, members of ethnic minorities and citizens of developing countries may certainly appear, but predominantly in 'white' roles or activities. They may be portrayed, but in minor, passive, derogatory, subservient or peripheral roles. Developing countries may appear only in the context of natural disasters, such as starvation, floods, earthquakes, drought, typhoons, or as inhabitants of countries whose historical tradition and contemporary culture is subject to interpretation only as an adjunct and in the context of metropolitan culture and history. Particular attention should be paid to the portrayal of the life styles of minorities and foreigners, their dress, food and style of habitation. Beware in particular of the 'grass skirts' and 'curry' syndrome.

Check the language. Particular care needs to be taken with the use of the English language, bearing in mind the fact that so many words encountered by English-speaking children in their early socialization are loaded with insulting, dehumanizing or derogatory overtones and implicit assumptions, especially when used in reference to minorities or Third World people. Some of these words are rarely used to describe white people, their qualities or actions. Children's action rhymes, singing games, sayings, tongue twisters and puzzles demand special scrutiny for their implicit racism and sexism. Check the process of naming within the book and make sure that characters of colour are neither left nameless nor given funny names, nor referred to exclusively by their first name when others are known by two names.

Particular difficulties attach to the words black and white, with black tending to be used in a negative manner and white in an exclusively positive manner – a comment which also applies to the many synonyms. Special attention needs to be paid to the patronizing use of qualifying adjectives, where through over-compensation a prejudiced assumption is reinforced. In this way, adjectives which are not themselves racist or sexist can reinforce the stereotypes on which racism and sexism are built. 'A well-dressed Black' or 'a well qualified Black' may be a way of implying that most Blacks are not well dressed or well qualified. Teachers and children should also be aware of the assumptions underlying value judgments about minorities and Third World people. For example, the term 'economically disadvantaged', when applied to Third World countries, could more realistically be replaced by the words 'economically exploited'. The use of the term non-white, for example, implies that the point of reference and major descriptor of all peoples should be their whiteness and it implies that persons of white skin are in a majority in the world.

Check the story. Particular care needs to be taken with individual and class readers whose story may sometimes inadvertently create negative characterizations of minorities or citizens of Third World countries. The negativism may take a very subtle form, as for example where all the problems are solved by males or by Whites or by citizens of developed countries, or where it is implied that the values of some groups or countries are unsuited to a modern scientific or technological context, or that a girl has to prove herself against boys' values, and black characters, often depicted in ghettos, are successful, only if they show preference for white culture and white values. Does the storyline accurately describe the struggles of minority groups for justice and equality or does it omit them from relevant historical locations?

Check the authenticity. Text and reading books should be checked for their historical accuracy and or any stereotypes, distortions, omissions and under- or over-representations of the history, traditions and culture of minority or Third World people. Questions should be asked about whether an anglocentric or eurocentric perspective on the lives and histories of other countries is the only one presented, whether minority cultures and customs are trivialized or whether alternative life-styles are presented as legitimate and acceptable. Is, for example, the only legitimate life-style presented that of white middle-class suburbia? Is there balance in the presentation of national and international heroes from different cultures and countries. Are the achievements of women and girls adequately represented, or is a glamorous stereotype of womanhood the only one portrayed? Issues of migration and settlement are particularly sensitive in this respect and it is important to check that the full historical array of motivations is included, such as slavery, economic exploitation, expulsion, oppression, etc.

Check the characterization. Often the characterization of Blacks and people from developing counties is related to traditional occupational stereotypes such as labourer, chauffeur, cook, maid, waiter and other menial positions; many times such people are portrayed in negative ways where the Black is always the 'bad guy' or speaks broken or non-standard English. Sometimes, too, dialect or slang is used in order to indicate the 'beyond the pale nature of Black culture and society'. Words such as 'girl' are used to describe adult females and 'boy' to describe any Black male. Such subtle stereotypes can also reach into the clothing, hair-styles and habitations associated with Blacks and Whites. Characters may sometimes be limited in their portrayal by the settings in which they appear and the behaviour which may be implied to be normally expected of them. It may be implied, for example, that Asians place less value on human life, Blacks on an orderly and peaceful environment, women on career progress, etc.

Check the sense of audience. Teachers should ask themselves what kind of audience sensitivity their materials show. Are there, for example, any subliminal messages in their texts or material which may damage the self-image of girls or minority students or reinforce stereotypical representations or attitudes which are rife in the broader society. What kind of relationships between people, between men and women, between different ethnic groups and between different nations are implied in the reading and other material which the students encounter. Remember that broader literature as well as textbooks carry a hidden message to their audience and that the interaction of student and text may serve to reinforce feelings of inferiority and superiority on the part of the students. In this sense, materials may strengthen or weaken that essential self-confidence which students use as a baseline for their learning. If, for example, they find that people of their kind never appear in the material they read or see, they may assume themselves to be from a less important group and therefore not full members of the learning community of the school.

Local Resources

There are many advantages to be gained from a recognition of the valuable reservoir of resources which are to be found at local level, among the school staff, the parents, in places of religious worship, among the local community and not least among the students. Thus, a recognition of the legitimacy of students' cultural contribution to the school can also be of assistance in both recognizing them as resources and in gaining access to community resources, which might otherwise remain inaccessible or unknown. Clearly, care is needed and all items will need to be subject to scrutiny for their appropriateness to the school's overall policy and to avoid awkward moments. It must be appreciated that it is the school which ultimately decides what is exhibited, utilized or included in its library or stock of readers. Such a strategy also provides a useful linkage between local studies and the global dimension of a school's work, and is a further means of encouraging the exploration of students' own ideas and opinions and of tapping into the very necessary citizen action dimension of the curriculum by, for example, undertaking surveys or responsibly supporting local causes or services.

More co-operative modes of working and a more democratic classroom ambience, too, may be expected to realize a veritable Aladdin's cave of rich resources among the students as well as evoking a pride in and preference for helping behaviour in the classroom and a carry-over into collaborative project work (Sharan, 1989), not least where many children may be visiting relatives abroad or experiencing overseas countries during the holidays or on exchanges. Community and student involvement in the appraisal of appropriate resources, the acquisition of minority language material, the translation or summarizing of written material for the library or resource centre are not only functional in themselves, but are also a very powerful symbolic manifestation of the schools policy.

Local museums and libraries often have staff who have experience in the education system and a special responsibility for liaison with schools. Many local voluntary organizations of a charitable kind can provide materials, links and visiting speakers in connection with each of the three foci: cultural diversity, global perspective and human rights. Then, too, many of the centres referred to above are, in any case, predominantly local, but even the most homogeneous of catchment areas will usually be able to yield people, perhaps from local charitable organizations, who may have particular cultural experiences and insights they could contribute to a school's curriculum. Thus, community involvement can be a two-way process for the school in this area of the curriculum, opening up new resources and making the local community feel that it is appreciated and its diversity of cultures fully recognized.

Evaluating Test and Assessment Materials

One aspect of bias review, to which especial importance needs to be attached, is that of the material used to make professional judgments in the form of tests and assessments. Because such assessments derive from majority and metropolitan cultures, their language, content, illustrations, underlying assumptions, subject matter and geographic, historic and cultural location are products of perceptions of the dominant culture. They represent, in other words, a different frame of reference from that of minority children, even though the language used may be the same. In the socioeconomic experiences demanded, they make assumptions about the cultural biography of minority children that are often wide of the mark.

Sometimes such material is taken from textbooks and sometimes it is manufactured by teachers or provided by official examinations boards. Without care in the choice of materials of this kind, not only can injustice arise but also a further damaging of the self-image of minority students. Teachers should scrutinize any material they intend to use for the purpose of making or recording professional judgments. Research indicates that racism and sexism in the content of tests may have an adverse effect on life chances. Even in apparently objective subjects, such as mathematics or science, the content may adversely affect the performance of girls and members of minorities. This applies even when the same skills would be required to answer questions where the content is slanted against girls and minorities. Format and rubric demand particular attention and an attmept should be made to balance different modes of testing performance including essay type and multiple choice questions. The cumulative effect of racism and sexism may have a specially negative effect on girls from minority groups. For this reason, 'test' material should be evaluated against combined criteria, such as:

- Are males and females, minorities and majorities, people from industrialized and developing countries portrayed in a variety of roles, activities and occupations?
- Is there a balance in terms of numbers of males and females used in the test items?
- Is the language used in the rubric, format and question content within the experience of all children?
- Is the validity of test items and materials established against proportionate numbers of majority and minority students?
- If the material is being used for selection purposes, is it equally valid and reliable for members of all cultural groups?
- Are the same or different norms used to assess the performance of male and female students?
- If the question is of an essay kind, does it include situations that are within the cultural experience of all students?
- Is care taken to arrange assessments at times and dates convenient to all cultural groups?
- Does test material include the 'great names' from different cultures?
- Is the material historically balanced in its portrayal of alternative perceptions and experiences of the same event by different cultural groups?
- Is the picture of developing countries balanced, up-to-date and fair?

As I pointed out in the earlier sections on assessment, evaluation does not simply comprise the testing and examination of students. Thus, each school will need to include the three major dimensions of the global multicultural curriculum in its evaluation strategy for the whole institution's resource commitment and allocation. Here there are sometimes difficult questions to be resolved, such as the justification of expenditure, where multicultural materials may be in competition perhaps with additional equipment for information technology or consumables for workshops. Those advocating the further development of a global multicultural dimension, inclusive of a commitment to human rights, will need to keep in mind that it is only to the extent that they can convince colleagues that such a commitment is central to the major goals of the school that they are likely to obtain the necessary resources to fulfil their goals. Thus the mutually reinforcing linkage between social equity and academic excellence is an important 'card' in their hands. Certainly, it would be important that any evaluation strategy should include criteria about the attentiveness of the policy and the materials to issues of cultural diversity at home and abroad and to human rights.

Chapter Summary

In this chapter I have tried to provide a very brief starter pack of information, resources, sources, ideas and principles which would enable teachers to begin the process of selecting and appraising resources for the implementation of a global multicultural curriculum, with a major commitment to human rights. I have concentrated on those materials which could enable teachers to make their own collection, rather than imposing on them my own collection. At the same time, I have indicated the importance of having a policy, including explicit criteria for the evaluation of materials and texts. The first section of the chapter on accessing resources included both manual and computer access. I have stressed from the start the initial and personal nature of the resources proposed, underlining the fact that it was in no sense comprehensive.

Next, lists of useful organizations, development education centres, ActionAid centres and journals and periodicals were referred to. A section on appraising material for bias included a simple list of principles for appraising books, illustrative materials and audio-visual aids under the headings of: date of publication, illustrations, language, story, authenticity, characterization, and sense of audience. A brief section alerted the reader not to underestimate the valuable resources available at local level. A concluding section concerned the evaluation of test and assessment materials and included a series of questions against which to examine proposed papers and questions.

In Chapter 6 we turn to the fundamental but problematic issue of the professional staff development, necessary to implement the kinds of changes outlined in this book. For, the changes in professional practice, implicitly recorded in this book in curriculum, assessment, evaluation and materials, will make heavy demands of teachers, their professionalism, flexibility and self-confidence. And, without succumbing to the concept of a deficit approach to staff development, the final chapter seeks to draw a line between the assumption that teachers should have total control over the curriculum, on the one hand, and the contrary view, on the other, that teachers are merely concerned with implementing a hand-me-down curriculum.

I shall, therefore, be seeking, in Chapter 6, to identify the changes necessary in the teacher's repertoire of skills and expertise if the global multicultural curriculum, committed to human rights, is to become even a partial reality. Linking with the theme of Chapter 4, teachers will also need to scan and garner resources for their own in-service education in this field. So, building on the work accomplished in the earlier part of the book, Chapter 6 proposes a series of principles which could guide the construction and implementation of a programme of professional development, which will be sensitive to strengths and needs and the ever-present demands of other curriculum innovations on teachers' time and energies, yet which is attentive to the values associated with a human rights centred curriculum for students and for staff. A set of proposed objectives for such a programme are advanced and the chapter concludes with a sketch of the content of such a programme, seen from both substantive and pedagogical perspectives.

Chapter 6

Learning for Teaching

In Chapter 5 we considered some of the material resources necessary to achieve the aims and objectives compiled in Chapters 1 and 2, and to deliver effectively the kind of curriculum described in Chapters 3 and 4. this exercise has been made more complex by the diverse nature and location of the materials, and the lack of cohesion among the cognate curriculum areas, from which this book has selectively drawn. Moreover, the fact that different schools and different teachers will have different needs has meant that there is little 'off-the-peg' material which unifies the literature of the three major foci of this book – multicultural education, a global dimension to the curriculum and human rights education – all of which are viewed as both content and value base for the curriculum. This limitation applies equally to materials for the initial and in-service education of teachers, and particularly to materials for school-based professional staff development.

Nonetheless, in Chapter 5, I emphasized the need for a policy of rigorous selection of material resources for teaching, measured against explicit criteria, for which the teacher may be called to account by colleagues, parents, students, administrators and politicians – and even legally. We considered the ways in which teachers could access information about resources, including computerized access, indicating the kinds of descriptors or key words under which material may be sought. Next, a brief list of useful organizations (local, regional and international) was referred to, together with lists of Education Development Centres and Action Aid centres. Periodicals and journals of relevance to the approach advocated were also referred to, and linking in with the bias review procedure proposed in Chapter 2, specific criteria for checking for bias of a racial, gender, credal or social class kind were suggested. Reference was made to the valuable resources available at local level from both official and voluntary sources and within the school itself and its community. Finally, the need for evaluating test and assessment material was highlighted and exemplary questions were posed to reveal potential bias, which could not only put certain students at a disadvantage academically, but might also have a detrimental effect socially on their confidence and self-image and the way they are perceived by other groups.

The parallel to that brief excursion in Chapter 5 into the material resources required to launch the global multicultural curriculum successfully is the need for systematic and on-going policies for human resource development, in the form of professional development of teachers, at individual, collegial and institutional levels, and their formulation and implementation in a way which is both realistic and helpful to teachers. For, there can be no fundamental curriculum development without an accompanying teacher professional development. It has been the argument of this book that it is in the excellence of their everyday teaching and personal relationships with students and each other than teachers can most clearly manifest their commitment to a global multicultural education centred firmly on human rights. So, the emphasis has been firmly on the improvement of existing professional practice, through a process of pushing back the frontiers of professional perception and by expanding and extending the criteria by which teachers measure themselves against those objectives. For such a task, it cannot be doubted that an appropriate professional staff development is essential. But there are many styles and approaches to staff development. Which approaches are most appropriate for our purposes?

It is very important that any such provision is built on the foundations of good educational practice, or, as we saw earlier with measures for prejudice reduction, it can be useless or even counterproductive. In a sense, we are very fortunate in being able to drawn on the development of action research and case study approaches, which has taken place over the past two decades. These approaches have utilized methodologies for planned educational change and curriculum development, which have been accompanied by evaluation of a kind variously described as illuminative (Parlett and Hamilton, 1972), holistic (Macdonald, 1975) or responsive (Stake, 1978). While such ethnographic approaches have been much criticized for their vagueness, lack of rigorous methodology and poor scholarly characteristics, they build strongly on well established traditions of anthropological study, which are both manageable by teachers and very appropriate to planned change in schools, where it is recognized as a change of paradigm or meaning rather than a mere structural change. It is of such evolution in meanings and perceptions and mutual reconstruction of reality that I have been writing about in this book. It is a concept of change, moreover, where we are speaking of growth through process rather than possession of any final product.

For this reason, in this chapter we shall be considering issues of the kind of professional development of teachers which is necessary on a continual basis, if they are to implement a global multicultural curriculum, core-committed to human rights as the value base and as part of the curriculum content. Firstly, we shall be looking at some baseline issues for 'starters'. From these issues and the earlier aims and objectives for the curriculum as a whole, we shall formulate a set of goals for the professional development of staff. We shall then compile a set of procedural principles to guide implementation and, subsequently, I shall make a number of suggestions about the substantive and pedagogical content of such a programme, based on a predominantly school-located provision, but weaving together the needs of the individual teacher professionals with those of the school. Finally, I shall suggest the need for an agreed 'covenant' for the staff development of the whole school as well as individual teacher professionals within it, in order to clarify for all parties what exactly it is that they are involved in and what part they have to play.

Some 'Starter' Issues

It will be apparent that individual teachers and individual schools will commence from a different baseline in terms of their current expertise and its congruence with the demands expressed by a global multicultural curriculum. Many teachers are already strongly committed to the implementation of a global or world studies, or development education or a human rights curriculum. Some few are seeking to implement a peace studies dimension to the existing curriculum. A few may even be attempting to unite all those areas into a coherent curriculum. Others are committed to a narrower concept and ideal which they term anti-racist education, while others still do not feel that their area of subject expertise or curricular responsibility has anything to offer either multicultural or human rights education, let alone needing to be enhanced by those two areas. This book addresses the needs of all these groups of teachers.

A number of promising ideas have been proposed about what multicultural teacher education may look like and what content and processes would be involved. Some even specify ideal-type lists of qualities which teachers should possess if they are to deliver a multicultural curriculum, although it is not quite clear what happens if they do not measure up to these 'qualities'. Some too, adopt a kind of mechanistic deficit paradigm to teacher professional development and assume that teachers should only be concerned with means and not with ends. I call this the 'NCO role'! Many of these proposals, moreover, address initial teacher education, whereas our concern here is with the in-service professional development of teachers, closely allied with curriculum and teaching development. Further, even where the in-service education of teachers for multicultural education is addressed, the other two dimensions of our focus in this book – a global dimension to multicultural education and human rights education – are usually not included. Then, too, there is an assumption that teachers are teachers of multicultural education rather than of students and other subject matter, which is regarded by the school staff, the students, their parents and prospective employers as much more important than any evidence of having studied multicultural education.

A variety of approaches and models has been proposed, often depending on the perspective of the individual writer, but usually assuming that all teachers have the same needs. This unitary focus on teacher needs often excludes an institutional perspective, let alone guidelines for a holistic school policy. For these and other reasons, educators such as Banks suggest that it is premature to think in terms of any one model of multicultural teacher education (Banks, 1985). So, it is important to emphasize that there is no one design, process or content of teacher professional development which is going to deliver all that is required to stretch multicultural education to include a global dimension and to include a commitment to and knowledge of human rights. What we can do, however, is to set down the overall goals of such a policy, according to which it can be designed and developed, and identify the major skills and knowledge areas required for the process of planning for improvement in professional action.

To start with, it is necessary to set down some ideas about the very important process of scanning and garnering of relevant information, before we begin the process of planning. In Kemmis' model (1980) this would be the preliminary fact-finding and analysis phase of a model envisaging a spiral of cycles. Perhaps the cycle could be commenced by a process of informal interviewing of colleagues and students, which could lead to the establishment of study or working groups, underpinned with legitimacy from the staff as a whole. This would give rise within a professional culture (Whitty, 1985) to progressive focusing on an agreed action plan and eventually to a school policy and staff development action although of course the early phrases of discourse are in themselves staff development. Such a collaborative model of staff development was developed by Troyna and Ball (1985) who were concerned with the enhancement of the professional effectiveness of staff at 'Milltown High School'. They point up the fallacious assumption that drawing teachers' attention to the discrepancy between their declared theory and the theory they actually implement will result in greater congruence between the two. They also usefully raise the issue of what constitutes effectiveness in multicultural settings, an issue we have addressed in detail earlier in this book. Stallings (1981) pulls the various factors together into what he terms a 'staff development mastery model' with four phases: pre-test (observation and starting where colleagues are now); information (link theory, practice and teacher experience, provision of good examples of the direction of change); organization and guidance of practice (integrate into existing behaviour; and, post-test (provide feedback). Whatever the model, for effective change, collaborative planning and implementation are essential (Fullan, 1985).

So, there are a large number of dilemmas to be faced by teachers wishing to advocate and collaboratively plan a phased programme of staff development for a global multicultural curriculum, centred on human rights, and it may be that some of these issues could constitute the initial agenda for discussion. Certainly whole school change will necessitate a whole school policy, resting on as much consensus as can be mustered. But, towards what provisional goals?

The Goals of Staff Development

In Chapter 1, I formulated a provisional set of master aims for a global multicultural education, which espouses human rights as both basic values and content for the curriculum. Those master aims were:

- The creative enhancement of cultural diversity, not solely the maintenance of existing cultures.
- The achievement of social justice in the form of equality of educational opportunity for all regardless of sex, race, class, creed or ethnicity.
- The propagation of a sense of shared values, rights and access to political power, and legitimate economic and human satisfaction.

Later in Chapter 1, I formulated a more detailed set of educational objectives and a series of procedural principles for the educational achievement of those objectives. The goals of a holistic, school-based professional staff development emerge naturally from the aims and objectives, which were drafted and allowed to flow into a curriculum design in the earlier chapters of this book. For, not surprisingly, a global multicultural curriculum, core committed to human rights, demands an analogous staff development. Even from the point of view of logical consequences, it is evident that a teacher cannot deliver his or her curriculum in a way that is expressive of a commitment to human rights, cultural diversity and a global dimension and sensitivity to in his or her teaching and learning, unless the teacher is committed to those ideals. Moreover, if the commitment is at the level of a purely external formalism, and the teacher has not clarified and internalized the values, underlying the commitment, those principles will not be manifest in the teaching.

In some cases there may be teachers who already have a high level of commitment, come from social science backgrounds and have meaningful encounters with members of minority communities and people from developing countries, but even where that is the case, and such teachers are an invaluable resource, they are only a minority and our task is to pervade the whole curriculum and all staff and students not only with the ideals, but also with the necessary professional knowledge, attitudes and skills. Certainly, not every teacher will possess all of the necessary personal and professional qualities, some will possess few of the necessary skills. They are probably, like the majority of teachers, dedicated and effective professionals, who are used to responding to new ideas and are 'of good will'. It is crucially important not to alienate such teachers or to turn them off by an inappropriate approach to staff development.

But the needs are very different too. In one case, the teacher with pastoral responsibility may need additional information about particular ethnic minorities and new skills in cross-cultural communication to relate to students and their parents as well as for record-keeping purposes. In another case a teacher of history may need new specialisms and expertise to realign the history taught and the way that it is taught. A teacher of religious or moral education may need new, cross-culturally reliable, means of assessing the moral maturity of students. All may need specific information and new techniques of teaching associated with the more central location of human rights education in the school and an intensified commitment to more co-operative modes of teaching and learning. The school librarian may need specific information about minority literature or assistance with the cataloguing of mother-tongue materials. All will need the reinforcement of collegial understanding and support in taking on new roles and new values.

Moreover, different aspects of staff development will need differing modes of engagement: some with means, some with goals, some with both. The means of delivery will also need to vary. Where new value acquisition is required, only sensitive working through of the issues in discussions, simulations, presentations and principled discourse is likely to leave room for clarified and reflective value movement to put teachers onto a modified moral auto-pilot. Where new teaching techniques and approaches are concerned, teachers probably learn best from other teachers, and through demonstration and trial and error. Where specific information is required, such as an updating or an initial mapping of the cultural biography of the catchment area, an individual teacher may combine that task with study for a higher degree. Where a sensitizing process to the life-styles and chances of people of colour or in the Third World are concerned, vicarious means such as films, slides and video presentations may be the most appropriate means.

Then, too, there is the question of the strategy to be adopted. So often enthusiasts work on the assumption that this is the only or most important demand facing teachers. As a consequence many other teachers are alienated by the (to them) unrealistic nature of the demands and claims. So, it is important to ask such questions as: Should one individual have responsibility for the planning and preparation of this aspect of in-service work, as the servant of the staff? Should a group undertake responsibility for planning on behalf of the staff meeting or academic board? In what ways can collaborative planning be used in order to engage as many staff as possible? How can the existing skills and knowledge of staff be shared more effectively and used as a springboard for the staff development of all? In what way can that crucial first step be achieved most sensitively and effectively? Should there be a joint committee with the school governing body?

Sometimes opportunities can be used which are not necessarily or exclusively labelled multicultural. For example, can informal opportunities, such as school dances or parties or other functions with parents be utilized as opportunities for learning new perceptions? Would a special resource centre be a useful way of concentrating materials and support, or would it permit all other staff to feel easy in forgetting about the issue? How can economies be made and involvement be increased by dovetailing this provision with other in-service tasks, where they may be common goals or overlap in techniques and approaches? What outside inputs will be necessary? Will such inputs necessitate a budget and, if so, how much and where will it come from? What proportion of that budget and indeed of total time available for staff development is it realistic to request for this dimension of the work of the school? Over what period of time (for example, one school year or several) should the plan be drawn up for?

So, a basic question is how to formulate goals for a staff development programme which can engage the differential perceptions and existing skills of all staff and their goodwill, in an exercise that will address all the varying needs of different subject specialists, with often very different training and cultural backgrounds, at different stages of career development and with differing political and ideological perspectives on life and different aspirations, and will nonetheless be realistic and be seen to be realistic by staff and the authorities, bearing in mind that this is only one aspect – truly a very important aspect – of the school's goals. Let us try!

For a school to be responsive to its own cultural diversity, expressive in its curriculum and policies to human rights and attentive to the need to prepare citizens of the world as well as of the nation, it will need to espouse the following staff development goals, which seek to advance the cognitive, affective and conative skills of teachers:

- Provide basic, accurate and up-to-date data concerning the facts of cultural diversity, of similarity and difference in human kind and life-styles, and of international interdependence.
- Develop a knowledge and understanding of human rights instruments, covenants and agreements to which the country is signatory and the main organizations concerned.
- Develop clarified values and reflective commitments among staff to the infusion of human rights principles into their teaching and curricula, where possible.
- Assist staff in the acquisition of new approaches to teaching with an emphasis on co-operative group and student-centred methods.
- Provide staff with new skills of assessment and evaluation, appropriate to the expression of cultural diversity among the students, in the curriculum and in the resources and other material used.
- Enable staff to inter-learn with each other, their students and the local community.
- Provide opportunities for staff to inter-visit in an atmosphere of professional confidence and confidentiality.
- Provide information and example about how to adopt teaching approaches that reduce prejudice and stereotypes.
- Enable staff to generate and collect materials which are expressive of a multicultural, human rights commitment in their teaching, whatever their subject.
- Assist staff to improve their skills of intercommunication with

different cultural groups.
● Provide staff with clear guidance on how to deal with racist incidents and racism in the school.

Clearly, some of the above goals address predominantly cognitive objectives, others have an attitude and value dimension, others focus on teaching and associated skills, and yet others combine all three. All are realistic goals for all staff, but differentially, depending on the role and responsibility of staff in school and the extent to which teachers assist each other in carrying the burden and achieving economies of effort by sharing expertise and resources. But how can those goals be implemented? In the next section I want to set out a series of procedural principles which respond to the basic ethic of the curriculum teachers will themselves be implementing and to the teachers' sense of professionalism.

Principles for Implementing Staff Development

Firstly, however, what are the procedural principles which might underlie a policy of staff development necessary for the growth of the existing curriculum which takes greater account of cultural diversity locally, nationally and worldwide and is, at the same time, attentive to and expressive of human rights education. Certainly, any staff development that hopes to assist teachers to evoke in students a commitment to respect for persons and their human rights cannot rest on coercion. In that sense, any policy will need to rely on professional and social support, and the legitimate pressure which can come from persuasion and shared norms and objectives, and which recognizes the centrality of the teacher in the process of curriculum development. Proposals for staff development will, therefore, need to appeal to the professional judgment of prospective participants and to involve teachers as much as possible in decisions about their own profile of staff development.

Secondly, and arising from the objectives and aims of the curricular approach, both policies and procedures will need to draw a balance between commonality and difference. To use the terminology we utilized earlier, the approaches will need to eschew over-emphasizing social category salience (Miller and Harrington, 1989). This is particularly important in 'selling' the changes because, although some teachers will immediately see the relevance of the approach being proposed to the needs of their students and to their area of expertise, others may rightly be expected to be sceptical and dubious about its possible effects on children's learning and examination results and, therefore, the students' life-chances. Any strategy will, thus, need to take into account the misgivings and genuine professional concerns of colleagues and adopt a predominantly normative–re-educative approach to curricular and broader educational change, and to recognize what is in effect an invitation to teachers to begin to reconstruct their professional reality. Any strategy will also need to recognize the affective or feelings dimension of the change being proposed, and that attitude change in adults is a slow but not impossible process.

In this respect, also, there will need to be a manifest balance between continuity and change. I have repeated on a number of occasions in this book that there is no *carte blanche* in introducing the new curriculum and that we need to take into account what already exists. The same principle also applies to teacher professional development. Moreover, there will be other in-service demands at the same time, with which any programme to train teachers for an extended multicultural commitment will need to be attentive. The commitment to cultural diversity at home and abroad, and to human rights, is only one aspect of the overall aims of a school, and 'subject imperialism' on its part will be unlikely to facilitate its absorption into the life of the school, its staff and students.

A gradualist philosophy of change will be essential to success if colleagues are not to become frustrated by demands for over-rapid movement, not least in their teaching approaches. Teaching is strongly linked to a teacher's personality and it will serve no useful purpose if teachers' confidence and sense of personal and professional competence is undermined. Then, too, teachers will need to be prepared for the frustrations inherent in trying out new teaching content, teaching approaches and assessment techniques. For, even in the best of all possible worlds, everything will not always turn out in the way that is planned. This is particularly so where new expectations are being levied of the students and they, in their turn, may become frustrated or even over-exercise their new-found freedoms until they learn to use them responsibly.

A sensitivity to language in planning and delivery of the staff development will be essential if misunderstandings are to be avoided. just as, at one remove, we are expecting teachers to adopt greater inter-communicative competence and to be more sensitive to the vocabulary they use and avoid inadvertent hurtfulness in their communications with students and parents, so a model of good communication in the process of staff development can be worth a thousand admonitions. Then, too, a gentle approach will need to be adopted to changing verbal repertoires, if feelings of social and professional discomforture are to be avoided because of a too sudden and vigorous challenging of what has been the accepted culture of the staff and not least the staffroom.

The preponderance of the professional development required will have to be provided by the school staff themselves, but there will be many occasions when inputs from 'experts' will be necessary. Where possible, for example, and particularly for difficult issues, which are likely to be controversial, it is a good idea to bring in a 'dynamic external' – a speaker or lecturer who can broach difficult, even embarrassing topics and issues and draw the initial antipathy of staff before they tackle the issue themselves. Such external inputs can take the form of lectures, workshops, role-playing and simulation exercises, discussion groups, etc., either with the whole staff or with smaller specialist groups.

Care is clearly needed in the selection of such persons and their perceived professional credibility and personal pedigree. Then, too, networking of schools, particularly where the school is small, can provide scope for discourse and inter-learning, which would not otherwise be available. There will need, however, to be an acknowledgement that it cannot be a matter of sending one member of staff on a course, as a kind of 'sin-eater' to eradicate the deficit of the whole institution, nor is it likely that any outside contributor will have 'the' solution to offer.

Staff development should be planned on a coherent, longitudinal basis, and 'one shot' solutions should be avoided. There should be a variety of different activities, including opportunities to observe each others' practice, and staff should be encouraged to 'inter-visit' each others' classes on an invitational and confidential basis. Timetable planning should facilitate this kind of activity and encourage teachers in achieving a more detailed and accurate picture of their own practice. Teachers seem to learn professional skills and expertise best form other teachers. There should also be demonstrations, trials of new approaches and curricula, and a built-in system for feedback to the planners of the programme and to individual teachers.

Any staff development will need to be able to take into account the diversity of disciplinary background of the teachers, present in all schools, but perhaps more marked in secondary schools, where there is a strong commitment to subject specialization. It should be noted that teachers are socialized by their previous studies into distinct subgroups with differing orientations to knowledge and teaching (Bernstein, 1972). Recent research has shown the extent to which teachers' ideas and attitudes about knowledge, as an objective body of information or as a function of personal experience and interpretation, and their classroom behaviour, is related to their academic training into a particular subject system (Yaakobi and Sharan, 1985). It is also unlikely that many members of staff will have had even an initial teacher education which included a strong commitment to a global multicultural commitment and to human rights. Then, too, some teachers may be subconsciously working on the basis of knowledge paradigms about people of colour, or girls, or linguistic and ethnic minorities, or perhaps people from developing countries, which are deeply embedded in western society. Put another way, some colleagues may have 'folk' preconceptions about particular culture groups, their cultures and traditions and suitability for studying particular subjects. Few, if any, will have had any training in cross-cultural communication, including the all-important non-verbal cues. This 'cultural diversity' among the school staff makes it all the more important that the underlying assumptions and values behind teachers' current practice are sensitively considered, and that a flexible approach to responding to teachers' own definitions of their needs is adopted.

It is inconceivable that the wide variety of substantive, attitudinal and methodological needs can be responded to by the same single programme for all staff, covering the same content and experiences. For this reason it is important to envisage a common core of knowledge and expertise, surrounded by alternate and optional components, mediated by a variety of different approaches, ranging from direct, purposeful experience of cultural phenomena to vicarious approaches through the literature, lectures, simulation exercises, films, video and audio clips, visits and visiting speakers. Moreover, just as it is essential for pupils to work out, clarify and internalize their own values, so also there is a sense in which professional colleagues must make the new values 'their own', before they can operationalize them.

Finally, in this list of procedural principles, it is important for any programmes of staff development to empower participants to take into account and come to terms with themselves, their own values, attitudes, self-image and professional identity. No such programme is going to be successful unless it empowers teachers to achieve new cultural and ethnic dimensions for their 'selves', attaining a more positive attitude and values to other ethnic and cultural groups. This does not imply the need for self-critical, racism awareness training as an isolated component, intended to evoke feelings of guilt on the part of participants. Where, for example, such an objective is linked with new pedagogical experiences, such as small group teaching, undertaken over a longer period of time, on a coherent and systematic basis, with the teachers exercising personal choice, it would appear that not only are there pedagogical 'pay-offs', but also attitudinal ones, not least with regard to the teacher's perceived need for control in the classroom, receptivity to the affective dimension of learning and the permissibility of feelings in the classroom, risk-taking and social orientation (Sharan and Hertz-Lazarowitz, 1982).

Let us now recapitulate the list of principles which could helpfully underpin a school's attempts to provide a programme of in-service professional development for its staff:

- Full involvement of teachers in decisions at all stages.
- Balance of emphasis between similarity and difference.
- Need for a balance between continuity and change.
- Strategy adopted will need to be a gradualist one.
- Where possible, INSET activities should be shared with other areas.
- Need to manifest a sensitivity to language.
- Need for a diversity of approaches.
- A coherent, longitudinal programme.
- Staff encouraged to observe each others' practice.
- Demonstrations, trials and feedback.
- Programmes to take into account the disciplinary diversity of staff and concomitant socialization.
- Supportive opportunities for staff to clarify their own values and identities.

Having set down the principles for the implementation of an appropriate staff development, I should like now to turn to the issue of the content of such programmes, bearing in mind that no one programme will meet in toto the needs of every teacher in the school and that what we are looking for is a programme which recognizes the needs of the teaching professional alongside those of the school (and the system).

The Content of Professional Development

In considering a suitable programme of staff development, we need to seek a conceptual framework which neither assumes a totally technical role for teachers, nor does it assume that teachers have total and exclusive control of the ends of the curriculum. Further, an appropriate staff development will neither assume the supremacy of curriculum development, nor of teacher development, but will acknowledge the dynamic interaction between the two. In seeking to sketch the outline of such a programme, it is necessary to differentiate between substantive considerations of new knowledge, skills and attitudes needed by the teacher, and the pedagogical means to deliver that content in the classroom and outside. One way of addressing this issue is to construct a checklist of knowledge, skills, attitudes and values demanded by the kind of curriculum I am advocating. This can then be juxtaposed with those strengths in those areas that already exist among the school staff, which leads in turn to the identification of the needs that should be considered for inclusion in the staff development programme. Provided that there is negotiation and discourse about the specific needs and how they are responded to, recognizing that the actual curriculum teachers create in their classrooms is unique in some senses and common in others, this need not necessarily divest teachers of their professional responsibility for engagement with aims as well as means.

In terms of substantive content there will need to be a gradation of expertise on as interlocking a basis as possible among the school staff. Those with responsibility for pastoral care, for example, may need to know more about the conventions and customs of cultural groups and about the bilingualism of students than others, and thereby be in a position to 'put the others straight' if and when necessary. The same may apply to the headteacher and knowledge of legislation and local regulations, or to the history teacher and a knowledge of the facts of colonialism and slavery, or to the geography teacher and the facts of international or local pollution. In other words the main criteria for more detailed knowledge in particular areas is whether it impinges on that teacher's field of action.

But all teachers in the school will need to know some of the above to some extent. All those with responsibility for report writing or communicating with parents in any way should become acquainted with the facts of local, national and global diversity across the dimensions introduced earlier in this book: cultural, social, economic and environmental. They should be acquainted with the names, languages and religions of the main cultural groups in their own society and more generally across the world. They should recognize any naming conventions which apply to particular cultural groups and the time and title of their main festivals. No teachers should be using generalizations such as Asian as denominators of judgment and professional decision, and they must be aware of the dangers of overcategorization and injustice in doing that. All teachers concerned with the fostering of good oral and written communication will need to have a sober, level-headed and unromantic understanding of the need for good standard English and of the economically impoverishing function of non-standard and dialect English.

All teachers will need to know about statutory organizations involved in race and gender equity at both local and national levels, and about any codes of practice or legislation in those areas and how that might affect their work. Naturally, the fact that some teachers will need to know about the above areas in greater detail than others does not absolve all teachers from having a map within which greater detail can easily be sketched. All, for example, will need to know school policy with regard to dealing with racist incidents and violence, including the reporting procedure and the members of staff to whom they should be referred in the first instance. There are also of course pedagogical implications of race and gender policy vis-à-vis the curriculum and assessment, to which I shall be making reference later in this section.

Teachers should also know about the interdependence of developed and developing countries and the ways in which the 'North' has developed a relationship with the 'South', which involves economic and environmental exploitation and cultural hegemony. They should have a balanced view of colonialism, including an appreciation of the different traditions of different nations in this respect and the on-going cultural legacy of their own country's tradition. A knowledge of the enslavement, which many peoples have endured (including the history of the Holocaust) is essential to the understanding of the history, genesis and the meaning of prejudice and the ways in which it leads to discrimination in education and the wider society. Some detail and understanding of the consequences of that discrimination for minority and majority communities is also desirable. They will need to be aware of the subconscious way in which they, in their teaching and in the fulfilment of other professional functions, may inadvertently perpetuate prejudice.

They will also need to know about the various human rights instruments, covenants and agreements, the national and international organizations fostering those rights, and about the structures constructed for the supervision and monitoring of human rights. They should have an opportunity to engage in discussion about some of the famous cases of human rights abuse in their own country and abroad, and should know a little about the importance of law-related education, and should appreciate its importance in educating students to participatory and responsible citizenship.

In the pedagogical realm there are a large number of items that are consequential on the content and process of the multicultural curriculum and assessment procedures, which need to be taken into account and, in some cases, demand new knowledge, expertise and skills. If, for example, the teacher is going to be expected to steer his or her teaching more towards the democratic classroom ambience and co-operative group work described in Chapters 3 and 4, there will be a need for information about how to do this, including a rationale to justify and legitimate such a move. But there will also need to be opportunities to see the methods demonstrated, to practice those methods and to professionally and critically appraise the new methods as they develop. Thus, as mentioned earlier, staff development of that kind becomes a multi-mode approach which permeates the everyday practice of the school and of the individual teacher. Of course, there is a resource dimension too, and collegial collaboration will be necessary if the right material is to be acquired and maximally utilized without unnecessary duplication.

The same applies to other new objectives or the refinement of older ones. The emphasis on skill development, including skills of reasoning, problem solving and decision making, contain new pedagogical imperatives for the teacher, the style of teaching, the necessary preparation and the availability of appropriate materials. Each of the learning experiences and knowledge components outlined as comprising the global multicultural curriculum in Chapter 2, has similar implications for the staff development of teachers, both its style and its content. How can teachers be expected, for example, to foster students' ability to brainstorm or to syndicate work if they have had no experience of it themselves? They would lack the essential 'inside' story which yields the insights into the how it actually 'feels' to do it.

Then, too, new approaches to the assessment of students, such as those advocated in this book, will similarly require both new knowledge and expertise, and the opportunity for teachers to monitor each other's practice in this respect. It will be recalled that the issues in assessment were seen not just as a matter of the content and rubric of tests, examinations and assessments, but also of the style, procedures and mode with the need for greater diversity of approaches and the appraisal of a broader profile of cultural expertise. Then, too, new teaching objectives such as greater co-operative emphasis necessitate new criteria of assessment and, according to the maturity of students, the opportunity to participate in the definition of criteria and assessment processes to some extent. Teaching for higher order cognitive gains also means testing for those gains on both an on-going and terminal basis.

Evaluation strategies also have implications for staff development. Where a school is moving from a predominantly monist concept of education and the curriculum, to one imbued with a cultural diversity not limited within national frontiers and including a commitment to human rights education, that clearly has deep implications for staff development and the kind of expertise which staff need to generate, if such evaluation is to be a useful source of feedback and improvement. It will need to be appreciated that such evaluation, institutional, collegial and institutional, is a complex matter demanding new skills on the part of the teacher. It involves skills of review of what currently exists, diagnosis of the issues, problems, needs, challenges 'unearthed', of the planning of appropriate corrective action and its implementation in an appropriate form, and of the monitoring of the perceived effects, leading back into a repetition of the cycle.

Inevitably, the process is not quite so simple as the linear description given above may seem to imply. Cross checking or triangulation of the process and its outcomes need to be in-built and it is here that the interpersonal perceptions of different parties, through the perspective of their own culture, need to be taken account of. Triangulation does not only imply different sets of evidence, but also different sources for the evidence and varying approaches to its collection. Moreover, the launchpad of reporting back leading to action also needs to be one which is informed by cultural diversity, with differently packaged oral, written or mixed reports for different groups. For example, where students are encouraged to appraise their own work and even to evaluate co-operative lessons, or in other cases where student or parent perceptions are an essential part of institutional evaluation, the cultural presentation needs to take account of audience. The same argument also applies for professional reasons in some cases.

Naturally, the skills and techniques associated with such a complex task cannot be acquired overnight, but on the other hand neither are they exclusive to the global multicultural dimension of the work of the school. So, here is a good example where the staff development needs of this area can be dovetailed with appropriate training for all other ares of school activity, and both academic and social dimensions of the school's functioning. Of course, the particular orientation and values of the kind of curriculum represented by this book will help to shape the process and content of that evaluation, and its criteria and outcomes. A commitment to human rights education and understanding of their permeation into all facets of the school's life has implications for the kind of curriculum content and process planned, but is also has important implications for the administration of the school, record-keeping, and transmission and pastoral care, as well as the involvement of parents.

Then there is the question of the role of the outsider in evaluation and, therefore, the outsider's involvement in appropriate staff development, with the range of possible partners very wide indeed, and the confidentiality dimension looming correspondingly larger as the circle grows wider, and the threshold of accountability is drawn ever closer to the point of praxis. Here it is important to underline the need for an advance 'contract' with outsiders who are going to be involved in training where confidential information is to be utilized or generated. In some cases, where the process and information may be of a more sensitively professional or cultural kind, a useful outsider may even be a colleague from another school, a governor, an academic or an adviser, provided that the terms of reference are clearly formulated, shared and carried out. In other cases, it may be possible, even essential, to involve parents, community leaders, other professionals, local business people, members of local religious associations and others from voluntary organizations. With all it would be important to emphasize that the purpose is the improvement of the school's present service to its students, which quite naturally comprises both strengths and weaknesses.

In a sense there will be a reflexivity in this part of staff development, which does not apply to the same extent and in the same way to other parts. For, the package of staff development, agreed and implemented by the staff, will itself need to be subject to evaluation and the result of that evaluation may well be an agreement to improve the staff development programme to better provide for the acquisition of skills of evaluation! But, although the profess is cyclical, it is not a pointless treadmill, but rather the means to the improvement of professional practice, in a fully professional way, which, in turn, will lead to an improvement in the students' learning and new opportunities for them in their future lives and relationships.

A Staff Development Covenant

A great deal is going to depend on the way in which any package of professional development activities is presented and the light in which it is perceived by the teachers. It is only natural, that if there is any suggestion of coercion or a 'wizard hunt', or an attempted imposition by those whose professional credibility is low, teachers are not likely to be inclined to actively participate. On the other hand, there is much in the outline of activities presented above which could be very attractive to teachers and could capture their idealism, interest and enthusiasm. But such features need highlighting and selling to the staff. These and similar considerations lead us quite naturally to the concept of a staff development covenant, addressing the construction and implementation of the necessary in-service activities, to develop the existing curriculum to become more sensitive to cultural diversity, to a global dimension to that diversity and to human rights, but making it equally evident to all concerned, but particularly to the teacher professionals, what the pay-off is for them and their students – in other words, making explicit the purposes and outcomes which might be legitimately expected to accrue. Teachers would need to be assured that the purposes of such activities, so costly in terms of their scarce time, were in line with the purposes and prospective outcomes, listed below:

- To increase the teacher's professional satisfaction and esteem.
- To improve the teacher's professional skills.
- To facilitate greater synergy of expertise among staff.
- To gradually enable the implementation of a more up-to-date, relevant and functional curriculum.
- To improve the quality of service offered to all students.
- To afford greater equity among students.
- To improve human relationships and respect for persons in the school and its community.
- To endorse and highlight the strengths of the school, and to improve and correct the weakness.

Making explicit such purposes could well make all the difference between a successful 'take-off' and a crash landing which would spoil the field for quite some time. So, as we said earlier, the initial legitimation of the initiative is a vital precursor to success, not a tiresome prelude that has to be played! Indeed, teachers should understand that there are many personal and professional benefits which could accrue to them and make their lives easier, if such a curriculum, and its accompanying staff development, is implemented successfully. After all, a greater commitment to human rights education and respect for persons means teachers' rights and respect for teachers as well! Closer and more understanding relationships with the local community includes a more understanding, helping and supportive relationship in times of strife and tension. Greater success for more students cannot be bad news for the school, for the students or for the teachers. The danger is in the assumption of some educational missionaries that it is obvious why teachers should co-operate in responding to cultural diversity, and of other educational 'politicards' that teachers are naïve enough to be manipulated in an endeavour which is *a priori* committed to propaganda rather than to education. What is needed is, on the contrary, explanation, justification and persuasion. And it is on the basis of those three principles that this chapter on professional staff development has been constructed – and, indeed, the whole book.

Chapter Summary

In this concluding chapter we have explored some of the professional staff development implications of introducing a multicultural curricu-lum, which manifests a global perspective and is expressive of human rights education. We have come a long way in our joint curricular journey since we first set out with our major criticisms both of the state of multicultural education and the contemporary curriculum of our schools and its cultural veracity, accuracy and usefulness. Sounding like an organ note throughout our journey have been the master aims of justice, diversity and common values, which we set out at the beginning and which have been the baseline for this chapter too.

We have drawn on aims and objectives, as well as the procedural principles, which we constructed in earlier chapters, and we have sought to take into account pre-existing factors such as the teacher's previous training, as well as the fact that different teachers have different needs, as do different schools, and that they are at different levels of sensitivity and different degrees of proximity to the issue. The intensity and immediacy of the challenge also varies from one school catchment area to another; each school's cultural profile is in many ways unique, although compris-ing similar components. In such circumstances no one model would fit all needs, even supposing that knowledge of multicultural education were at a more mature stage of development than in fact it is . For this later reason if for no other, the work of this final chapter has been a pencilling-in rather than a once-and-for-all definitive statement.

A professional approach has been espoused for staff development which eschews both propagandist and deficit models of in-service education, but also acknowledges that teachers are not totally auton-omous and that they also have other pressing in-service needs. Discourse was seen as the major means, therefore, of planning, designing, constructing, implementing and evaluating an appropriate programme of activities, which could be legitimated among staff and does not work on unrealistic assumptions about the supremacy of multicultural goals in a school's overall mission, but seeks to dovetail those goals with the school's other aims and objectives. A differentiation was introduced between the substantive knowledge required by teachers, including both cognitive and affective dimensions, and the additional pedagogical expertise which teachers will need to develop if they are to implement the new principles effectively.

In a 'starter' section, general principles were identified prior to the formulation of goals for staff development. The goals were tailored to take into account the differential 'fields of action' of teachers and the consequent need for more detailed exposition and learning in some cases than in others, as well as the different levels of commitment and previous expertise and experience. Attention was drawn to the need for differing modes of engagement according to the substance being dealt with; the uses and pitfalls of such strategies as inviting external speakers were discussed. On the basis of these preliminaries, eleven major goals were formulated for school-based, professional teacher development, which could serve the needs both of teachers and of schools, and assist in improving the quality of the service offered by the school to the students.

Procedural principles were then constructed to keep the learning of staff on course with the underlying moral direction and values of the kind of multicultural curriculum being advocated. Particular emphasis was placed on the desirability of a coherent, longitudinal programme, drawing on the participation of staff in the identification and definition of their own agenda at all stages. Attention was drawn to the need to firmly exclude coercion and to avoid the augmentation of social category salience. The need for a gradualist and differentiated approach was advanced which is sensitive to the use of language and the need for opportunities for teachers to begin to review their personal and professional value systems in a socially supportive, principled and professional atmosphere. The chapter then proceeded with outline details of the substantive and methodological content of such programmes, giving an indication of the extent of specialization necessary for different roles. The chapter concluded with a suggested covenant for staff development which could make clear to all parties what was envisaged, what the purpose was and what the prospective outcomes were.

Appendix I: List of Useful Organizations

Africa Bureau, Montague House, High Street, Huntingdon, Cambs. PE18 6EP

American Bar Association, Clearing House on Law-Related Education, 750 North Lake Shore Drive, Chicago, IL 60616 (Also ABA Special Committee on Youth Education for Citizenship at the same address)

Amnesty International, Tower House, 8–14 Southampton Street, London WC2E 7HF (British Section, Education Department, 5 Roberts Place, London EC1 0EJ)

Anti-Defamation League of B'nai B'rith, 823 United Nations Plaza, New York, New York 10017

Association for Supervision and Curriculum Development, 125 N. West Street, Alexandria, VA 22314

Associated Schools Project (Unesco ASPRO), Jordanhill College of Education, Southbrae Drive, Glasgow G13 1PP

Association for Teaching the Social Sciences, Didsbury Faculty, Manchester Polytechnic, Wilmslow Road, Manchester M20 8RR

Association pour la recherche interculturelle (ARIC), Institut de Psychologie, Route des Fougeres, CH–1700 Fribourg

Bradford School of Peace Studies, Bradford University, West Yorkshire DB7 1DP

British Film Institute, 127 Charing Cross Road, London WC2H 0EA

Campaign Against the Arms Trade, 5 Caledonian Road, London N1 9DX

Campaign for Nuclear Disarmament, 11 Goodwin Street, London N4

Catholic Fund for Overseas Development, 21a Soho Square, London W1Y 6NR

Catholic Institute for International Relations, 1 Cambridge Terrace, London NW1 4JL

Centre for Applied Research in Education, University of East Anglia, Norwich NR4 7TJ

Centre for Education in World Citizenship, Seymour Mews House, Seymour Mews, London W1H 9PE

Centre for Global Education, University of York, Heslington, York YO1 5DD

Centre for Multicultural Education, London University Institute of Education, 20 Bedford Way, London WC1H OAL

Centre for Peace Studies, St Martins College, Lancaster LA1 3JD

Centre for Teaching about Peace and War, 754 University Center Building, Wayne State University, Detroit, MI. 48202, USA

Centre for Teaching International Relations, University of Denver, Denver, Colorado 80208, USA

Centre for World Development Education, Regent's College, Inner Circle, Regents Park, London NW1 4NS

Central Film Library, Government Building, Bromyard Avenue, Acton, London W3 7JB

Central Office of Information, Publications Section, Hercules Road, London SE1 7DU

Center for Teaching International Relations, University of Denver, Denver, Colorado 80208

Children's Legal Centre, The, 20 Compton Terrace, London N1 2UN

Childrens Rights Workshop, 4 Aldebert Terrace, London SW8

Christian Aid, PO Box No 1, London SW9 8BH Commission of European Community, 20 Kensington Palace Gardens London W8 4QQ

Commission for Racial Equality, 10–12 Allington Street, London SW1E 5EH

Commonwealth Institute, Kensington High Street, London W8 6NQ

Commonwealth Institute, Scotland, 8 Rutland Square, Edinburgh EH1 2AS

Concord Films Council, Nacton, Ipswich, Suffolk IP3 9BJ

Conservation Trust, 246 London Road, Earley, Reading RG6 1AJ

Contemporary Films Ltd, 55 Greek Street, London W1V 6DB

Council for Education in World Citizenship, 26 Blackfriars Lane, London EC4V 6EB

Council of Europe, F67006 Strasbourg

Council for Environmental Education, School of Education, University of Reading, London Road, Reading RG1 5AQ

Development Education Centre, Selly Oak Colleges, Bristol Road, Birmingham B29 6LE (see also the selected list of Development Education Centres in Appendix II)

Educational and Television Films Ltd, 247 Upper Street, London N1 1RU

Education Materials Service Centre (EMSC) 144 Railroad Avenue, Suite 233, Edmonds, Washington 98020, USA

EMI Special Films Unit, 135 Wardour Street, London W1

Equal Opportunities Commission, Overseas House, Quay Street, Manchester M3 3HN

ERIC Clearing House on Teacher Education, Number One Dupont Circle, NW, Washington DC 20036

ERIC/CRESS Appalachia Educational Laboratory, 1031 Quarrier Street, PO Box 1348, Charleston, West Virginia 25325

ERIC Clearing House for Social Studies/Social Science, Indiana University, 2805 East Tenth Street, Suite 120, Bloomington, Indiana 47045

Friends of the Earth, 9 Poland Street, London W1V 3DG

Future Studies Centre, 15 Celso Road, Leeds LS2 9PR

Global Development Studies Institute, PO Box 522, Madison, New Jersey 07946, USA

Global Perspectives in Education, 218E 18th Street, New York, NY 10003, USA

Inner London Education Authority (ILEA) Learning Resources Branch, Marketing and Publicity Section, Television and Publishing Centre,

Thackeray Road, London SW8 3TB

Institute of Development Studies, University of Sussex, Brighton BN1 9RE

Institute for World Order, 1140 Avenue of the Americas, New York, NY 10036, USA

International Association for Intercultural Education, PO Box 14007, 3508 SB Utrecht, The Netherlands

International Defence and Aid Fund, 2 Amen Court, London EC4M 7BX

Jordanhill Project in International Understanding, Jordanhill College of Education, Glasgow G13 1PP

Mid-America Program for Global Perspectives, 513 North Park Avenue, Bloomington, Indiana 47401, USA

Minority Rights Group, 36 Craven Street, London WC2N 5NG

Multiculturalism in Education, Department of the Secretary of State of Canada, Ottawa, Ontario, K1A OM5

National Anti-Racist Movement in Education, PO Box 9, Walsall, West Midlands WS1 3SF

National Association of Development Education Centres, 6 Endsleigh Street, London WC1H 0DX (see also the selected list in Appendix II)

National Anti-Racist Movement in Education, 86 Station Road, Mickleover, Derby DE3 5FP

National Association for Race Relations, Teaching and Action Research, 22 Laneham Close, Bessacarr, Doncaster

National Centre for Alternative Technology, Llwyngwern Quarry, Machynlleth, Powys, Wales

National Council for Civil Liberties, 186 Kings Cross Road, London WC1X 9DE

One World Trust, 24 Palace Chambers, Bridge Street, London SW1

Overseas Development Institute, 10 Percy Street, London W1P 0JB

Oxfam, 274 Banbury Road, Oxford OX2 7DE

Pax Christi, St Francis of Assisi Centre, Pottery Lane, London W11 4NQ

Politics Association, 16 Gower Street, London WC1E 6DP

Richardson Institute for Peace and Conflict Research, Fylde College, University of Lancaster, Lancaster LA1 4YF

Runnymede Trust, 178 North Gower Street, London NW1 2NB

Save the Children, 17 Grove Lane, London SE5 8RD

School of Oriental and African Studies, University of London, Malet Street, London WC1E 7HP

Scottish Central Film Library, 74 Victoria Crescent Road, Glasgow G12 9JN

Slide Centre Ltd, 143 Chatham Road, London SW11 6SR

Social Science Education Consortium, 855 Broadway, Boulder, Colorado 80301, USA

Student Recordings Ltd, 88 Queen Street, Newton Abbot, Devon

Teachers for Peace, 22–24 Underwood Street, London N1 7JQ

Third World First, 232 Cowley Road, Oxford OX4 1UH

Third World Foundation, New Zealand House, 80 Haymarket, London SW1Y 4TS

UNICEF, 46 Osnaburgh Street, London NW1 3PU

United Kingdom Centre for European Education, University of London

Institute of Education, 18 Woburn Square, London WC1H 0NS
United Nations Association 3 Whitehall Court, London SW1A 2EL
United Nations Children's Fund, 55 Lincolns Inn Fields, London WC2A 3NB
United Nations Information Centre, 20 Buckingham Gate, London SW1E 6LB
Voluntary Service Overseas, 9 Belgrave Square, London SW1X 8PW
War on Want, 467 Caledonian Road, London N7 9BE
World Bank, 1818H Street NW, Washington, DC 20433, USA
World Development Movement, Bedford Chambers, Covent Garden, London
    WC2E 8HA
World Education Centre, 1730 Grove Street, Berkeley, California 94707, USA
World Education Fellowship, 33 Kinnaird Avenue, London W4 3SH
World Future Society, PO Box 30369, Bethesda Branch, Washington, DC
    20014, USA
World Studies Teacher Education Network, Westminster College, North
    Hinksey, Oxford
Worldwatch Institute, 1776 Massachusetts Avenue, NW Washington, DC
    20036, USA
World Without War Publications, 67 East Madison, Chicago, Illinois 60603,
    USA

Appendix II: List of Development Education Centres

The address of the National Association of Education Centres is 6 Endsleigh Street, London WC1 0DX

Bangor World Development Education Centre, School of Education, St Mary's College, Lon Pobty, Bangor, Gwynedd LL57 1DZ

Bath Development Education Centre, 7 Barton Buildings, Bath, Avon BA1 2JR

Belfast One World Centre, 4 Lower Crescent, Belfast BT7 1NR

Berkshire WEB Bus Project, Haymill, 112 Burnham Lane, Slough, Berks SL1 6IZ

Birmingham Development Education Centre, Gillett Centre, Selly Oak Colleges, Birmingham B29 6LE

Brighton Development Education Group, Brighthelm Church and Community
Centre, North Road, Brighton

Bristol BREAD, 84 Colston Street, Bristol BS1 5BB

Cambridge Harambee Centre for Environment and Development Studies, 20 Burleigh Street, Cambridge CB1 1DG

Canterbury Development Education Group, c/o 40 Old Dover Road, Canterbury

Cheltenham Centre for World Development Education, c/o 13 Priory Terrace, Cheltenham, Gloucestershire GL52 6DS

Cleveland World Studies Group, c/o Greystone, Carlton, Stockton, Cleveland TS21 1DR

Cork Development Education Network, University College, Cork, Ireland

Coventry Development Education Centre, 300 Walsgrave Road, Coventry CV2 4BL

Cumbria Schools World Development Project, 38 Kirkgate, Cockermouth, Cumbria CA13 9PJ

Derry World Development Education Centre, 12 London Street, Derry BT48 6QR

Dorset World Development Education Centre in East Dorset (DEED), South-East Dorset Teachers' Centre, Lowther Road, Bournemouth, Dorset BH8 8NR

Dudley One World Resource Centre, c/o 32 Newfield Drive, Kingswinford, West Midlands D76 8HY

Dundee One World Centre, Blackness Project Office, 1 Westport, Dundee

Edinburgh MAC (Multi-agency Centre), Old Playhouse Close, Moray House College of Education, Holyrood Road, Edinburgh EH8 8AQ

Edinburgh SEAD (Scottish Education and Action for Development), 29 Nicholson Square, Edinburgh EH1 ELT

Exeter Third World Centre, c/o St David's Hill, Exeter, Devon

Exmouth Centre for International Studies, Box 18, Exmouth, Devon

Glasgow Centrepeace, 143 Stockwell Street, Glasgow G1

Hampshire Development Education Centre, Mid-Hants Teachers' Centre, Elm Road, Winchester, Hampshire

Hull Development Education Centre, c/o Flat 5, 4 Park Avenue, Hull HU5 3HR

Ipswich and District One World Centre, c/o Christian Resource Centre, Diocesan House, 13 Tower Street, Ipswich IP1 2BG

Lancashire Development Education Centre, Room 1, Avenham Building, Avenham Lane, Preston PR1 3SS

Leeds Development Education Centre, 151–3 Cardigan Road, Leeds LS6 1LJ

Leicester World Development Centre, Traidfair, 26 Belgrave Gate, Leicester LE1 3PG

Liverpool World Development Studies Centre, Liverpool Institute of

Higher Education, St Katharine's College, Stand Park Road, Liverpool L16 9JD

London (North) Women's International Resource Centre, 173 Archway Road, London N7

London Africa Centre, 38 Kings Street, Covent Garden, London WC2 8JT

London (North West) Development Education Centre, c/o 26 Cressy Road, London NW3 2LY

London (South) Ujamaa Centre, 14 Brixton Road, London SW9

London (East) Tower Hamlets International Solidarity, Oxford House, Derbyshire Street, London E2

Manchester Development Education Project, c/o Manchester Polytechnic, 801 Wilmslow Road, Disbury, Manchester M20 8RG

Milton Keynes World Development Education Centre, Block A, Bridgewater Hall, Stantonbury Campus, Milton Keynes MK14 6BN

North Staffordshire Development Education Centre, Newcastle under Lyne College, Liverpool road, Staffs ST5 2DF

Nottingham Mundi, c/o YMCA, 4 Shakespeare Street, Nottingham, Notts.

Norwich Education and Action for Development, Church Alley, Redwell Street, Norwich, Norfolk, NR2 4SN

Oxford Development Education Centre, 33a Canal Street, Jericho, Oxford OX2 6BQ

Pendle Centre for Development and Peace, Unit 20, Coln Commercial Centre, Exchange Street, Coln, Lancs. BB8 0SQ

Rochdale Alternative Development Education Centre, 187 Yorkshire Street, Rochdale, Lancs.

Saffron Walden (Brandt Development Education Centre), Saffron Walden County High School Audley End Road, Saffron Walden, CB11 4UH

Southampton Tools for Self Reliance, Netley Marsh Workshops, Southampton SO4 2GY

South Yorkshire World Development Education Centre, Burngreave Middle
   School, Earldom Road, Sheffield S4 YEJ
Stevenage Urban Studies Centre, Pin Green School Site, Lonsdale Road,
   Stevenage, Herts. SG1 5DQ
Warwickshire World Studies Centre, 32a Bath Street, Leamington Spa,
   Warwickshire.
Wolverhampton Development Education Centre, Darlington Street
   Methodist Church Buildings, 24 School Street, Wolverhampton WV1 4LF

Appendix III: List of ActionAid Education Services

Head Office
(Sue Guide) Hamlyn House, Archway, London N19 5PG.
(Tel. 01 281 4101)

Cambridgeshire
Essex
Hertfordshire
Norfolk
Suffolk
(Yao Agbesi) 17 Malta Road, London E10 76JT
(Tel. 01 299 3041)

Avon
Berkshire
Gloucestershire
Isle of Wight
Wiltshire
(Cliff Allen) ActionAid, The Old Church House, Church Steps, Frome, Somerset BA11 1PL
(Tel. 0373 73128/61623)

Kent
London (South and East)
(Jane Burnett) 30 Albany Road, London E17 8DA
(Tel. 01 521 9870)

Bedfordshire
Buckinghamshire
Northamptonshire
Oxfordshire
Warwickshire
West Midlands
(Chris Davey) 48 Clarence Avenue, Kingsthorpe, Northampton NN2 6NZ
(Tel. 0604 721272)

Channel Islands
East Sussex
West Sussex
Surrey
Overseas
(Sue Davison) 2 Eastbourne Road, Brighton, East Sussex BN2 4DL
(Tel. 0273 673499)

Scotland
(Richard Dietrich) ActionAid, 15 Windsor Street, Edinburgh EH7 5LA
(Tel. 031 556 5443)

Northern Ireland	(Olwin Duglas) ActionAid, 118 University Street, Belfast, Northern Ireland BT7 1HP (Tel. 0232 324483)
Cheshire Greater Manchester Merseyside South Lancs. Staffordshire	(Audrey Hill) 252 Park Lane, Macclesfield, Cheshire SK11 8AA (Tel. 0625 34521)
Hampshire	(Andi Holliday) 10 Graham Road, Yapton, Nr. Arundel, West Sussex (Tel. 0243 551912)
Wales Salop	(Helen Jones) 3 Bloomfields Road, Blackwood, Gwent NP2 1QB (Tel. 0495 225210)
Cleveland Cumbria Durham Humberside Isle of Man North Lancs. Northumberland Tyne and Wear North Yorkshire West Yorkshire	(Gavin Keir) ActionAid, 51 Walmgate, York YO1 2TY (Tel. 0904 51383)
Cornwall Devon Dorset Somerset	(Ed Macalister–Smith) ActionAid, The Old Church House, Church Steps, Frome, Somerset BA11 1PL (Tel. 0373 73128/61623)
Derbyshire Leicestershire Lincolnshire Nottinghamshire South Yorkshire	(Roger Parsons) Aintree Cottage, Hurnbridge Road, New York, Lincolnshire LN4 4XT (Tel. 020 573 5623)
Herefordshire Worcestershire	(Theresa Tooth) 4 Knights Buildings, Masons Ryde, Pershore, Worcestershire WR10 1JG (Tel. 0386 555655)
London (North and West) Middlesex	(Susan Treacy) ActionAid, Hamlyn House, Archway, London N19 5PS (Tel. 01 281 4101)

179

Appendix IV: List of Journals and Periodicals

Action for Development — Centre for World Development Education

Arena — Newsletter of NAME

Broadsheets — Council for Education in World Citizenship

Bulletin — Interracial Books for Children

Bulletin of Environmental Education

Children's Book Bulletin — Town and Country Planning Association

Childright — Children's Rights Workshop

Cultures — Children's Legal Centre

Cultures Canada — UNESCO

Development Forum — Secretary of State for Multiculturalism, Ottawa

Education and the Law — Centre for Economic and Social Information

Education in Human Rights Network Bulletin — Longman

Ethnic and Racial Studies — Human Rights in Education Network

IDS Bulletin — Routledge

Impact — Institute of Development Studies

International Association for the Study of Cooperation in Education Newsletter — UNESCO/HMSO

Journal of Development Studies — IASCE

Journal of Multilingual and Multicultural Development — Frank Cass

Mentor — Multilingual Matters Ltd

— Newsletter of the National Advisory and Coordinating Committee

Australia Multicultural Education Abstracts	Carfax Publishing Company
Multicultural Teaching	Trentham Books Ltd
Multiracial Education	Commission for Racial Equality
MOST	Modern Studies Association, Scotland
New Community	Commission for Racial Equality
New Era	World Education Fellowship/World Studies Project
New Internationalist	Oxfam/Christian Aid
Newsletter	World Studies Teacher Education Network
Outlook	War on Want
Prospects	UNESCO
Race and Immigration	Runnymede Trust
Social Education	National Council for Social Studies
Social Studies	Heldref Publications
State of Affairs	Jordanhill College
Teaching Politics	Politics Association
Third World Quarterly	Third World Foundation
UNESCO Courier	UNESCO
World Development Reports	World Bank
World Studies Journal	Centre for Global Education, York

Bibliography and References

ACTION AID (1988) *GCSE Standard Grade Project*, London, Action Aid Education Service.

ADELMAN, C. and ALEXANDER, R.J. (1982), *The Self Evaluating Institution*, London and New York: Methuen.

ALLPORT, G.W. (1954) *The Nature of Prejudice*, Reading, Mass.: Addison-Wesley.

AMIR, Y. and SHARAN, S. (with the collaboration of RACHEL BEN-ARI) (1984) *School Desegregation*, Hillsdale, New Jersey: Lawrence Erlbaum Associates.

ASSOCIATION FOR VALUES EDUCATION AND RESEARCH (1978) *Prejudice*, Toronto, The Ontario Institute for Studies in Education.

ASSOCIATION FOR VALUES EDUCATION AND RESEARCH (1978) *Prejudice* (Teachers manual), Toronto: Ontario Institute for Studies in Education.

BAEZ, A.V., KNAMILLER, G.W. and SMYTH, J.C. (eds) (1987) *The Environment and Science and Technology Education*, Oxford: Pergamon.

BARNES, D. (1976) *From Communication to Curriculum*, Harmondsworth: Penguin.

BANKS, J.A. (1985a) *Teaching Strategies for the Social Studies*, 3rd ed., White Plains, New York: Longman.

BANKS, J.A. (1985b) 'Multicultural teacher education: knowledge, skills and processes', paper prepared for the Conference on Intercultural Training of Teachers, sponsored by the National Swedish Board of Universities and Colleges, June.

BANKS, J.A. (1987) *Teaching Strategies for Ethnic Studies*, 4th ed., Boston: Allyn and Bacon.

BANKS, J.A. (1987) 'The social studies, ethnic diversity, and social change', *The Elementary School Journal*, 87(5), 531–43.

BANKS, J.A. (1988) *Multiethnic Education: Theory and Practice*, 2nd ed., Boston: Allyn and Bacon.

BECK, C. (1983) *Values and Living* (Learning Materials for Grades 7 and 8), Toronto: The Ontario Institute for Studies in Education.

BECK, C., McCOY, N. and BRADLEY-CAMERON, J. (1980) *Reflecting on Values* (Learning Materials for Grades 1–6), Toronto: The Ontario Institute for Studies in Education.

BECKER, J. (1979) 'The world and the school: A case for world-centred education', in BECKER, J. (ed.) *Schooling for a Global Age*, New York: McGraw Hill.

BERNSTEIN, B. (1972) 'On the classification and framing of educational knowledge', in YOUNG, M.F.D., *Knowledge and Control*, London: Collier-Macmillan.

BLOOM, B.S. (1984a) 'The search for methods of group instruction as effective as one to one tutoring', *Educational Leadership*, 41(8), 4–17.

BLOOM, B.S. (1984b) 'The 2 sigma problem: the search for methods of group instruction as effective as one-to-one tutoring', *Educational Researcher*, 4–16.

BOULDING, E. (1988) *Building a Global Civil Culture*, New York: Teachers College, Colombia University.

BRITISH BROADCASTING CORPORATION (BBC) (in association with the SECONDARY EXAMINATIONS COUNCIL) (1987) *Oral English for GCSE and Standard Grade*, London: BBC.

BROWN, C. (1988) 'Curriculum responses to ethnic minority groups: a framework for analysis', *Educational Review*, 40(1), 51–68.

BROWN, J. (1983) 'Students' rights', in RAY, D. and D'OYLEY, V., *Human Rights in Canadian Education*, pp. 38–52, *op. cit.*

BULLIVANT, B.M. (1984) *Pluralism: Cultural Maintenance and Evolution*, Clevedon, Avon: Multilingual Matters Ltd.

CAMBRIDGESHIRE COUNTY COUNCIL EDUCATION DEPARTMENT (1988) *Learning Now: The Cambridgeshire Experience.*

CAPPS, F. KLINE (1986) 'The search for global perspectives in social education's history articles, 1937–1982', *International Journal of Social Sciences*, 1(2), 90–8.

CHILDREN'S LEGAL CENTRE (1983) 'Children's charters', *Childright*, 1, 11–14.

CHILDREN'S LEGAL CENTRE (1986) 'Rights of the Child', *Childright*, 32, 17–20.

CHILDREN'S LEGAL CENTRE (1987) *Education Rights Handbook*, London: The Children's Legal Centre.

COMMISSION FOR RACIAL EQUALITY (1978) *Books for Under Fives in Multi-Racial Britain*, London: CRE.

COUNCIL FOR EDUCATION IN WORLD CITIZENSHIP (1980) *World Studies Resource Guide*, London: CEWC.

COUNCIL OF EUROPE (1984) *Human Rights Education in Schools: Concepts, Attitudes and Skills*, Strasbourg.

COUNCIL OF EUROPE (1984) *The European Convention on Human Rights*, Strasbourg.

COUNCIL OF EUROPE (1985) Committee of Ministers, *Recommendation No. (85) 7 of the Committee of Ministers to Member States on Teaching and Learning about Human Rights in Schools*, Strasbourg.

COUNCIL OF INTERRACIAL BOOKS FOR CHILDREN (n.d.) *Guidelines for Selecting Bias-Free Textbooks and Storybooks*, New York.

CRAFT, A. and KLEIN, G. (1986) *Agenda for Multicultural Teaching*, London: Longman for the School Curriculum Development Committee.

DEPARTMENT OF EDUCATION AND SCIENCE (1977) *Education in Schools: A Consultative Document*, London: HMSO.

DEPARTMENT OF EDUCATION AND SCIENCE (1985) *The Curriculum from 5 to 16*, London: HMSO (Curriculum Matters 2).

DEPARTMENT OF EDUCATION AND SCIENCE (1988a) *The Curriculum from 5 to 16* (The Responses to Curriculum Matters 2), London: Department of Education and Science.

DEPARTMENT OF EDUCATION AND SCIENCE (1988b) Assessment of

Performance Unit, *Attitudes and Gender Differences*, Windsor, Berkshire: NFER-Nelson.

DEPARTMENT OF EDUCATION AND SCIENCE (1988c) Assessment of Performance Unit, *Pupils Attitudes to Writing*, Windsor, Berkshire: NFER-Nelson.

DEPARTMENT OF EDUCATION AND SCIENCE (1988d) Assessment of Performance Unit, *Pupils Attitudes to Reading*, Windsor, Berkshire: NFER-Nelson.

DEPARTMENT OF EDUCATION AND SCIENCE (1988e) Assessment of Performance Unit, *Science Progress Report 1977–78* (List of Science Concepts and Knowledge), London.

DUNLOP, J.P. (1983) *International and Multicultural Education Programme, Working Papers*, Glasgow: Jordanhill College of Education.

EDUCATION IN HUMAN RIGHTS NETWORK (1987) *Bulletin No 1*, Scarborough: North Riding College.

ELKIN, J. and GRIFFITH, V. (eds) (1985) *Multi-Racial Books for the Classroom*, Birmingham: The Youth Libraries Group of the Library Association.

ELKIN, J. and TRIGGS, P. (eds) (1986) *Children's Books for a Multi-Cultural Society*, London: Books for Keeps.

ENVIRONMENTAL EDUCATION ADVISERS ASSOCIATION (1981) *Environmental Education in the Curriculum*, Manchester Education Offices.

EVANS, C.S. (1987) 'Teaching a global perspective in elementary classrooms', *Elementary School Journal*, 87, 554–5.

FISHER, S. and HICKS, D. (1982) *Planning and Teaching World Studies: An Interim Guide*. London: Schools Council.

FISHER, S. and HICKS, D. (1986) *World Studies 8–13: A Teachers Handbook*, Edinburgh and New York: Oliver and Boyde.

FRAZER, M.J. and KORNHAUSER, A. (eds) (1986) *Ethics and Social Responsibility in Science Education*, Oxford: Pergamon.

FULLAN, M. (1982) *The Meaning of Change*, Colombia: Teachers College Press.

GORDON, M. (1964) *Assimilation in American Life: The Role of Race, Religion, and National Origins*, New York: Oxford University Press.

GRIMSHAW, J. (1986) *Feminist Philosophers*, Brighton: Wheatsheaf Books.

HEATER, D. (1986) 'The politics of political education', *Westminster Studies in Education*, 9, 33–44.

INDEPENDENT COMMISSION ON INTERNATIONAL DEVELOPMENT ISSUES (1980) *North-South: A Programme for Survival*, London: Pan Books.

INNER LONDON EDUCATION AUTHORITY (1988) *Educational Materials for a Multiethnic Society*, London: ILEA.

INTERNATIONAL ASSOCIATION FOR THE STUDY OF COOPERATION IN EDUCATION (September 1988) *Newsletter* 9(3/4) (Recent Research in Cooperative Learning: Implications for Practitioners).

JEFFCOATE, R. (1979) *Positive Image: Towards a Multiracial Curriculum*, London: Writers and Readers Publishing Cooperative.

JOSEPH, K. (1986) 'Without prejudice: education for an ethnically mixed society', *Multicultural Teaching*, 4(3), 6–8.

JOHNSON, D.W., MARIYAMA, G., JOHNSON, D., NELSON, D. and SKON, L. (1981) 'The effects of cooperative, competitive and individual goal structures on achievement: a meta-analysis', *Psychological Bulletin*, 89, 47–62.

JOYCE, B. and WEIL, M. (1986) *Models of Teaching*, 3rd ed., Englewood Cliffs, New Jersey: Prentice-Hall.

KEHOE, J.W. (1982) 'Multicultural Canada', in WILSON, D.C. (ed.), *Teaching Public Issues in a Canadian Context*, Toronto: OISE Press.

KEHOE, J.W. (1984) *A Handbook for Enhancing the Multicultural Climate of the School*, Vancouver: The University of British Colombia.

KEHOE, J.W. and TODD, R.W. (1978) 'The effects of principal testing discussions on student attitudes towards selected groups subjected to discrimination', *Canadian Journal of Education*, 3(4), 73–80.

KEMMIS, S. (1980) *The Action Research Planner*. Geelong: Deakin University Press.

KLEIN, G. (1985) *Reading into Racism*, London: Routledge.

KOHLBERG, L., LEVINE, C. and HEWER, A. (1984) 'The current formulation of the theory', in KOHLBERG, L., *Essays on Moral Development* (Volume II), San Francisco: Harper and Row.

LEWIS, J.L. and KELLY, P.J. (eds) (1987) *Science and Technology Education and Future Human Needs*, Oxford: Pergamon Press.

LIBRARY ASSOCIATION, Youth Libraries Group (1985) *Multiracial Books for the Classroom*, London.

LYNCH, J. (1983) *The Multicultural Curriculum*, London: Batsford Academic.

LYNCH, J. (1986) *Multicultural Education: Principles and Practice*, London: Routledge.

LYNCH, J. (1987) *Prejudice Reduction and the Schools*, London: Cassell; New York: Nichols Publishing Company.

MACDONALD, B. (1975) *The Programme at Two*, Norwich: The Centre for Applied Research in Education.

MARC GOLDSTEIN MEMORIAL TRUST (1988) *Teaching Resources for Education in International Understanding, Justice and Peace*, London: University of London Institute of Education, 2nd ed. updated.

MANCHESTER CITY COUNCIL EDUCATION COMMITTEE (1988) *Education for Peace in Manchester* (Guidelines).

MICHIGAN DEPARTMENT OF EDUCATION (1979) *Bias Review Procedure*, Lansing, Michigan.

MILLER, N. and HARRINGTON, J.H. (1989) 'A situational identity perspective on cultural diversity and teamwork in the classroom', in SHARAN, S. (ed.), *Cooperative Learning: Theory and Research*, New York: Praeger.

MORTIMORE, P., SAMMONS, P., STOLL, L., LEWIS, D. and ECOB, R. (1988) *School Matters* (The Junior Years), Wells, Somerset: Open Books.

NATIONAL UNION OF TEACHERS (1984) *Education for Peace*, London.

NATIONAL YOUTH BUREAU (1988) *Social Education: Resources and Sources Information Pack*, Leicester: NYB.

OLIVER, H. (1987) *Sharing the World – A Prospect for Global Learning*, Toronto: Ontario Institute for Studies in Education.

OVERSEAS DEVELOPMENT ADMINISTRATION (1986) *Overseas Development and Aid*, London: ODA.

PARKER, W.C. (1988) 'Why ethics in citizenship education?', *Social Studies and the Young Learner*, 1(1) Sept.–Oct., pp. 3–5.

PARLETT, M. and HAMILTON, D. (1972) 'Evaluation and illumination', in

HAMILTON, D. (ed.), *Beyond the Numbers Game*, London: Macmillan.

PERROTT, E. (1982) *Effective Teaching*, London: Longman.

PIKE, G. and SELBY, D. (1988) *Global Teacher, Global Learner*, London: Hodder and Stoughton.

PORTER, N. and TAYLOR, N. (1972) *How to Assess the Moral Reasoning of Students*, Toronto: The Ontario Institute for Studies in Education.

RAMSEY, G.P. (1987) *Teaching and Learning in a Diverse World*, New York and London: Teachers College, Colombia University.

RAO, A.N. (ed.) (1987) *Food, Agriculture and Education*, Oxford: Pergamon.

RAY, D. and D'OYLEY, V. (1983) *Human Rights in Canadian Education*, Dubuque, Iowa: Kendall/Hunt Publishing Company.

SCHMUCK, R.A., RUNKEL, J.P., ARENDS, J.H. and ARENDS, I.R. (1977) *The Second Handbook of Organisation Development in Schools*, Palo Alto, California: Mayfield Publishing Company.

SCHNELLER, R. (1988) 'The Israeli experience of crosscultural misunderstanding: insights and lessons', in POYATOS, F., *Cross-cultural Perspectives in Nonverbal Communication*, Toronto: C.J. Hografe.

SCHOOL CURRICULUM DEVELOPMENT COMMITTEE/LAW SOCIETY (1987) *Curriculum at the Crossroads*, London, SCDC.

SCHOOL CURRICULUM DEVELOPMENT COMMITTEE/LAW SOCIETY (1988) *Law in Education: News*.

SELBY, D. (1987) *Human Rights*, Cambridge: Cambridge University Press.

SECRETARY OF STATE FOR EDUCATION AND SCIENCE (1985) *Report of the Committee of Enquiry into the Education of Children from Ethnic Minority Groups* (Education for All), London: HMSO (The Swann Report).

SECRETARY OF STATE FOR CANADA (1987) *Canadian Multiculturalism Act*, Ottawa: House of Commons.

SHARAN, S. (1980) 'Cooperating learning in small groups: recent methods and effects on achievement, attitudes, and ethnic relations', *Review of Educational Research*, 50(2), 241–7.

SHARAN, S. et al. (1984) *Cooperative Learning in the Classroom: Research in Desegregated Schools*, Hillsdale, New Jersey: Lawrence Erlbaum Associates.

SHARAN, S. and HERTZ-LAZAROWITZ, R. (1982) 'Effects of an instructional change program on teachers' behaviour, attitudes and perceptions', *Journal of Applied Behavioral Science*, 18(2), 185–201.

SHARAN, S. and SHACHAR, H. (1988) *Language and Learning in the Cooperative Classroom*, New York: Springer-Verlag.

SHARAN, S. (1989) 'Cooperative learning and helping behaviour in the multi-ethnic classroom', in FOOT, H., MORGAN, M. and SHUTE, R. (eds), *Children Helping Children*, London: John Wiley and Sons.

SIMONS, H. (ed.) (1988) *The National Curriculum*, Kendal: British Educational Research Association.

SINGH, B.R. (1986) 'Human rights and multicultural education', *Journal of Further and Higher Education*, 10(3), 76–85.

SLAVIN, R.E. (1985) 'Cooperative learning: applying contact theory in desegregated schools', *Journal of Social Issues*, 41(3), 45–62.

SOLOMAN, W. (1987) 'Improving students' thinking skills through elementary social studies instruction', *The Elementary School Journal*, 87(5), 557–69.

SOUTHERN EXAMINATION GROUP (1988) *Decision Making: Social and Life Skills*, Guildford: SEG.

STAKE, R. (1978) 'The case study method in social enquiry', *Educational Researcher*, 7, 5–7.

STALLINGS, J. (1981) 'What research has to say to administrators of secondary schools about effective teaching and staff development', ERIC ED209348.

STARKEY, H. (1986) 'Human rights: the values for world studies and multicultural education', *Westminster Studies in Education*, 9, 57–66.

STARKEY, H. (1988) 'Practical activities for teaching and learning abut human rights in schools', Oxford: Westminster College (cyclo. in draft form).

STENHOUSE, L. (1975) *An Introduction to Curriculum Research and Development*, London: Heinemann Educational Books.

STEVENS, R., MADDEN, N., SLAVIN, R. and FARNISH, A.M. (1987) 'Cooperative integrated reading and composition: two field experiments', *Reading Research Quarterly*, 22(4), 433–54.

TARROW, N. BERNSTEIN (1988a) 'Human rights education: a comparison of Canadian and US approaches', paper presented at the Comparative and International Education Society, Western Regional Conference, Sacramento, CA, 21 October.

TARROW, N. BERNSTEIN (1988b) *Human Rights and Education*, Oxford: Pergamon Press.

TAYLOR, C. (ed.) (1987) *Science Education and Information Transfer*, Oxford: Pergamon.

TETREAULT, M.K.T. (1985) 'Feminist phase theory: an experience-derived evaluation model', *Journal of Higher Education*, 56(4), 363–84.

TROYNA, B. and BALL, W. (1985) 'Resistance rights and rituals: denominational schools and multicultural education', *Journal of Educational Policy*, 2(1), 15–25.

UNITED KINGDOM CENTRE FOR EUROPEAN EDUCATION (1986) *Europe as a Resource for Education in International Understanding*, London: University of London Institute of Education.

UNITED NATIONS (1978) *Human Rights: A Compilation of International Instruments*, New York: United Nations.

UNITED NATIONS EDUCATIONAL, SCIENTIFIC AND CULTURAL ORGANISATION (174) *Recommendation Concerning Education for International Understanding, Cooperation and Peace and Education Relating to Human Rights and Fundamental Freedoms*, Paris.

UNITED STATES DEPARTMENT OF EDUCATION (1986) *What works* (Research About Teaching and Learning), Washington, DC.

UNITED STATES DEPARTMENT OF JUSTICE (1987) *Law-Related Education: Making a Difference*, Washington, DC.

UNITED STATES OFFICE OF EDUCATIONAL RESEARCH AND IMPROVEMENT (1988) *Class Size and Public Policy: Politics and Panaceas*, Washington, DC.

WALBERG, H.J. (1984) 'Improving the productivity of America's schools, *Educational Leadership*, 41(8), 19–27.

WHITEHEAD, W. (1988) *Different Faces* (Growing up with Books in a Multi-Cultural Society), London: Pluto Press.

WHITTY, G. (1985) *Sociology and School Knowledge*, London: Methuen.

WILSON, D.C. (ed.) (1982) *Teaching Public Issues in a Canadian Context*, Toronto: The Ontario Institute for Studies in Education.

WINTER, R. (1986) 'Fictional critical writing', *Cambridge Journal of Education*, 16(3), 175–83.

YAAKOBI, D. and SHARAN, S. (1985) 'Teacher beliefs and practices: the discipline carries the message', *Journal of Education for Teaching*, 11(2), 187–99.

Index

Action Aid Education Service, 140
Adelman, C., 99
aid agencies, 139–40
Alexander, R.J., 99
Allport, G.W., 39, 61
Amir, Y., 115, 138
Amnesty International, 70
Arends, I.R., 10
Arends, J.H., 10
assessment and test material,
    evaluating, 146–8
Association for Values Education and
    Research, 62

Ball, W., 153
Banks, J.A., 3, 21, 138, 153
BBC (British Broadcasting
    Corporation), 97
Beck, C., 123
Becker, J., 22
behavioural systems family, 108
Best, Francine, 71
bias, checking for, 140–45
Bloom, B.S., 120, 121
Boulding, E., 71
Bradley-Cameron, J., 123
Brandt Report, 15
British Assessment of Performance
    Unit for Science, 93
British Environmental Advisers
    Association, 23
Brown, C. or J., 75
Bullivant, B.M., 5, 6

Cambridgeshire County Council, 55
Canada, human rights in, 70–71, 83
Capps, F. Kline, 13
Children's Legal Centre, 75, 76
children's rights, 73–87
co-operative and collaborative group
    work, 38–40, 114–21
Commission for Racial Equality, 138
Council for Education in World
    Citizenship, 137
Council of Europe, 16, 20, 85
    Committee of Ministers of, 84

Council on Interracial Books for
    Children, 142
Court of Human Rights, European, 70,
    71
Craft, A., 137
cultural/ethnic diversity, 4–9, 35–43,
    116–17
curriculum goals, levels and dimensions
    of, 3–4
data bases, 138
Department of Education and Science,
    15, 16, 34, 52, 93
development education centres, 139
Dewey, John, 110, 114
drama/theatre, use of modes of, 125–6
Dunlop, J.P., 23

ethnic/cultural diversity, 4–9, 35–43,
    116–17
    curriculum response to, 42
European Commission, 71
Evans, C.S., 88

Fisher, S., 16, 137
Fullan, M., 154

Gillick case, 86
global approach, of multicultural
    education, 43–9
    delivering a, 104–31
    evolution of concepts in, 13–14
    planning a, 1–33
    procedural principles, 27–30
    resourcing, 132–49, esp. 135–9,
        145–7
    setting operational goals, 18–30
    teaching goals of, 30–1
    see also cultural/ethnic diversity
Gordon, M., 8
group teaching/learning, 40

Hamilton, D., 151
Harrington, J.H., 11, 158
Heater, D., 20
Hertz-Lazarowitz, R., 115, 162
Hewer, A., 124

Hicks, D. 16, 137
human rights, 20–21, 67–103
  the core values, 69–73
  facilitative approaches for, 91
  see also children's rights; human
    rights education
human rights education, 77–82
  bias, prejudice and discrimination
    review, 99–103
  curricular policy for, 87–96
  evaluating and monitoring, 97–9
  school policy for, 82–7

Independent Commission, 15
information-processing family, 107
International and Multicultural
  Education Programme (IMEP), 22

Jeffcoate, R., 36
Johnson, D.W., 115
Joyce, B., 92, 107, 108, 130, 138

Kehoe, J.W., 122, 123, 128
Kemmis, S., 153
Klein, G., 138, 141
Kohlberg, L., 124

Levine, C., 124
Library Association, Youth Library
  Group, 138
Lynch, J., 30, 36, 136, 138

McCoy, N., 123
Macdonald, B., 151
Machalksi, 137
'Man A Course of Study' programme,
  138
Manchester City Council Education
  Committee, 11, 22
Marc Goldstein Memorial Trust
  (Institute of Education, University of
  London), 136, 137
Michigan Department of Education,
  102, 142
Miller, N., 11, 158
'Milltown High School', 154
Mortimore, P., 85
multicultural curriculum,
  attitude development, 61–2
  category salience and curriculum
    planning, 50
  developing skills, 59–61
  knowledge components, 53–9
  and learning experiences, 49–53
  see also ethnic/cultural diversity
multicultural education
  assessment and evaluation, 62–5
  folkloric, 36
  goals of, 2
  setting master aims, 10–19
  see also assessment and test material;
    bias; curriculum goals; global
    approach; human rights;
    multicultural curriculum; teaching;
    values education; whole school
    teaching

National Association of Development
  Education Centres (NADEC), 139
National Council for Social Studies, 13,
  21
national organizations, 137
National Research Centre (France), 71
National Science Foundation studies, 88
National Union of Teachers, 16
National Youth Bureau, 137
Norway, children's rights in, 76

One World Trust and the Centre for
  Peace Studies, 16
Ontario Institute for Studies in
  Education, 123
Overseas Development Administration,
  137

Parlett, M., 151
peace project, 22–7
Perrott, E., 127
personal awareness family, 107
Pike, G., 19, 138
Plowden Report, 118
pre-assessment, 127–9
principle testing, and values education,
  122–5
professional development *see* staff
  development

Ramsey, G.P., 138
role play, 125–6
Runkel, J.P., 10

Schmuck, R.A., 10

School Curriculum Development
   Committee/Law Society, 21
Selby, D., 19, 138
Shachar, H., 114, 115
Sharan, S., 38–9, 114, 115, 138, 145,
   161, 162
Singh, B.R., 72
Slavin, R.E., 39, 115
social studies, 21
Soloman, W., 94
staff development, 154–8
   content of, 162–7
   covenant, 167–9
   implementing, 158–62
Stake, R., 151
Stallings, 154
Starkey, H., 20, 138
Stenhouse, L., 31 , 123
Swann Report, 2, 15
synergetic social family, 107–8

Tarrow, N. Bernstein, 78, 79, 84
teaching,
   learning for, 150–70
   models of, 107–8
   a philosophy of, 108–27
   'starter' issues, 152–4
   see also staff development
test and assessment materials,
   evaluating, 146–8
theatre/drama, use of modes of, 125–6
Todd, R.W., 123
Troyna, B., 153

Unesco (United Nations Educational,
   Scientific and Cultural Organisation),
   82, 83
Unicef (United Nations Children's
   Fund), 75
United Kingdom, human rights in, 71
United Nations, 75, 76
United States,
   Department of Education, 85
   human rights in, 71

values education, and principle testing,
   122–5

Walberg, H.J., 12
Weil, M., 92, 107, 108, 130, 138
Whitty, G., 153

whole class teaching, 30–1, 116–21
world studies, objectives 27 + prev
World Studies Project, 16, 18–19
World Studies Teacher Training
   Project, 19

Yaakobi, D., 161
Youth Library Group, Library
   Association, 138